ISSUES IN POLITICAL THEORY

Political Theory has undergone a remarkable development in recent years. From a state in which it was once declared dead, it has come to occupy a central place in the study of Politics. Both political ideas and the wide-ranging arguments to which they give rise are now treated in a rigorous and analytical fashion, and political theorists have contributed to disciplines as diverse as economics, sociology and law. These developments have made the subject more challenging and exciting, but they have also added to the difficulties of students and others coming to the subject for the first time. Much of the burgeoning literature in specialist books and journals is readily intelligible only to those who are already well-versed in the subject.

Issues in Political Theory is a series conceived in response to this situation. It consists of a number of detailed and comprehensive studies of issues central to Political Theory which take account of the latest developments in scholarly debate. While making original contributions to the subject, books in the series are written especially for those who are new to Political Theory. Each volume aims to introduce its readers to the intricacies of a fundamental political issue and to help them find their way through the detailed, and often complicated, argument that that issue has attracted.

PETER JONES
ALBERT WEALE

ISSUES IN POLITICAL THEORY

Series Editors: PETER JONES and ALBERT WEALE

Published
David Beetham: **The Legitimation of Power**
Tom Campbell: **Justice** (3rd edition)
John Horton: **Political Obligation** (2nd edition)
Peter Jones: **Rights**
Albert Weale: **Democracy** (2nd edition)
Kerri Woods: **Human Rights**

Forthcoming
Raymond Plant: **Equality**

ISSUES IN POLITICAL THEORY SERIES
Series Standing Order

ISBN 978–0–230–54394–2 paperback
ISBN 978–0–230–54393–5 hardback
(outside North America only)

You can receive future titles in this series as they are published by a placing a standing order. Please contact your bookseller or, in the case of difficulty, write to us at the address below with your name and address, the title of the series and one of the ISBNs quoted above.

Customer Services Department, Palgrave Macmillan Ltd,
Houndmills, Basingstoke, Hampshire RG21 6XS, England, UK

Human Rights

Kerri Woods

palgrave
macmillan

© Kerri Woods 2014

First published 2014 by
PALGRAVE MACMILLAN

Palgrave Macmillan in the UK is an imprint of Macmillan Publishers Limited, registered in England, company number 785998, of Houndmills, Basingstoke, Hampshire RG21 6XS.

Palgrave Macmillan in the US is a division of St Martin's Press LLC, 175 Fifth Avenue, New York, NY 10010.

Palgrave Macmillan is the global academic imprint of the above companies and has companies and representatives throughout the world.

Palgrave® and Macmillan® are registered trademarks in the United States, the United Kingdom, Europe and other countries

ISBN 978-0-230-30274-7 hardback
ISBN 978-0-230-30275-4 paperback

This book is printed on paper suitable for recycling and made from fully managed and sustained forest sources. Logging, pulping and manufacturing processes are expected to conform to the environmental regulations of the country of origin.

A catalogue record for this book is available from the British Library.

A catalog record for this book is available from the Library of Congress.

Typeset by Cambrian Typesetters, Camberley, Surrey, England, UK

Printed in China

For Lola and Maya

Contents

Acknowledgements

I have always thought that, for all the significance of individual contributions, the pursuit of political philosophy, like the protection of human rights, is really a collective endeavour. I am thus very happy to have the opportunity to record my numerous debts in relation to this project, and to warmly thank all those who have helped me along the way. I would not have got this far on my own.

First, I am grateful to all at Palgrave Macmillan who worked on this book, particularly my cheerful editor Stephen Wenham, who was kind enough to overlook my perennial inability to stick to agreed deadlines. Second, I am much indebted to the British Academy for the award of a postdoctoral fellowship, which gave me time and resources to research and teach human rights theory at the University of York – without that opportunity, this book would never have been begun.

I also thank my former colleagues in Political Philosophy at York for the intellectually vibrant environment that they created. Sue Mendus, my 'mentor' at York, deserves particular thanks for all her advice and encouragement, and most of all for her thorough feedback on much of what I've written for the past five years. Tim Stanton also deserves special thanks for (a) being sane and (b) patiently answering a thousand questions along the way. Since moving to the School of Politics and International Studies at the University of Leeds I have been warmly welcomed by my new colleagues, particularly my fellow theorists Jonathan Dean and Derek Edyvane, and I thank them all for their generous help and support.

A number of friends and colleagues read drafts of various chapters of this book and I am tremendously grateful for their thoughtful comments and probing criticisms: thanks to Peter Balint, Chris Berry, Elizabeth Cripps, Stewart Davidson, Jonathan Dean, Derek Edyvane, Tim Fowler, Simon Hope, Christopher M. Hays, Monica Mookherjee and Sue Mendus. Rowan Cruft helped by answering some questions via email, and James Chalmers pointed me in the direction of some useful literature. I am also grateful to seminar audiences at the University of Leeds and the Netherlands Research School for Practical Philosophy for giving thoughtful feedback on parts of the book presented in their midst. Peter Jones supported the project from the beginning and gave enormously helpful feedback on a draft of the entire manuscript, and I am hugely grateful to him for all his help. The book is much improved for all of this input, and for feedback from two anonymous readers, and I am deeply thankful for it. Of course, I claim for myself credit for remaining errors.

I am also grateful to students at the University of York and the University of Leeds who opted for my courses on human rights theory; I learned a great deal from teaching them. I must again thank Chris Berry at the University of Glasgow for teaching me much of what I know about good teaching. A longer-standing debt of gratitude is owed to Peter McCaffery and Nigel Dower at the University of Aberdeen for their indulgence of my first ill-formed thoughts about human rights theory as an undergraduate.

Two personal debts: first, I thank my good friend Julie Sheker for being a voice of reason, humour and justified anger in an often bewildering world. And most importantly, I thank my partner Cristina Johnston, who read the entire manuscript (on a train, no less) as well as drafts of individual chapters, and without whom this book, and much else besides, would never have been anything at all.

Finally, while I think that human rights theory *matters* – indeed, I think it matters a great deal – I have enormous respect and admiration for those who give their time (and sometimes their lives) to human rights activism. My royalties from this book are donated to Amnesty International.

Edinburgh   KERRI WOODS
November 2013

List of Abbreviations

CEDAW	Convention on the Elimination of All Forms of Discrimination against Women
ECHR	European Convention on Human Rights
ICC	International Criminal Court
ICCPR	International Covenant on Civil and Political Rights
ICESCR	International Covenant on Cultural, Economic and Social Rights
LGBT	lesbian, gay, bisexual and transgender
MNC	multinational corporation
NGO	non-governmental organization
OHCHR	Office of the High Commissioner for Human Rights
UDHR	Universal Declaration of Human Rights
UN	United Nations
UNESCO	United Nations Educational, Scientific and Cultural Organization

Introduction

'The philosophical interest of a question of human rights is not strictly proportional to its real-life importance.' (Nagel, 1995, p. 83)

Human rights have become *the* authoritative language in which to advance moral and political claims. If I say that you have violated my human rights, I am taken to be saying something important, something that indicates a grave wrong on your part, and implies duties, certainly on your part, and perhaps for other people as well. Human rights are claims about what ought to happen in the real world.

Human rights quite obviously exist in the real world. They are proclaimed in the International Bill of Rights, that is, the Universal Declaration of Human Rights (1948), the International Covenant on Civil and Political Rights (1966) and the International Covenant on Cultural, Economic and Social Rights (1966). They also exist in the protests and claims and affirmations of political activists and non-governmental organizations (NGOs) engaged in all manner of campaigns, from fights against oppressive governments to claims for the right to same-sex marriage to defences of the right to clean water.

Many, perhaps most, political philosophers, affirm a commitment to human rights, both in theory and in practice. But many are also puzzled, sometimes troubled, by the very idea of human rights. They raise some difficult questions, such as: why do humans have human rights? Do all and any and only human beings have human rights? What should properly be the content of human rights? Who has duties with respect to human rights? What are the limits of human rights? Thomas Nagel notes, in the quote above, that these puzzles and problems can appear to be disconnected from the urgent real world politics of human rights. But it is not only philosophers who turn out to be puzzled, and sometimes troubled, by some of these questions. Political actors, whenever they draw on human rights, are appealing to the idea of some universal moral

1

standard, but both the existence and the content of that standard are, in the real world, deeply contested.

So it is important that we answer these, and other, philosophical questions about human rights. The persistence with which scholars pursue these questions may well seem intensely irritating to activists. When lives are at stake these sorts of questions no doubt seem a privileged indulgence. But not only are these questions deeply interesting, they also speak to our need for clarity and certainty when we seek to make weighty moral claims, which is something that we often want to do when lives are at stake. So while it seems that Nagel is right that the importance of philosophical questions about human rights may not be strictly proportional to their real-life importance, they are important nevertheless.

The sorts of philosophical questions that arise, then, in the field of human rights, are the subject of this book. In pursuing many of the debates considered within this book, and many beyond the scope of it, people – politicians, activists, political scientists and political theorists – take for granted the privileged moral status of human rights as normative claims. They assume that human beings are beings of unique moral value who have rights entitling them to certain protections or certain goods. It would not be too unjustly damning to say there is a degree of complacency about human rights talk – it seems obvious to everyone that human rights are what they are, and that they are important.

A brief foray into the search for philosophical foundations for human rights reveals that much of what we take for granted about the justification for human rights is not obvious at all. There is deep disagreement about what rights are, why we have them, why and whether and how they entail duties, who exactly has those duties, and what are the contents of the rights and the duties. Theorizing about human rights raises questions about the nature of human beings and the nature of morality. Studying the history of the idea of human rights reveals to us the extent to which the answers to those questions have changed, and the extent to which they have remained remarkably similar, in the few hundred years that people have been thinking in terms of things that might recognizably be described as human rights.

The book is organized as follows. In the first chapter I address the question: what is a human right? I do not propose a definitive answer; rather, I introduce some ways of conceptualizing rights in general, and human rights in particular, that can help with the challenge of understanding what a human right is, and with ruling out claims that are not human rights. In the second chapter I give a brief introduction to the history of human rights via a focus on three historical moments of particular importance for the development of ideas about human rights. The third chapter evaluates some of the many attempts that have been made to find philosophical foundations that can furnish an answer to the question: why do we have human rights? In Chapter 4 I address those critics who doubt that there is a coherent answer to this question at all, and instead defend what is often called a 'political view' of human rights.

There then follow three related chapters. The first of these, Chapter 5, tackles two sets of questions in relation to religion and human rights: to what extent a conflict exists between human rights understood in secular terms and human rights understood from a religious perspective; and the possibilities and tensions of an Islamic conception of human rights. This raises some questions about the validity of universal values, further explored in Chapter 6, which tackles the debate between universalism and relativism. In this chapter I draw particular attention to feminist critiques. Chapter 7 continues with some of this material in relation to ideas about group rights, multiculturalism and the human rights claims of minorities.

The penultimate two chapters focus on current debates in human rights theory: global justice (Chapter 8) and environmental human rights (Chapter 9). These are areas where there have been significant developments in recent years. Debates in these chapters raise questions about the extent and allocation of counterpart duties to human rights, and whether future generations can be said to have human rights that impose duties on us now. In the conclusion I reflect on the central challenges in human rights theory and how these have evolved.

1 What is a Human Right?

'[T]he more the fight for human rights gains in popularity, the more it loses any concrete content, becoming a kind of universal stance of everyone towards everything, a kind of energy that turns all human desires into rights.' (Kundera, quoted in Mendus, 1995, p. 13)

If we are to resist the confusion that Milan Kundera describes here, we will need to be clear about what, precisely, is a human right. What is the difference between a desire, a need, a duty, a right, a human right? What is it about human rights that makes them important as moral claims and political practice? What sorts of agents can be rights-bearers? What are the implications of conflicts between rights? In this chapter, I aim to clarify human rights as a concept, which should, I hope, make the questions that we address later in the book – questions about why we have human rights and what we have human rights to – that bit easier to get to grips with.

In some respects it is possible to be specific about what human rights are, but a familiar worry, to which Kundera alludes, is that there is a protean quality to human rights. That is to say, they evolve and change, and multiply and disappear for a while to re-appear later in a slightly different form. So a definitive answer to the question 'what is a human right?' may be more than we should hope for. What I am aiming for here is to establish some parameters, to set markers, in terms of which to make sense of the claims that people make when they say, 'this is a human right', or, indeed, 'this is *my* human right'.

Rights: general, positive, moral, human

As a citizen of the United Kingdom, I have certain rights, for example the right to vote in elections to the UK parliament. I do not have the right to vote in France or America, and I do not have the unqualified right to go and become a French or American citizen (though I may be able to become a French or American citizen in time, subject to particular qualifications). If I promise you that I will help you with your essay, you have a right against me that I keep my promise. If I have not made such a promise, then it might be nice if I helped you, but I am not duty bound to do so. (If I have made such a promise, I am not myself at liberty to release myself from the obligation – only you can do that.) As a consumer, I also have certain rights, for example, the right not to be lied to about the ingredients in a pizza; these rights arise by virtue of consumer law. It is only because of the positive existence of statutes regulating the behaviour of companies that we have consumer rights. We might also note that in legal terms, you do not necessarily have to be a human being to have rights – for example, if someone in their will bequeathed a sum of money to be held in trust to fund a student bursary for a particular university, in legal terms, the trust would have certain rights against the university (that is, that it be used to fund students' maintenance and not spent by the university faculty on their Christmas party), though of course only a human being would be able to claim the rights on behalf of the trust.

Rights spoken of in these terms depend upon there being some identifiable status or relationship that positively exists; there must be some qualification entailing my right, for example:

Rights in virtue of citizenship (status)
Rights in virtue of promise or contract (relationship)
Rights as consumers (positive law)

Human rights, in contrast, are said to be rights which are held by virtue of nothing other than our humanity. We do not look for evidence of them in contracts, status, relationships, or positive law; they are, as the American Revolutionaries told us, 'self-evident truths'. More recently, the Office of the High Commissioner for Human Rights tells us:

Human rights are rights inherent to all human beings, whatever our nationality, place of residence, sex, national or ethnic origin, colour, religion, language, or any other status. We are all equally entitled to our human rights without discrimination. These rights are all interrelated, interdependent and indivisible. (OHCHR, no date)

The Universal Declaration of Human Rights (UDHR), an important document in the history of human rights, declares in its preamble that 'the inherent dignity and ... the equal and inalienable rights of all members of the human family is the foundation of freedom, justice and peace in the world'. Which is to say, these rights 'inhere' in us, they exist in human beings insofar as we human beings exist ourselves, and they are inalienable in the sense that we cannot alienate these rights from ourselves – we cannot sign a contract that says that we give up our human rights; no court would recognize the contract as valid. Importantly, they are also equal rights.

So, whereas rights in general, say citizenship rights, depend upon a particular status or relationship, and are thus not always, nor even often, equal, human rights are said to be both equal and universal; they apply to, or are held by, all persons in all places equally, irrespective of any discriminating or particular characteristics of each person. Rights in general can also be variously weighty or trivial (my civil right to vote seems more important than your promissory right that I help you with your essay), whereas human rights are said to represent especially morally weighty claims. The right to vote is a right held by citizens of a country because of their status as citizens of that country, but it is also a human right, set out in Article 21 of the UDHR:

(1) Everyone has the right to take part in the government of his country, directly or through freely chosen representatives.
(2) Everyone has the right of equal access to public service in his country.
(3) The will of the people shall be the basis of the authority of government; this will shall be expressed in periodic and genuine elections which shall be by universal and equal suffrage and shall be held by secret vote or by equivalent free voting procedures.

But we do not usually think that human rights exist only because they are written down in national constitutions, like the US Bill of Rights, or agreed in regional conventions, such as the European Convention on Human Rights (ECHR), or proclaimed in declarations, like the UDHR. I say we do not usually, but one way of understanding human rights does take the fact of human rights' existence in positive law to be foundational – I will discuss this in Chapter 4.

Human rights do of course exist in positive law, notably in the International Bill of Rights (that is the UDHR of 1948 and the International Covenants on Civil and Political Rights, and on Economic,

Social and Cultural Rights of 1966), as well as in regional and national human rights charters. While the UDHR is declaratory in character, and thus is not legally binding, some human rights instruments are legally binding and enforceable, including, in principle, the two international covenants, and, in practice, the ECHR, as well as human rights constitutionally guaranteed by national governments. Human rights law is itself a complex and intriguing field of study which I will touch upon in this book, but only insofar as doing so is necessary to understand the conceptual and philosophical questions that are our primary focus (for a useful introduction to human rights law see, *inter alia*, Sieghart (1985) and Alston et al. (2007)).

For the most part, though, human rights are not understood to be conceptually dependent on the legal recognition of human rights claims. Indeed, human rights are often asserted *precisely because* the recognition of the rights claimed is being denied by governments or legal authorities. But we do not accept that because some authority refuses to recognize a human right, the human right does not exist. On the contrary, we take the authority to be making some kind of moral error. Thus understood, human rights are, in an important sense, *moral* rights, and their being recognized in positive law is rather an affirmation of their legitimacy than a proof of their existence (Wellman, 2011). Human rights are moral rights in the sense of resting on moral argument for their legitimacy.

This moral foundation for human rights gives rise to a degree of ambiguity. Whereas the content of positive rights – those that exist in law – can be identified simply by consulting the relevant statute, moral human rights are those that can be justified in moral reasoning. The contrast is not quite so sharp as this suggests, since laws, even those that are written down, have to be interpreted. Hence, constitutional lawyers and human rights lawyers equally make their living arguing that the rights being claimed by their clients are consistent with the best interpretation of constitutional rights or human rights. But philosophers, activists and politicians can deliberate as to what *moral* human rights are without the aid of an agreed foundational text to interpret.

This helps to explain the protean character of human rights already alluded to – how are debates about what is and is not the object of a moral human right to be decided? I will say more about the possibilities for justifying human rights understood as moral rights in Chapter 3. For now we should note that arguments from moral rights, even those that become recognized in law, can be vulnerable to the charge that they are utopian fictions (as can the whole idea of human rights itself – again see Chapter 3 for Alasdair MacIntyre's critique).

In an article now famous within human rights theory, Maurice Cranston (1967) dismisses some rights recognized in the UDHR as 'manifesto rights', which, he claims, are not real rights at all (cf. Raphael, 1967). Real rights are those rights that meet two tests: they protect interests that are of paramount importance, and they are practicable, that is, they imply obligations that can be met. His critique is symptomatic of a wider concern with the practicality, or perhaps the usefulness, of human rights from the point of view of their claimants. It seems that universal human rights imply duties on all of us, to at least some extent. But duties of all are about as useful as duties of none, for the rights-bearer does not know against whom she can press her claim.

In fact the structure of human rights as affirmed in the International Bill of Rights presupposes that states are the primary duty-bearers – and it is the difficulties facing poor and weak states, in terms of their capacity to honour these obligations, that lead Cranston to doubt that all accepted human rights would pass the practicability test. But even if we accept that human rights need not imply that states are the only duty-bearers and that individual citizens or corporations may have obligations as well, indeterminacy with respect to the allocation of duties is not fatal to the coherence of human rights as a normative framework:

> It is important to emphasize that the recognition of human rights is not an insistence that everyone everywhere rises to help prevent every violation of every human right no matter where it occurs. It is, rather, an acknowledgement that if one is in a plausible position to do something effective in preventing the violation of a human right, then one does have an obligation to consider doing just that … Imperfect obligations have to be distinguished from perfect obligations, which are more specific and more specified, but they must not be confused with no obligations at all. (Sen, 2012, p. 5)

We will return to these thoughts and say more about perfect and imperfect duties in Chapter 8. For now, the important thing to note is the interesting dynamic at work in the relationship between moral human rights and legal or positive human rights. One way of thinking about human rights suggests that human rights are claimed when they are denied, and that they are in effect claims for legal recognition of a moral right:

> Claims of human rights thus ultimately aim to be self-liquidating, giving the possession paradox a distinctive twist. Human rights claims characteristically seek to challenge or change existing institu-

tions, practices, or norms, especially legal practices. Most often they seek to establish (or bring about more effective enforcement of) a parallel 'lower' right. (Donnelly, 2003, p. 12)

This idea of a paradox does seem to capture an important feature of human rights practice. Formal legal recognition is one part of the target of a claim of a human right, effective enforcement is another. Formal recognition and substantive enforcement do not always automatically coexist, as is illustrated in the mismatch between formal acceptance of human rights treaties by governments worldwide and the protection and enjoyment of the world's citizens.

An emerging feature of human rights theory puts human rights to a slightly different purpose than that which Donnelly is describing. In contemporary debates about global justice and climate change we find arguments drawing on the moral authority of human rights to justify the allocation of duties beyond the state to address the underfulfilment or prevent the future violation of human rights (see Chapters 8 and 9).

As well as being moral rights, human rights are also important political concepts. They serve as markers for the just terms of relationships between the citizens and the state; they are also often understood to serve as markers for just terms of action between states (Rawls, 1999; Donnelly, 2003), and to set limits to the legitimate actions of corporations (MacLeod and Lewis, 2004). The systematic violation of human rights has been argued to be a justification for humanitarian intervention (Wheeler, 2000). Understood in this way, human rights set a 'standard of civilisation' (Donnelly, 2007) that justifies sovereignty; if states fall below this standard they are not entitled to the respect of their right to self-determination that sovereignty implies (Jackson, 2000).

Human rights, then, are founded in arguments from normative principles, but as realized in the International Bill of Rights they also presuppose a normative global structure divided into sovereign states. This gives rise to another paradox: human rights both affirm cosmopolitan principles of justice – the principle that a single standard of justice is universally valid, and that the violation of that standard anywhere is a legitimate concern of any citizen of the world – and at the same time, human rights affirm the right to self-determination, which the sovereignty-based international order is conceived to realize. Louis Henkin (1995, 1999) calls this the 'sovereignty paradox'. We will return to this in Chapter 4.

'Cosmopolitan' is a term originally found in Stoic thought in Ancient Greece, and it literally means citizen of the world. Today it denotes a universalist approach to political ethics that is frequently endorsed by some supporters of human rights who see human rights as the expression of the idea that all humans comprise a single moral community (see, *inter alia*, Brock and Brighouse, 2005). However, as Hannah Arendt (1971) was acutely aware, in practice the condition of statelessness is among the most dangerous positions for a human being to be in. To lack the protection of a specific government is typically to be extremely vulnerable in today's world. Arendt thus thought of human rights as a 'right to have rights' within a specific polity.

This territorial division of the world into political communities also points towards the link between human rights and constitutional rights. Many human rights advocates argue that human rights ought to be enshrined in national constitutions, as they are in the US Bill of Rights. In the UK, the ECHR has been incorporated into British law via the Human Rights Acts of 1998 in Scotland and 2000 in the rest of the country – the British government is thereby required to ensure that all its actions are consistent with the rights of citizens as set out in the ECHR (though as I write this, the idea of withdrawing from ECHR and instead instantiating a UK Bill of Rights is under discussion). Constitutional rights provide for the protection of universal human rights in national law (Wellman, 2011). On the other hand, the potential for the ossification of human rights norms when enshrined in constitutions leads some to sound a note of caution here:

> A legal right that finds protection in a Bill of Rights finds it under the auspices of some canonical form of words in which the provisions of the charter are enunciated. One lesson of American constitutional experience is that the words of each provision in the Bill of Rights tend to take on a life of their own, becoming the obsessive catch-phrase for expressing everything one might want to say about the right in question. (Waldron, 1993, p. 26)

Again, this points us to the protean character of rights that Kundera alluded to above – rights claims have a habit of proliferating (Glendon, 1994), and we should remember that this can be true not only of moral rights claims, but also where rights are authoritatively set out in legal documents. The practice of interpretation of legal proclamations of rights can lead to divergent claims, just as can the practice of deliberation about the normative justifications of human rights.

To sum up where we have got to so far, human rights are especially important moral rights that (i) are distinct from general rights, legal rights, and so on, but are sometimes recognized in positive law (and sometimes not) and in constitutions; (ii) have counterpart duties that may or may not be determinate and may or may not be assigned to particular agents; and (iii) serve political functions as normative markers of relations of agents within and between states.

Understanding human rights

We have made some progress in clarifying the concept of a human right, but one point that needs to be unpacked is what a *right* is; this can tell us something about the ways in which human rights, like other rights, register claims, entitlements, prohibitions and duties. Wesley Hohfeld's (1919) classic work remains the authoritative starting point for addressing this question. Hohfeld understood that people at times mean different things by the single term 'rights'. He created a typology of the sorts of entitlements and obligations that specific types of rights give rise to (see Jones, 1994, pp. 12–25, for a very useful overview).

The most easily recognizable of these is the claim right – a claim right is a claim that the rights-holder is entitled to some X that is the object of the right. Claim rights can be further divided into positive or negative claims. A positive claim right is an entitlement to some good or service. A negative claim right is an entitlement to non-interference with respect to the object of the right. So, for example, the human right to education entitles me to access to the provision of schooling. The human right to freedom of conscience entitles me to demand of others that they respect (that is, do not interfere with) my practice of my faith. Note that this neat separation into positive and negative claims is not always, nor often, so distinct. The right to education, for example, can be understood in both positive and negative terms, as implying both an entitlement to provision of the good of education (positive), and as a claim that I not be prevented from accessing education on arbitrary grounds (negative).

Claim rights impose corresponding duties on others to fulfil the claim. If these duties are not performed that will count as a violation of my right. The violation of a right *per se* will not always be serious. If I have promised to help you with your essay, you have a claim right against me, which places me under a duty (in virtue of the promise). Only you could release me from my promise, but if I fail to honour the promise, though I have violated your right, it is a fairly trivial violation of a right. The violation of human rights, however, is in principle a very serious matter. Human rights are entitlements to goods or freedoms that are particularly morally weighty. The violation of a duty to honour a human right would thus be a correspondingly morally weighty failure. It is conceivable, though, that a person could fail to honour a (human) right but for various reasons not be blameable for that failure; perhaps because they were constrained from acting or because there were multiple rights claimants and inadequate resources to meet all claims. In these circumstances, we might distinguish between the violation of a right and the infringement of a right (Gewirth, 1984, p. 92).

Most human rights theorists understand human rights to be claim rights (for example, Shue, 1980; Pogge, 2002; Donnelly, 2003; Griffin, 2008). Carl Wellman argues that this is a mistake, and that human rights are also sometimes other types of rights:

> [T]here are other important moral human rights that are not claim-rights. For example, the moral human right to liberty is, as its name suggests, a liberty-right. Its defining core is the general moral liberty of acting as one chooses as long as so acting does not violate any contrary moral obligation. Although it also contains a moral duty of others not to hinder or prevent one from acting freely without strong justification, it is a misinterpretation to reduce the moral human right to liberty to this negative duty. This duty serves to protect the core moral liberty of this right, not to define its essential content. (Wellman, 2011, pp. 23–4)

Liberty rights in Hohfeld's scheme are the entitlements that arise from the absence of a constraining rule. For example, the seventeenth-century natural rights theorist Thomas Hobbes (1984) affirms the principle that where the law is silent men are free. This is an example of a liberty right. It is an entitlement to do as one pleases. There are no corresponding duties to liberty rights; there is simply the absence of a claim. This gives us reason to think that Wellman's claim that the human right to liberty should be understood as a liberty right in Hohfeld's sense of the term is problematic, because it is hard-wired into the moral architecture of human rights that they represent moral norms that ought to be respected. To assert my right to liberty is implicitly to say that others ought to recognize themselves as being under a (negative) duty to respect it. So, Wellman may be right that the negative *claim* right to liberty (freedom) does not define its essential content, but it seems true that the right to liberty must be a claim right, in Hohfeld's sense, as well as a Hohfeldian liberty right, that is, a right that entails that others do not have a legitimate claim to restrict the right-holder's freedom.

Thus, for the most part within human rights theory we will be dealing with claim rights – rights that assert an entitlement to some good, service, or freedom that is the object of the right, which right places others under a corresponding duty to respect the claim, either positively by meeting it, or negatively by not interfering with the agent's access to it – though we may recognize that liberties that are commonly treated as human rights, for example, freedom of expression, freedom of religion, freedom of association, would normally be understood as conjoining liberty rights and claim rights in Hohfeld's sense of these terms. Human rights may also involve other sorts of Hohfeldian rights as well, such as powers and immunities, but primarily we will be concerned with claim rights.

Two rival conceptual frameworks that may help us make sense of the sorts of rights that are human rights are will or choice theory and interest theory. These theories give distinct answers to the question of the relation between rights and duties. Will theory defines rights in terms of the rights-holder having a power over the duty-bearer to hold (or not) the duty-bearer to the performance of some action (Hart, 1967). If we return to my promise to help you with your essay – I, as the duty-bearer, am not free to release myself from my promise, whereas you, as the right-holder, do have the power to choose to let me go and watch rugby instead (or whatever it is that I wish to do). The point here is that whether or not someone is required to perform a duty correlated to a particular right depends on the 'will', or the choice, of the right-holder.

This is in some sense a useful mechanism for analysing legal rights and contractual rights. With respect to human rights, this theory has been applied to debates about the scope and extent of human rights – advocates of a will-theory approach to conceptualizing human rights typically claim that insofar as there are any human rights, these are more limited than the current lists found in international agreements like the UDHR, because only in those rights where we find a perfect correlation between right-holder and duty-bearer do we really have a right – perhaps only the rights to life and liberty (Hart, 1967; cf. Lercher, 2007). In other cases, we might have some sort of moral obligation, but it does not have the status, and thus the moral weightiness, of a fundamental right.

In contrast, interest theorists (for example, Nickel, 2005) claim that human rights are rights to protect particularly important and morally weighty and universal human interests. Further, for the interest to be a right, it has to be a sufficiently weighty right to give rise to a duty (Raz, 2007), though this need not entail a clear specification of who the duty-bearer is. Insofar as these interests are recognized to be fundamental and universal, then, they are the subject of a human right, even where there is not a perfect correspondence between rights-holders and duty-bearers, as there is in the will theory account. This allows interest theorists to present a greater range of issues and claims in terms of human rights; anything that is a fundamental human interest is potentially the object of a right. This is controversial because it seems as though there are some things that are fundamental human interests but that may not be best protected by rights. For example, any child has a fundamental interest in being loved by her parents, but we would find it odd to say that a father ought to love his child because he has a duty to do so, even though we may think that morally a father ought to love his child (cf. Liao, 2010). Nevertheless, interest theory is the more dominant way of conceptualizing human rights, and can be used to clarify both the justification for human rights (see Chapter 3) and the contents of those goods that should properly be the object of a human right (see examples in Chapters 8 and 9). I will say more about the range of goods and freedoms that can be thought of as objects of human rights below.

Another feature of rights theory in general that is particularly salient in the context of human rights is the idea that rights can act as 'trumps', as Ronald Dworkin put it – they override decisions based on general or aggregate well-being. For much of the nineteenth and the first half of the twentieth centuries moral and political liberal thought was dominated by utilitarianism. Utilitarianism, very broadly speaking, may be understood as endorsing principles which maximize overall utility or happiness or well-being. There are, thus, no right or wrong actions *per se*, rather the moral appropriateness of an action is a function of the outcome it can be reasonably expected to produce.

This is undoubtedly a powerful approach to normative ethics. It is intuitively compelling to think that the right thing to do is often the thing that produces the best outcome for the greatest number of people, and in everyday moral thinking we very often do evaluate choices and actions in terms of their consequences. However, since the revival of political philosophy in the latter half of the twentieth century, beginning with John Rawls' seminal work, *A Theory of Justice*, many scholars have called into question the earlier primacy of utilitarian thinking, and this critique is significant for understanding the current dominance of rights- (and particularly human rights-) based approaches to moral and political ethics.

A central part of the critique of utilitarian thought is that it fails to register the moral significance of individuals (Williams, 1973). For example, it might be true that greater overall utility could be secured by enslaving a small number of people to do particularly difficult or labour-intensive work that produced necessary goods for the rest of society. But to do so seems fundamentally wrong. We might explain this in terms of it being inconsistent with widely held beliefs about the moral equality of all human beings. These beliefs are well captured in rights-based reasoning. If we accept the validity of human rights, held equally and inalienably by all, then we have reason to reject the idea that we can disregard the interests of some to produce greater goods or utility for the majority. The concept of rights captures the thought that the majority is not entitled to disregard the moral standing of any member of society.

An oft-discussed example, which I will briefly return to in Chapter 7, is the torture of people suspected of terrorist offences. The utilitarian may argue that we have plausible grounds for thinking that the torture of a person, if we have reason to believe she has important, potentially life-saving information, may sometimes be justified (cf. Shue, 2012). What the concept of human rights expresses is well captured by Dworkin:

> We want to say that the decision is wrong, in spite of its apparent merit, because it does not take the damage it causes to some into account *in the right way* and therefore does not treat these people as equals entitled to the same concern as others. (Dworkin, 1984, p. 166, emphasis added)

It is not that the utilitarian calculates incorrectly when weighing the merits of different courses of actions and their likely consequences; rather, it is that the utilitarian makes a categorical mistake in failing to take note of the fact that individuals have a legitimate claim never to have their interests disregarded for the sake of others.

Human rights need not be the only component of a morality – indeed, there are good reasons to think that a wholly rights-based morality would be deficient in important respects (Mackie, 1984; cf. Chapter 9) – but they do seem to be an important part of morality. What human rights signal is that human beings have equal moral status and a *prima facie* claim to be respected as such.

We should note, however, that it does not follow from this, nor from the preceding critique of utilitarian thought, that human rights are absolute. Hillel Steiner (1994) has argued for a fully 'compossible' set of rights, by which he means rights that are mutually possible and do not conflict with one another. For the most part, though, human rights theorists expect to find conflicts between competing human rights claims (see, for example, Griffin, 2008), so while it is the case that human rights trump general considerations (such as overall utility), we still face the prospect of trade-offs *between* human rights. For example, the human right to freedom of expression does not extend to the right to incite others to violence; that would compromise another's right to physical security. But in the scales of deliberation about what to do, human rights will weigh as extremely important reasons.

We now have a fuller picture of the concept of a human right. Human rights are especially weighty moral claims that generate corresponding duties, they are typically justified by appeal to universal human interests, they trump competing general claims. In the next section I will say more about the sorts of goods that have been claimed as human rights, and the sorts of agents that might be held to be rights-bearers.

'Three generations' of rights

Human rights are sometimes spoken of in terms of three generations of rights: first-generation rights are, broadly speaking, civil and political rights, second-generation rights are social and economic rights (in some versions, social, economic and cultural rights), and third-generation rights are collective rights and group rights, or sometimes 'solidarity' rights (Wellman, 2000). This division is suggestive of a parallel with the French Revolutionary slogan 'Liberty, Equality, Fraternity'. Historically the first generation of rights is linked with seventeenth- and eighteenth-century struggles for recognition of natural rights, which are thought to be predominantly negative rights. The second-generation social and economic rights are linked with nineteenth-century struggles for social equality and a decent minimum standard of living for the working classes in the context of European industrialization. The third generation of rights is associated with later twentieth-century struggles for the recognition of group claims and rights to self-determination.

The division between first-, second- and third-generation rights in part reflects the separation of the two International Covenants, which implies that there is a conceptual difference between civil and political rights on the one hand, and cultural, social and economic rights on the other – a position rejected by a number of human rights theorists (see Chapter 2). Since 1966 there have been additional claims for new rights to be recognized, such as the right to protection for cultural groups, the right to development, and the right to a safe environment. The 1981 African Charter on Human and Peoples' Rights represents a departure from earlier human rights declarations in giving substantial weight to 'peoples' rights' as well as individual rights (though note that 'peoples' rights' were first raised in the International Covenants). The 2007 Declaration on the Rights of Indigenous Peoples is a further example in this direction.

However, as the discussion in the next chapter suggests, the picture of rights divided into generations oversimplifies a very complex history. Moreover, the purported correspondence between historical moments and particular conceptions of rights is often over-stated. At least some seventeenth- and eighteenth-century natural rights theorists accorded an important place to social and economic rights insofar as they recognized a right to subsistence, and the nineteenth-century struggles for rights were also importantly focused on the campaign to abolish the transatlantic slave trade and the extension of the franchise, classic civil and political rights issues.

Yet, there is some value in this idea of generations of rights insofar as it offers an organizing principle to indicate the range of goods and freedoms that are recognized as human rights; since it is widely drawn on as a foundational text I will first draw attention to rights recognized in the UDHR. I also want to say something in particular in the remainder of this chapter about who can be a rights-bearer, which takes us into questions about the concept of group rights.

The first two articles of the UDHR and the preamble establish conditions of equal enjoyment of the rights set forth in the declaration and affirm the equal dignity of all human beings. There follow a further 28 articles.

Articles 3 to 22 affirm recognizably civil and political rights, including:

Rights to liberties or freedoms:
    (3) The right to life, liberty and security of person
    (4) Rights against slavery and an explicit prohibition on all forms of the slave trade
    (5) Rights against torture, cruel, inhuman and degrading treatment or punishment
  (12) A right to privacy
  (13) Freedom of movement within and between countries
  (14) A right to asylum
  (18) Freedom of conscience.

Civil rights including:
    (6) To recognition as a person before the law

     (7) Equality before the law
     (9) Against arbitrary arrest, detention or exile
    (10) To an independent trial and to know any charges against oneself
    (11) The presumption of innocence until guilt is proven.

  Political rights including:
    (19) Freedom of association (also a right to liberty)
    (20) Freedom of expression (also a right to liberty)
    (21) The right to participate in government, including the declaration that 'the will of the people shall be the basis of the authority of government; shall be expressed in periodic and genuine elections which shall be by universal and equal suffrage and shall be held by secret vote or by equivalent free voting procedures'.

Articles 22 to 26 affirm recognizably social and economic rights, including:

    (22) A right to social security
    (23) The right to work, including the right to equal pay for equal work and to belong to a trade union
    (24) The right to leisure
    (25) A standard of living adequate for health and well-being; Article 25 also recognizes special protections for motherhood and childhood and prohibits discrimination between children born 'in or out of wedlock'
    (26) Rights to education; Article 26 also recognizes the rights of parents to direct the children's education.

There are also articles that could plausibly be described as affirming third-generation rights: Article 27 declares a right to participate in the cultural life of the community. Article 29 includes this statement: 'Everyone has duties to the community in which alone the free and full development of his personality is possible.' Article 28 declares the right of all to 'a social and international order in which the rights and freedoms set forth in this Declaration can be fully realized'. The UDHR also protects property rights, which could be understood to be either a civil and political right, or an economic right.

  However, as noted above, human rights are fundamentally moral rights, so we should not expect that questions as to the content of human rights can be answered by reference to existing declarations alone. Rights not recognized in international law and practice are also affirmed as human rights, including the right to a safe environment, the right to same-sex marriage, rights to collective ownership of natural resources and the human right to water. Moreover, some of the rights recognized in positive law are attacked by some scholars and critics as not being human rights at all.

The majority of these rights are clearly individual rights. They may sometimes or often be exercised in concert with others, but they are rights held by individuals. For many human rights theorists, human rights are axiomatically individual rights – they are protections against the arbitrary use and abuse of power and authority. Rights held by groups, it is feared, could not be protected without risk to the rights of individuals. But this individualistic conception of human rights is much criticized, as I will discuss further in Chapters 5 and 6. Although perhaps the majority of human rights theorists – certainly those working within the liberal tradition that dominates the literature – tend not to be readily receptive to the idea of group rights (for example, Kukathas, 1992; Donnelly, 2003; and Tasioulas, 2010, all reject the idea for diverse, if overlapping reasons), there are those who defend a limited number of group rights or collective rights:

> Collective human rights are rights the bearers of which are collectivities, which are not reducible to, but are consistent with individual human rights, and the basic justification of which is the same as the basic justification of individual human rights. Some human-rights theorists argue either that there are no collective human rights or that there are collective human rights but all such rights are derivative from individual human rights. [But] there are non-derivative collective human rights which are justified by the grounding value of the interest that individuals have in the quality of their own lives. (Freeman, 1995, p. 38)

What Freeman has in mind here are the interests of a group in the maintenance of its culture. Despite the inclusion of peoples' rights in the African Charter, there is a fair bit of scepticism about the coherence of the idea of collective rights, and their justifiability from a story about universal interests. In the end, there may not be much distance between individually justified rights to collective goods that can only be achieved in groups, and collective rights that are justified via an account of the good that they have for individuals. If there is much difference, then the 'humanness' – the purported universality – of the rights is in question (Donnelly, 2003). I return to these issues in Chapter 7.

A different sort of collective right could be ascribed to future generations, based on the fundamental human interest in a safe environment, which passes the 'universal' test. This is of potential significance for debates about climate change, but in fact theorists of human rights and climate change have tended to follow the conventional route of understanding human rights to be rights held by individuals (see Chapter 9; cf. Wellman, 2000). In what follows, then, I will mostly be concerned with individual rights.

Conclusion

My aim in this chapter is to outline various ways of conceptualizing human rights in order to facilitate means of understanding the range of rights that are debated and the justificatory strategies adopted in the chapters that follow. My hope is that human rights are not, as Kundera worried, becoming meaningless, but it is certainly not the case that there is a single, simple, and widely agreed answer to the question: what is a human right?

In general, we can say that human rights are especially morally weighty claims that signal the moral equality and moral importance of all human beings. They are most often justified in relation to universal and important human interests. They are moral rights, in the sense of not being dependent on positive recognition in law for their validity. Human rights have counterpart duties or obligations, which may or may not be clearly allocated. They protect a significant range of goods and freedoms, which, when combined, express necessary, though not necessarily sufficient, minimum conditions for a good human life.

To be able to say more about what human rights are, and to approach the question of what might justify the claim that human beings have human rights, I turn in the next chapter to a brief history of human rights.

2 A Brief History of Human Rights

'It is true that the United Nations put the term "human rights" to new uses, but they did not just amputate its history. They combined new elements with old, both of which must be kept in mind in order to properly understand current thought about human rights.' (Griffin, 2011, p. 14)

Introduction

Human rights as they exist in the world today, in statute, international agreements, political claims and philosophical debates, are importantly influenced by the historical antecedents by which they have been shaped. As James Griffin points out above, human rights did not fall from the sky fully formed in 1948. The ideas and practices of preceding generations of scholars, lawyers, political leaders and citizen activists influenced and informed the text of the Universal Declaration of Human Rights and the claims and contestations of contemporary activists and theorists. This chapter explores some of the ways in which earlier concepts of natural rights and Western ideas about freedom, equality and justice have shaped contemporary understandings of human rights. It also reflects on the ways in which important historical events have inspired new developments in the concept of human rights. We may justly hold, with Griffin, that understanding these histories is crucial to understanding contemporary human rights.

If we look for them, we can find more and less substantial traces of ideas that cohere with the content of contemporary human rights in multiple religious and secular ethical traditions, from many times and places in human history. Many of the ethical claims at the heart of contemporary human rights norms, such as the idea that (human) life is sacred, that private property ought to be respected, that persons should enjoy equality before the law, that there is value in education for all, that religious freedom ought to be respected, are to be found in many different political, religious and ethical contexts, in recent and distant history (Hayden, 2001; Ishay, 2008). But if we want to explain whence emerged *human rights* as an idea, specifically an idea about the legitimate claims of individual citizens against their government, codified in legal declarations, and held individually and universally, then that story will be predominantly European and North American in its pre-twentieth-century history, whatever the contemporary cross-cultural appeal of such claims (Panikkar and Panikkar, 1982; Dower, 1996; Freeman, 2002; Ishay, 2004).

The story of the development of the concept of human rights that I tell here is necessarily highly selective. I focus on three moments in the history of human rights, and reflect on theorists and ideas that inform contemporary accounts of human rights. These moments are (i) the American and French Revolutions of the late eighteenth century and their proclamations of 'natural rights'; (ii) the socialist response to the industrial revolution of the nineteenth century and the international abolitionist movement; and (iii) the Second World War and subsequent development of a global human rights regime in the twentieth century. Different histories of the idea of human rights can be and have been told, histories that acknowledge in far more detail the rich and diverse tapestry of philosophical, legal and political ideas and events that have informed the concept of human rights (for example, Hunt, 2007; Ishay, 2004). In this brief historical overview, I single out some significant points of reference in a much more complex story.

Natural rights in the eighteenth century

The idea that individuals have inalienable rights that inhere in them simply in virtue of their humanity may not strike contemporary readers as particularly startling or controversial. In recent decades human rights have become *the* authoritative language in which to advance moral claims in many political contexts. But it was not always like this. The concept of individual human rights emerged from a set of ideas about natural rights and about the limits of government authority and the legitimate claims of citizens and subjects. The practice of proclaiming the content of such entitlements, and thus prescribing the limits of sovereign authority, in a single authoritative document, goes back at least as far as the English Magna Carta of 1215. The 1789 French *Declaration of the*

Rights of Man and the Citizen, and the 1791 American Bill of Rights continued this tradition, and were important precursors to the 1948 UDHR. Note, however, that the Magna Carta, like the 1688 English Bill of Rights, referred to the 'Ancient Rights of Englishmen', rather than men or humans in the abstract, in contrast to the Declarations of 1789 and 1948. The universality and abstraction of contemporary human rights are distinctive features that we first encounter in eighteenth-century proclamations of rights.

Both the French *Declaration* and the American Bill of Rights should be seen in the context of eighteenth-century Enlightenment thought, a heady mix of ideas about the human capacity for reason and the insights and knowledge advanced through empiricist approaches that informed an explosion of ideas about the social and political world. This rationalist approach was particularly evident in the French Enlightenment, while Scottish Enlightenment ideas about the nature of man, man's capacities for sympathy and the institutional character of commercial society had a greater influence on American thinkers and leaders. The Enlightenment in all contexts was also informed and influenced by remarkable social and political upheaval across Europe and North America. The political and religious calls for freedom that emerged in this period were themselves importantly informed by post-Reformation debates about toleration and the proper use of state power over the spiritual lives of citizens. The state's paradoxical role as both guarantor of rights and as power against which the protections of rights are needed, is already evident in seventeenth-century conceptions of natural rights, just as it is in contemporary theories of human rights.

John Locke (1632–1704), a key figure in the development of ideas of toleration and natural rights, had a significant influence on Enlightenment philosophy in a number of fields, including political philosophy. As a 'social contract' theorist, he used a particular structure to explore questions about the proper limits of government authority and the natural rights of individual citizens. He imagines men existing in what he calls a 'state of nature', with no government, no laws, no judges or police, nor formal civil or political institutions of any kind, and tries to imagine the sort of freedom that men would have in that pre-institutional state. He finds that in the absence of government three specific 'inconveniences' emerge: there are no settled laws, there is no impartial judge, and there is no independent executioner to punish transgressions. As a result, conflict is inevitable, and thus progress is stunted, because progress depends upon stability and security, and, as Locke tells us, God gave the earth to 'the industrious and the rational', so it is humans' duty to pursue God's plan (1988, V, 34). Thus, Locke concludes, it is rational to submit to government so as to avoid the inconveniences of the state of nature, but it is only rational to consent to such government as will preserve our natural rights, specifically, our rights to 'life, liberty, health and possessions' (1988, II, 5). Only a government that upholds natural rights is legitimate; indeed, the function of government is to secure our natural rights. (These natural rights set the limits of the legitimate 'social contract'.) This paradoxical role for the state also arises in contemporary human rights.

Locke was responding to the modernist ideas of his near contemporaries Thomas Hobbes (1588–1679) and Robert Filmer (1588–1653), whose pre-modernist defence of the divine right of kings was influential in his day. Hobbes and Filmer were in turn responding to the political crises that emerged in the years of the English Civil War and the Thirty Years' War in Europe. However, Locke's argument resonated significantly with the ideas of the later *philosophes* of eighteenth-century France, and with the American Revolutionaries who sought and won independence from colonial Britain; indeed, the American Declaration of Independence of 1776 echoed Locke's terminology and endorsed his ideas when it proclaimed:

> We hold these truths to be self-evident, that all men are created equal, that they are endowed by their Creator with certain unalienable Rights, that among these are Life, Liberty and the pursuit of Happiness – that to secure these rights, governments are instituted among men, deriving their just powers from the consent of the governed. That whenever any form of government becomes destructive of these ends, it is the right of the people to alter or abolish it.

More on the Enlightenment

The Enlightenment was a period of intense philosophical and scientific discovery, which coincided with, and was connected to, the radical political change, and ultimately revolution, in North America in 1776 and France in 1789. Both the French and American Revolutions emerged against a backdrop of significant economic and social change, as well as from a period of intellectual innovation.

Isaac Newton (1642–1727), the founder of modern physics who was mythologized by the poet Alexander Pope ('Nature and nature's laws lay hid in night/ God said, "Let Newton be", and all was light'), was a hero to Enlightenment philosophers as well as to later scientists. He applied reason to the problem of understanding the natural world and in doing so overturned existing ideas, wiping away religiously informed 'superstitions' or 'prejudices' about the nature of the world. We might also remember that Newton was a committed alchemist, so his status as the champion of modern rational empiricism is interesting. Nevertheless, he was held to embody the enlightened approach that eighteenth-century thinkers sought to apply to the social world as well as the natural world.

What this approach suggests is that if we can understand the truth of human nature, then it should be possible to create institutions that would solve common human problems like poverty. Socially engaged philosophers, such as the English thinker Jeremy Bentham (1748–1832), held that, via the application of reason and scientific investigation, we could ultimately free ourselves from all the superstitions and prejudices that impede progress. Note that the logic of this project presupposes that people are fundamentally the same everywhere, that there *is* such a thing as human nature (that is, receptive to pleasure and pain in relevantly similar ways, capable of reason in relevantly similar ways), which is universal, and which, once understood, holds the key to a formula for social peace, harmony and progress, whether in America, France, India or anywhere.

Bentham, we should note, was a sufficiently committed empiricist to reject the idea of natural rights as 'rhetorical nonsense - nonsense upon stilts' (Waldron, 1987). For Bentham, laws necessarily emanate from a sovereign authority. The idea of natural rights is nonsensical because they claim authority for a set of rights in abstraction from any sovereign. The hugely influential German philosopher Immanuel Kant (1724–1804) defended an account of moral philosophy grounded in the demands of reason, and offered the most systematic attempt to show, on the contrary, that principles of right could be justified without recourse to either worldly or divine authority. Kant's thought is another important marker in the development of ideas that shaped human rights.

Perhaps the most influential figure in the French Enlightenment, the Swiss philosopher Jean-Jacques Rousseau (1712–78), was rather less optimistic than many of his contemporaries about both the Enlightenment idea of progress and the promise of reason. Scottish Enlightenment philosophers, such as David Hume (1711–76) and Adam Smith (1723–90), were also rather more circumspect than many French *philosophes* about the limits of reason (Berry, 1997). Rousseau saw that our capacity for rationality had the potential to be dangerous, and though he thought that if directed in the right way it could lead to freedom, he had a particular understanding of freedom. Even in an apparently free society we can become corrupted by our desires, most of all our desire for social status, hence inequality in society is a pernicious evil (Rousseau, 1984). Nevertheless, he accepts some typically Enlightenment principles; he accepts the truth of there being a universal human nature and, from this, universally valid principles of government. For Rousseau, as for Kant, true freedom consists in following the law that you yourself have willed. This vision of freedom significantly informed the French Revolutionaries, who sought to remodel French society in radical ways, erasing centuries of religiously and culturally informed practice, a project that was at times brutally realized.

Article 6 of the *Declaration* includes Rousseau's phrase and sense of 'the general will', stating 'The law is the expression of the general will', and Rousseau is credited with the first use of the phrase '*droit de l'homme*', in print at least. Indeed, there is much to be said in favour of the view that Rousseau's political vision was the single most significant influence on the language of the *Declaration* (see Baker, 1988; van Kley, 1997).

On the other hand, it is also worth remembering the impact of Rousseau's epistolary novel, *Julie, or the New Héloïse*, an international bestseller that told a romantic story of lovers divided by class and parental expectations. Lynn Hunt argues persuasively that the birth of the idea of human rights owed a considerable debt to the concurrent emergence of the novel, and particularly the epistolary novel, as an enormously popular genre that encouraged and facilitated the empathetic identification of readers with people who were separated from them by thick boundaries of class, gender or nationality: 'reading novels created a sense of equality and empathy through passionate involvement in the narrative' (Hunt, 2007, p. 39). The imaginative identification fostered in novels prepared the ground for the shared moral community expressed in a proclamation of universal rights. The idea that our capacity for imaginative sympathy is crucial to the development of our moral senses is a central idea of Smith's thought, which is known to have influenced some of the key figures in the American Revolution.

We should note, however, the impacts of political and social realities as well as ideas. What began as a slave revolt in the French colony of Saint-Dominigue in 1791 became the Haitian Revolution, leading to the founding of Haiti as a state, the first state to be run by former African slaves who through revolution claimed their freedom. The significance of this landmark event is manifold. It was an assertion of freedom and personhood by black slaves on their own behalf. There were many slave revolts before and after this, but few can be said to have demonstrated so strikingly what the *philosophes* claimed in the abstract – that all men are free and equal. Of course, most *philosophes* understood 'men' to mean 'white men'. Though the radical new ideas emerging from the Enlightenment were undoubtedly influential, particularly on responses to the Haitian uprising in Europe and North America, the Haitian Revolution itself was first and foremost born of the appalling brutality of slavery and the striking injustices perpetrated by white plantation owners.

Before the descent into the Terror, the French Revolution embodied some remarkable achievements. The rights of women were debated, but not, in the end, instantiated in law. Torture was abolished, and legal punishments made more humane (for example, the guillotine, later a symbol of the horror of the Terror, was considerably less cruel than the erstwhile standard practice of breaking on the wheel or strangulation by hanging). Slavery was abolished, but later reinstated by Napoleon. We should not pretend that the abolition of slavery in the French colonies was purely an act of disinterested virtue on the part of the French deputies. On the contrary, turmoil in the colonies and war with rival colonial powers Britain and Spain made the abolition of slavery in the colonies strategically vital to holding on to the territories and the income they produced for France. Nevertheless, abolition would have been unimaginable had it not been for the *Declaration* and the claims of liberty and equality *for all men* contained within it (Singham, 1994; Hunt, 2007).

Another significant development was the recognition of Jews as entitled to citizenship rights for the first time. The development of citizenship rights for Jews illustrates what Hunt calls the powerful 'inner logic' of human rights (2007, p. 150), which we will observe again in later developments. Although questions of Jewish rights were debated publicly before the Revolution, and indeed were the subject of a commission established by Louis XVI in 1788, Deputies to the National Assembly at first thought only of granting religious freedom to Protestants. Calls for political rights for Protestants were defended on the grounds that Protestants, unlike Jews, were truly Frenchmen. When Protestants were granted civil and political rights, Jewish groups began petitioning for like rights for themselves, basing their claim on the inconsistency of proclaiming universal rights to the abstract categories 'man' and 'citizen', whilst excluding minorities from the definition of 'man' and 'citizen'. Similarly structured claims were made on behalf of excluded groups such as slaves, free black men and propertyless men, but rarely on behalf of women. A notable exception was Olympe de Gouges (1748–93), whose 1791 *Declaration of the Rights of Women and the Citizen* clearly drew on the language of the 1789 *Declaration*. She was executed during the Terror for her political activities.

Prior to this period the status of non-Europeans, Jews, women, homosexuals, religious minorities and poor people was very clearly inferior to the status of propertied Christian white men. Both formal law and informal social conventions reflect the conviction that some people were not fully human beings at all. In the course of the Enlightenment we find these assumptions begin to be challenged in light of emerging ideas about a universal human nature and the promise of reason. Calls for women's rights in this period include Mary Wollstonecraft's (1759–97) *Vindications of the Rights of Women* as well as de Gouges' *Declaration of the Rights of Women and the Citizen*. De Gouges was also a prominent abolitionist, who, along with philosophers such as Rousseau and Voltaire, published attacks on slavery. First-hand accounts of slavery written by freed slaves were also circulating in this period; amongst the most successful was Olaudah Equiano's (1745–97) *Interesting Narrative*, published in 1789, which contributed significantly to the development of a public re-evaluation of the status of slaves. In 1791 a new criminal code was approved in France that decriminalized sodomy for the first time in Western Europe, and in England Bentham was one of the first to publicly argue for the decriminalization of sodomy. These developments all owed something to the prominence of Enlightenment ideas which made possible the development of claims for rights.

Of course, the reality of the French Revolution was very far from an Enlightened ideal in many ways, but what has been of lasting significance is the universalism of the French *Declaration*; it proclaims the 'natural, inalienable, and sacred rights of man' (Preamble), and declares unequivocally, 'Men are born and remain free and equal in rights' (Article 1).

In response to events in France, and long before the height of the Terror, the Anglo-Irish philosopher and politician Edmund Burke (1729–97) published the hastily written and remarkably prescient *Reflections on the Revolution in France*, in which he savagely attacked the very idea of natural rights, and the principle of universal morality. In response to Burke's text, Thomas Paine (1737–1809), the English-born American Revolutionary, published *The Rights of Man*, a spirited defence of the idea of natural rights. Burke's attack and Paine's defence each establish positions that are echoed by critics and defenders of the idea of human rights in the twentieth and early twenty-first centuries.

Burke's Reflections

Above all, Burke is disenchanted with the Enlightenment fascination with reason. The idea that you could, by means of empirical investigation, discover the universal nature of man, and then, by reasoning (and by nothing other than reason), determine solutions to social problems everywhere, is, for Burke, an utter absurdity.

The *Declaration of the Rights of Man and the Citizen* purports to proclaim the natural freedoms of 'all mankind', the truth of which is evident to us by virtue of our capacity for reason. Although these rights and freedoms are sacred, we not need look for scriptural evidence for their validity, nor to the authority of kings or ancient philosophers, for we know it by our own processes of reasoning. The fact that previous generations and authorities have not come to the same conclusion shows not our faulty reasoning, but their limitations.

To Burke this is nonsense. Reason is limited, and each person's stock of reason is small. Moreover, each person, with self-interest to blind him, can very easily reach faulty conclusions that he claims to derive from 'pure reason'. Thus, Burke favourably compares 'the wisdom of ages' with the results of the reasoned conclusions of an individual. For Burke, the state is properly a partnership between the present generation, previous generations and future generations. A political settlement based on individual rights allows the present generation to tear up all its obligations and duties of honour to previous generations, and leaves a mess for future generations.

Two pointed attacks are particularly noteworthy. First, the category of 'man', in abstraction from his own particular circumstances, has no meaning for Burke. 'Government is not made in virtue of natural rights, which may and do exist in total independence of it, and exist in much greater clarity and in a much greater degree of abstract perfection; but their abstract perfection is their practical defect.' He goes on, 'What is the use of discussing a man's abstract right to food or medicine? The question is upon the method of procuring and administering them.' (Burke, 1987, p. 52) The key point here is that it is not the business of government to pontificate in abstraction but to meet concrete needs and administer the resources of the community for the sake of future generations and out of a sense of debt and honour to preceding generations; theorizing in abstraction about rights is of no practical use in achieving this.

Second, Burke defends the 'rights of Englishmen', validated by tradition and positive law, and credible because they are defensible and specific claims, in contrast to the 'rights of man', which exist only in abstraction and but are allegedly valid everywhere. On the contrary, Burke contends, these abstract rights have no authority, because authority must derive from tradition and convention, whereas the authority of the rights of man derives from nothing but proclamations; they are fictions, inventions, they have no standing in the world.

The abstraction of the idea of natural rights, the practical emptiness of natural rights claims, and the specious foundational authority of natural rights claims, are all significant attacks on the concept of natural rights that are echoed in later debates about human rights.

Paine's Rights of Man

Paine's rebuttal of Burke's argument, *The Rights of Man*, likewise, resonates with many contemporary defences of human rights. Burke says there are no 'rights of man' abstracted from his social and political context, only rights of Englishmen, or Frenchmen; rights of citizens of specific countries dependent upon the authority of the constitutions and conventions of those states. Against this, Paine asserts that Burke must either mean to deny that any man has rights anywhere, or that he is making a claim about the origin of rights. If the latter, Paine argues that the origin of civil rights – the rights of Englishmen or Frenchmen in Burke's terms – are ultimately to be found in natural rights. 'The error of those who reason by precedents drawn from antiquity, respecting the rights of man, is that they do not go far enough into antiquity. They do not go the whole way.' (Paine, Pt IV). While Burke thinks we have to look to the wisdom of preceding generations for an authoritative account of rights, for Paine, we must go back to the origin of man to find the origin of rights. The origin of both is found in God.

All religious doctrines agree that 'men are all of one degree, and consequently that all men are born equal, and with equal natural right' (Paine, Pt IV). As a matter of fact, not all religions do agree on that, but the majority of Paine's initial readers who professed a faith would have been Christians and Jews. From the Biblical account of creation, Paine notes that 'no distinction [is] implied' in the status of man, thus he claims divine authority for his doctrine of the equality of man (1999). Moreover, Paine claims, the laws of all countries acknowledge 'degrees in crimes but not in persons', which again affirms the principle of equality before the law, a principle under varyingly active debate since the Magna Carta at least.

Key to Paine's argument, then, is the relationship of civil rights to natural rights, and here we find very strongly the influence of Locke:

natural rights are ultimately an entail from God's creation of man. These rights are principally the rights of 'the intellect', that is, conscience and expression, and the 'rights of acting as an individual for his own comfort and happiness, which are not injurious to the natural rights of others' (Paine, 1999). This suggests the core character of natural rights as rights of non-interference, which are necessarily equal rights for all, since each has rights insofar as he does not infringe on the rights of others; logically, that implies the moral equality of human beings.

The religious character of the justification for natural rights in the work of thinkers like Locke and Paine is of course distinctly different from the typically secular justification of human rights. Later scholars looking for a secular foundation would often find it in a Kantian story about the dignity of man inhering in man's capacity for reason (see Chapter 3 for an example). What either strategy upholds is the claim that there is something morally significant about a man, *qua* man, such that he ought not to be treated in particular ways – this is particularly explicit in the French *Declaration*, which proclaims the rights of 'Man and the Citizen', thus does not confine itself to the jurisdiction of French territory. This is the universalism that Burke found spurious.

The ways in which men ought not to be treated in seventeenth- and eighteenth-century conceptions of natural rights are sometimes characterized as reflecting the rights of the political and economic agent (MacPherson, 1962). Arguably, this does not quite capture the whole story of either Paine's or Locke's account of natural rights: Locke's (1988) 'subsistence proviso', which limits the right to accumulate in the state of nature (such that 'enough and as good' is left for others), underwrites a commitment to the welfare of others that is grounded in our duties to God. Paine (1999) explicitly includes welfare rights in his account of the rights of man. Nevertheless, the principal rights defended both in philosophical tracts and in public declarations in this period are rights to hold property, rights to religious freedom, rights to equality before the law and rights to participate in government. And we should note that in practice many defenders of these rights for white Europeans were deeply disconcerted by such rights being claimed by black Africans.

If natural rights, like human rights, protect the inherent dignity of man, then we can read in these natural rights a story about the 'standard threats' to man's freedom, or to his dignity; despotic government and religious tyranny are the chief concerns of Enlightenment defenders of natural rights. This view of the kinds of threats against which rights are needed for protection itself discloses some assumptions about the nature of man. On this view, seventeenth- and eighteenth-century natural rights are the rights of the relatively privileged.

Social and economic rights in the nineteenth century

The next moment in our history of the concept of human rights is the Western European industrial revolution of the nineteenth century. Rapid industrial innovation both created a demand for labour in urban areas where factories were concentrated and displaced labouring people from rural areas in the wake of the mechanization of many industries. This industrial expansion was closely connected to the wealth produced by the transatlantic slave trade. Concurrently, social movements demanded the end of slavery internationally and the extension of the franchise domestically. Revolutionary movements across Europe led uprisings in 1848 (the overwhelming majority, ultimately, unsuccessfully), in the name of equality and democracy. We should also note the dramatic rise of nationalism as a social and political force in nineteenth-century Europe and beyond. Calls for the democratic equality of national groups sat alongside assertions of national pride and calls to deny rights to minorities within nations.

In this context of enormous social, economic and political upheaval, socialist ideas came to prominence. Political thought in the nineteenth century was notably characterized by a move away from the abstraction of rights claims towards the purportedly more scientific utilitarian thought championed by Bentham and John Stuart Mill (1806–73) in liberal circles, the dialectical idealism of the German philosopher G. W. F. Hegel (1770–1831), and the economic materialism of Karl Marx (1818–83) and his followers.

Karl Marx's 1844 essay *On the Jewish Question* is his most direct engagement with the concept of natural rights (his thought at this time owes a significant debt to Hegel, his later work is more markedly driven by his political-economic theory). It is a reply to work by Bruno Bauer in which the latter addresses the prospects for emancipation of the Jews. The 'Jewish question' was a topic that interested political and religious thinkers in an age that saw the consolidation of nation-states as the primary political unit. The status of minorities, and the potential for minority rights, remained as an anomalous feature in this political model, and thus represented a political problem (we will return to the issue of minority rights in Chapter 7). Although the French *Declaration* had granted citizenship rights to Jews for the first time, anti-Semitism remained a widespread formal and informal feature of European life. In this essay Marx critiques what he calls 'the so-called rights of man', exposing the falseness of the question of *political* emancipation for the Jews. Equal civil and political rights for the Jews would not, for Marx, realize their true emancipation, because civil and political emancipation is *not* human emancipation.

To understand that claim, it is necessary to analyse what is offered in civil and political rights, and, on Marx's reading, we find that what is offered is equality before the law, and what the law principally does is protect citizens' property. But property is unevenly distributed: the capitalists own the means of production, whilst the proletariat have only their labour to sell. These protections, then, far from granting us freedoms, serve to alienate us from our true selves, and thus the freedom offered in civil and political emancipation is a false freedom. Bauer saw that legal and political freedom for Jews would not equate to real freedom so long as the influence of organized religion, both in the state and society, persisted. But for Marx, this is only half the question of just what emancipation is. He writes:

> Let us notice first of all that the so-called rights of man, the *droits de l'homme* as distinct from the *droits du citoyen*, are simply the rights of a *member of civil society*, that is, the rights of egoistic man, separated from other men and from the community. (1978, p. 42)

The influence of Rousseau can be seen in Marx's belief that man is not naturally egoistic, but that he is socialiszd into this by corrupt commercial (in Marx's terms, capitalist) society. The separation of men from other men, and from the community, is characteristic of their alienation from themselves, their work, and their true sociable natures, all of which is a consequence of the competitive drive engendered by capitalism. The freedom offered under capitalism is an empty freedom: 'The practical application of man's right to liberty is man's right to *private property*.' (Marx, 1978, p. 42) But that freedom discloses an implicit understanding of the nature of the man thus protected by such rights: 'finally, it is man as a bourgeois, and not man as a citizen who is considered to be the *true* and *authentic* man' (Marx, 1978, p. 43). Thus, what is offered in the seventeenth- and the eighteenth-century project of natural rights is not emancipation at all:

> [M]an was not liberated from religion; he received religious liberty. He was not liberated from property; he received the liberty to own

property. He was not liberated from the egoism of business; he received the liberty to engage in business. (Marx, 1978, p. 45)

Marx's ambivalence towards political rights, and his insistence on the material foundations of true freedom, can be seen as having influenced the 1918 Bolshevik *Declaration of Rights of Working and Exploited People*, which embraced the universalism of the 1789 *Declaration* – it proclaimed rights for workers everywhere – but eschewed entirely the notion of democratic political rights. Marx's contemporary, the French socialist Louis Blanc (1811–82), is similarly dismissive of the freedom offered in the French *Declaration*:

> But the poor man, you say, has the *right* to better his position? So!
> And what difference does it make, if he has not the power to do so?
> What does the right to be cured matter to a sick man whom no one is
> curing? Right considered abstractly is the mirage that has kept the
> people in abused condition since 1789 ... Let us say it then for once
> and for all: freedom consists, not only in the RIGHTS that have been
> accorded, but also in the power given men to develop and exercise
> their faculties, under the reign of justice and the safeguard of law.
> (Blanc, 1848)

Whereas Marx foresaw the eventual withering of the state as a necessary condition of freedom, and the Russian anarchist Mikhail Bakunin (1814–76) saw in any process of institutionalization the incipient corruptive influence of state power, Blanc accepted a role for the state as a vehicle for achieving true emancipation. Blanc's evident scepticism about rights here is illustrative of a wider hostility to the concept of rights amongst some left-leaning critics. While Marx's near contemporary Pierre-Joseph Proudhon (1809–65), for example, accepted the majority of the rights proclaimed in the French *Declaration*, but rejected the right to private property – 'property is theft' he famously declared – Marx, on the other hand, was much more sceptical of the very idea of natural rights.

The Marxist attitude to natural rights as a concept, and the debates within socialism about the role of the state, could lead us to overlook the significance of Marxist and socialist thought in the shaping of the concept of human rights, which, in their twentieth-century incarnation, remain institutionally enmeshed in a network of sovereign states. What is undoubtedly important for the history of human rights is the emergence in these nineteenth-century debates of a fierce critique of the limited nature of the freedom afforded by natural rights as conceived in the American and French Revolutions and in the ideas of eighteenth-century defenders of these revolutions. If freedom and equality were at all connected, then material inequality was itself a barrier to universal freedom, a point accepted by Rousseau but not Locke. If that is so, then social and economic rights are a necessary corrective to the empty, or, at any rate privileged, freedom of civil and political rights.

This conclusion is the outcome of an 'immanent critique' of the concept of natural rights, undertaken by the left, that has been repeated by activists and scholars holding various perspectives, and which as a process has become a feature of the development of human rights (Stammers, 1999). Critics like Marx and his collaborator Friedrich Engels (1820–95), the Chartists and the Fabians in Britain, pro-democracy and anti-slavery campaigners in the USA, and French and Russian socialists of various stripes, all took the promise of freedom and equality in the idea of natural rights and applied it critically to the practice of rights as then entrenched in national laws. To whom did these rights accord freedom, they asked, and who was excluded?

Thus, we should not overlook the struggle for civil and political rights led by socialists, and informed by socialist thought, in the nineteenth century. An important example is the fight for universal suffrage, the final extension of a 'liberal' right, which was driven by socialist movements demanding an end to property qualifications for male voters in the nineteenth century, and towards the end of that century and into the twentieth century by early feminists who demanded the vote for women. Universal male suffrage was first introduced in France in 1850, but retracted within months when the National Assembly re-imposed a property qualification for voting. In the UK, the Chartist Petition of 1837 called for universal male suffrage, which was finally achieved in the Second Reform Act of 1867, though it would be 1928 before the Equal Franchise Act accorded votes to women and men on the same footing.

The call for an end to the transatlantic slave trade, and then to the practice of slavery itself in European countries, colonies and in the USA, was in an important sense a call for traditional liberty rights, but for those rights to be extended to a category of persons not hitherto (legally) recognized to be the moral equals of white men. In this and the previous example we see the 'inner logic' of human rights at work. Note, however, that while many commentators at the time presented the call for an end to slavery in terms of a moral imperative and the demands of justice (though relatively few phrased this in terms of rights), some historians (for example, Williams, 1944) have subsequently argued that the question of motives was more complex, and that economic self-interest played a role in the decisions to abolish both the trade in slaves and the practice of slavery. This point illustrates another contemporary issue in human rights debates – compliance with human rights standards is sometimes attacked as a matter of *Realpolitik*, a point we will return to in later chapters.

The international dimension of the anti-slavery movement, the internationally oriented socialist movements and the early feminist movement, all emerging against the backdrop of nineteenth-century nationalism, stand out as precursors of the global human rights movement that would achieve remarkable reach in the twentieth century. Though undertaken by many who were critics of the Enlightenment, these internationalist projects themselves owed something to Enlightenment visions of universalism, articulated most clearly as a political project in Kant's (1795) *Sketch for Perpetual Peace*.

Another example of this burgeoning internationalism, and a landmark development in the emergence of an international institutional apparatus of human rights, is the 1864 Geneva Convention, which established protections for wounded soldiers and immunity for those attending them. The Convention was inspired in significant part by the Swiss J. Henri Dunant's *Memory of Solferino*, his account of the horrors of the battle between Austrian troops and French and Italian troops at Solferino in 1859 and his attempts to alleviate the suffering of the wounded. Reportage of this kind was also hugely important in generating support for workplace safety rights, and particularly restrictions on children's working hours and conditions, a significant socialist project of the nineteenth century that informed the content of twentieth-century discourses of human rights.

The development of popular calls for the extension of rights to disenfranchised groups has owed as much, if not more, to the efforts of journalists and social and political campaigners, as it has done to philosophers (Stammers, 1999). Certainly, the idea of rights as legitimate claims that inhere in all persons individually and inalienably, and the content of the rights that are said to do so, is unmistakably shaped by the conceptions of freedom advanced by thinkers like Marx. Equally important, though, in fostering openness to the claim that such rights are universal was the idea of universal brotherhood, expressed in the French revolutionary triptych of '*Liberté, Égalité, Fraternité*', promoted both by socialist movements like the First and Second Internationale, and by socially engaged religious bodies like the Quakers, prominent in both the eighteenth-century American Revolution and the nineteenth-century abolitionist movement.

Nevertheless, in the latter half of the nineteenth century and into the early twentieth century natural rights as an idea was somewhat in the doldrums. The League of Nations, for example, contains no mention of either human or natural rights (Freeman, 2002). (The *Declaration of the Rights of the Working and Exploited People* (1918) proclaimed in the aftermath of the Bolshevik Revolution, is a notable exception, but as the Bolshevik project turned into Stalinist authoritarian rule, the promise of an international project of socialist rights was not realized.) The remarkable prominence of human rights claims today is largely a product of responses to the unimaginable destruction of the Second World War.

The Second World War and the Universal Declaration of Human Rights

The carnage of the Second World War, preceded by the horrors of the First World War and the misery of the Great Depression, attested to the remarkable failure of late nineteenth- and early twentieth-century strategies for ensuring international peace and prosperity. This paved the way for calls for open diplomacy and multilateral agreement, formally organized in an international institution, as a guarantor of collective peace. The 1948 Universal Declaration of Human Rights (UDHR) is thus part of a wider story about the international political response to the project of maintaining peace that built on the international institutional apparatus begun with the failed League of Nations and the more successful International Labour Organisation. But it is also a response to the sheer scale of the suffering that occurred in the Second World War, and the Nazi atrocities of the camps, in particular. As Hunt puts it:

> World War II set a new benchmark of barbarity with its almost incomprehensible 60 million deaths. Moreover, the majority of those killed this time were civilians, and 6 million of them were Jews killed only because they were Jews. (2007, p. 201)

The UDHR, then, is a political response to a particular historical moment, but it is deeply shaped by an earlier set of ideas about the moral significance of individual human beings held to be worthy of respect simply because they are human beings, and is informed by longstanding debates about the rights held by individuals by virtue of their humanity.

Human rights were not initially at the heart of proposals for the international organization that would become the United Nations (UN) –

pressure from smaller countries, from religious organizations, as well as from prominent human rights leaders such as Mahatma Gandhi and W.E. du Bois, led to the inclusion of protection of human rights as a central purpose of the UN as set out in the 1945 Charter. The Nuremberg Trials (1945–6) and the Tokyo Trial (1946) firmly established the concept of 'crimes against humanity' in public consciousness and established the important precedent of international legal accountability for crimes of this magnitude, wherever they were committed, by whomever. Today that principle of accountability is enshrined in the International Criminal Court (ICC), which sits permanently in The Hague.

The Human Rights Commission, established by the UN in 1947 and chaired by Eleanor Roosevelt, drafted the bill of rights that became the UDHR. The commission comprised 18 members, with representatives from Australia, Belgium, Byelorussia, Chile, China, Egypt, France, India, Iran, Lebanon, Panama, the Philippines, Ukraine, the UK, Uruguay, the USA, the USSR and Yugoslavia. Those most prominently involved in the drafting were Roosevelt (who was both chair and a member), the Chinese philosopher and diplomat and Commission vice-chair Pen-Chung Chang, the Lebanese philosopher and UN Ambassador, Charles Malik, and the French legal scholar and later Nobel Laureate René Cassin (Ishay, 2004). The UNESCO committee was also culturally, ideologically and nationally diverse, if overwhelmingly male (Maritain, 1948).

Critics have since argued that the origins of the UDHR and the UN human rights regime are thoroughly Western, and have thus decried the purported universality of contemporary human rights (for example, Hussain, 2001). Indeed, Michael Freeman argues that the structure of the rights defended in the UDHR are distinctly 'Lockean', and that it is therefore embedded in a Western and liberal tradition, which is thus 'doubly controversial: because it is Western, and because it is liberal' (Freeman, 2002, pp. 35–6). The fact that a significant number of contemporary countries, particularly in sub-Saharan Africa and parts of Asia, were under colonial rule at this time, is another factor that is cited as evidence of cultural bias built into the process of drafting the UDHR. Against this, some point to the diversity of the Commission and the UNESCO committee as evidence in favour of the universality of the UDHR (see, for example, Dower, 1996), though others question the substance of this purported diversity. For example, Abdulaziz Sachedina (2009, pp. 10–11) points out that most Muslim contributors were in fact secularly trained individuals deeply influenced by Western values. In contrast, Susan Waltz (2004) identifies a sustained Islamic and Arabic influence on the drafting of the International Bill of Rights between 1948 and 1966.

At the Commission's request, UNESCO invited a number of leading philosophers and theorists to reflect on the ideas and principles of human rights, in order to inform the debates that led to the Declaration. Of this process, one of the contributors, the Thomist philosopher Jacques Maritain, observed that they could agree on a list of rights, 'but on condition that no one ask us why' (1948, p. 1). From its beginning, framers and defenders of the UDHR sought to insulate the practice of human rights from philosophical controversies. As Freeman puts it, '[t]he declaration set aside the traditional, but controversial, foundation of natural rights, without putting any new foundation in its place' (2002, p. 35).

The UDHR consists of a preamble and 30 articles guaranteeing civil, political, economic, social and cultural rights (see Chapter 1). It was endorsed by the General Assembly of the United Nations on 10 December 1948 (48 states voted in favour, eight abstained (the Soviet bloc plus Saudi Arabia and South Africa), and none voted against), but as a declaration rather than a treaty it has no legal effect.

From its inception the UDHR was subject to ideological controversies concerning the indivisibility, or not, of the rights proclaimed, with positions soon dividing along Cold War lines. Cassin, for instance, insisted on the indivisibility of human rights, as do a number of contemporary theorists such as Henry Shue (1980), and in a different though related vein, the philosopher and activist Vandana Shiva (1999). The US government led by Harry Truman fully endorsed civil and political rights but was sceptical of social and economic rights, whilst the reverse was true of the government of the USSR. The UN Vienna Declaration of 1993 reaffirmed that '[a]ll human rights are universal, indivisible and interdependent and interrelated' (Article 5).

The plan to create a legally binding treaty of human rights predictably foundered on this tension, which was eventually resolved by the establishment of two separate treaties, the International Covenant on Civil and Political Rights (ICCPR) and the International Covenant on Economic, Social and Cultural Rights (ICESCR) in 1966. Together, these three documents are known as the International Bill of Rights.

Despite its declaratory nature, the long-term impacts of the UDHR are manifest and multiple. There are well over 200 legal human rights instruments worldwide. Not all explicitly appeal to the UDHR as a source of authority, but the precedent of the UDHR, and its success in securing near-universal formal assent from world governments, undoubtedly shapes the international arena in which proclamations of human rights have become an accepted part of legal and political practice. Powerful regional human rights regimes, such as the African Charter on Human and Peoples' Rights (1981), and the European Convention on Human Rights (1953), as well as global declarations of Women's Rights, Children's Rights, Indigenous Peoples' Rights, and draft declarations of environmental human rights, all owe a debt to the UDHR. Women's rights are protected in the Convention on the Elimination of All Forms of Discrimination Against Women (1979); children's rights are protected in the Convention on the Rights of the Child (1989). Both refer in their preamble to the fundamental equal rights and dignity of the human person, echoing the language of the UDHR. Most recently, indigenous peoples' rights are protected in the Declaration on the Rights of Indigenous Peoples (2007); the preamble to this declaration cites the two Covenants of 1966 as authorities. The institutionalization of human rights in the UN system also influenced the process of de-colonization: after the UDHR and the UN Charter established the right to self-determination as a human right, signatories struggled to defend the practice of colonialism. The admission of post-colonial states to the UN in turn influenced the focus of debates about human rights and in particular the status of social, cultural and economic rights.

In parallel with the inter-governmental and governmental affirmation of human rights, and building on the practice of campaigning groups in the nineteenth century, there is an enormous industry of human rights non-governmental organizations (NGOs) that has grown remarkably in the twentieth and twenty-first centuries, and today forms an acknowledged part of the global human rights regime. NGOs such as Human Rights Watch and Amnesty International are recognized authorities, if not uncontroversial ones, on the state of human rights protection in countries around the world.

One thing we should note about these declarations and covenants is that they both express and underpin an approach to ethics in which human rights have become *the* authoritative language in which to advance claims for social and political justice. In contrast to nineteenth-century thought, much contemporary moral and political thought today assumes an inherent connection between the concept of justice and individual rights. The prevalence of human rights norms and claims as instruments of legal and political practice suggests profound confidence about the status of human rights as moral standards to which every human being is entitled. With the end of the Cold War some theorists were adventurous enough to proclaim the triumph of liberalism (Fukuyama, 1989), and with it the triumph of human rights as a standard of civilization (Donnelly, 1998). Since 11 September 2001 and the advent of the 'war on terror', that confidence has been punctured somewhat, but the potency of human rights as a moral idea is in robust health. However, the content of human rights is in fact a matter of deep controversy amongst a range of political actors, and the status and content of human rights, as well as the connection between rights and justice, are deeply contested amongst political theorists and philosophers.

Conclusion

This chapter alights on three historical moments in the development of human rights: the late eighteenth century declarations of natural rights in North America and France, the emergence in the nineteenth century of claims for social and economic rights, and the institutionalization of human rights in the aftermath of the Second World War in the twentieth century.

Though a richer and more complex history of the development of human rights could certainly be told, each of these three moments is significant for the theory of human rights, both historically and in the present day. The declarations of the late eighteenth century were substantially informed by ideas about natural rights that were debated and refined by Enlightenment thinkers, and importantly shaped by Locke and Rousseau. These ideas established parameters for understanding human beings as special sorts of creatures, with a moral status that set limits on the authority of government, and that conceived of the limits of human freedom largely in terms of the power of the state. Nineteenth-century advocates of social and economic rights challenged both the idea of humanity and the conception of freedom at work in this view. Twentieth-century framers of human rights eschewed the philosophical foundations of natural rights as a means of securing political agreement, and argued for the indivisibility of civil and political rights together with economic, social, and cultural rights.

From the eighteenth century on, there have been critics of the individualism, atomism, and abstraction of human rights. The persistence of philosophical and political criticisms of both the concept and content of human rights has not been a barrier to the advance of the political and legal practice of human rights, but, on the other hand, the manifest popularity of human rights as a moral idea is not itself an answer to these philosophical questions. In the next chapter, we look more closely at contemporary attempts to provide a philosophical foundation for the concept of human rights, in contrast to the agnosticism of the framers of the UDHR on questions of theoretical underpinnings.

3 Philosophical Foundations for Human Rights

'The fundamental challenge to each and every human rights claim is a demand for reasons.' (Perry, 1998, pp. 30–1)

'It is logically and empirically possible to reject the philosophical foundations of human rights. One must make a nonrational decision either to accept or reject solidarity with humanity.' (Freeman, 1994, p. 514)

Introduction

The question of sound philosophical foundations for human rights continues to generate controversy amongst theorists, if not amongst many (perhaps most) of those who campaign for human rights in the real world. The latter may find frustrating the persistent scepticism of some human rights theorists about the normative foundations of human rights claims, though the overwhelming majority of moral, legal and political theorists in fact endorse human rights. Yet it seems to me that Perry is absolutely right to insist that a theoretical justification for human rights is practically necessary – whenever and wherever human rights are challenged in the real world, advocates of human rights need to be able to offer reasons in support of their demands. If an agent ought to do X because a theory of human rights says so, then the agent might reasonably ask why he should be guided by a theory of human rights – in other words, what are the grounds or foundations of human rights claims? This question matters, not least because, as Michael Freeman points out, 'rights without reasons are vulnerable to denial and abuse' (1994, p. 493).

43

Whether or not the reasons we offer in support of human rights must also be *foundations* is a matter we will take up in this chapter. In the quote at the head of this chapter, Freeman raises the thought that we could hang on to our support for human rights even if we ultimately reject philosophical foundations for human rights. However many theorists (including Freeman himself) are uneasy with this way forward. Debates about philosophical foundations disclose deep-seated tensions amongst those who are philosophically committed to human rights as a valid (and valuable) set of political or moral principles. And these tensions matter if we hold that human rights claims are, or ought to be, action-guiding, and if we also hold that agents can reasonably ask why they ought to do X.

A quite daunting variety of answers have been advanced by philosophers and legal and political theorists seeking to justify human rights. In this chapter we will primarily concern ourselves with three approaches to the project of providing philosophical foundations for human rights – the interest view (which we first met in Chapter 1), the idea of human dignity and the idea of personhood – as well as looking at two noted sceptics of this project. We should note both that other approaches are taken, and that there is a degree of overlap between the approaches considered here. The literature on the philosophical foundations of human rights is so vast that any attempt to summarize it will necessarily invite objections. But if we are to make progress with the task of understanding what human rights are, a grasp of these three approaches, and familiarity with some important criticisms, is essential.

The interest view

We first encountered the interest view in Chapter 1, where it was contrasted with the will or choice theory as a means of addressing the question: what is a human right? A basic version of the answer given by interest theorists would be that a human right is a claim that protects an agent's basic or fundamental interest. Many theorists of human rights adopt some variant of an interest view. Indeed, a remarkable number of theorists apparently find it unproblematic to argue from the premise X has an interest in Y, to the conclusion X has a human right to Y. Examples include Simon Caney (2010) and Derek Bell (2011) in relation to climate change (see Chapter 9). Another example is S. Matthew Liao's (2006; 2012) proposed right of children to be loved (cf. Cowden, 2012).

In the years since the signing of the UDHR there has been a striking proliferation of human rights claims (Glendon, 1994). The interest-based approach seems particularly amenable to an elastic understanding of the content of human rights. Anything that could be identified as a universal human interest could be claimed as a human right. Do we have human rights to free higher education? To dental care? Against social exclusion? To periodic holidays with pay? To be educated in one's native language, or to a clean environment? All of these, and more, seem to be important human interests.

Careful proponents of the interest view need not accept that all interests, nor even all universal human interests, give rise to a right. Following Joseph Raz's (1986) seminal work, the interest view holds that human beings have some universal interest, X, which is of sufficient importance to generate a duty in others not to frustrate access to it, or perhaps to provide access to it, and this duty is the corollary of a fundamental claim right. In fact, the duty is *grounded* in the right (Cruft, 2013). Raz tells us 'X has a right' if and only if X can have rights, and, other things being equal, an aspect of X's well-being (his interest) is a sufficient reason for holding some other person(s) to be under a duty' (1986, p. 166). The right is prior to the duty here, in that the duty would not exist were it not for the existence of the right, but the right is only a basic (or human) right insofar as it is one that gives rise to a duty. Thus the fact that a right serves as a sufficient reason for holding another agent to be under a duty helps us to identify which interests give rise to rights.

This definition, of course, gives rise to the question of what counts as a sufficient reason for holding another person to be under a duty. John Tasioulas argues that 'even though a right is prior to the duty it grounds, it is still not *fundamental* in the order of justification. That place belongs instead to the interest' (2004, p. 25). One response to this might be to say something about the societal or common-good interests that are served by recognition of rights. But this consequentialist move would undermine the individualistic character of a human right – a person is not entitled to have her human rights respected because of the good it brings to others, but because it is essential to her own good.

A more promising move will be to say that the interest view will need to be amplified by a further explanation relating to the moral weight of the given universal human interest. In attempting to tackle this step in the project of justification, one might take the view that some human interest is of intrinsic or ultimate value. Here, human rights in effect stand as 'intermediate conclusions that exist between ultimate values and duties' (Freeman, 1994, p. 512). But this intermediate condition is bothersome to some. The justification of human rights depends upon the justifiability of the ultimate value. Raz (1986) sees ultimate values as being subject to disagreement, and though that does not entail the claim that they are arbitrary or indefensible, it does present problems for the universality of human rights. Certainly, there is significant divergence in today's world about ultimate values. To ground an account of human rights in such contentious terrain may open up more problems than it solves.

Alternatively, we could say something about the moral weight that a right has from the individual's point of view, in terms of her wider projects and values (see, for example, Cruft, 2005a). This is distinct from the story about ultimate values, but in the end it is no less problematic. Suppose we face the question of whether or not a parent can be compelled to allow their child to receive a blood transfusion. The parent, on religious grounds, objects to the transfusion. Others concerned for the child's welfare point out that her life is in danger.

It is no good, if human rights are justified by individualistically held values, to say that objectively the value of being alive is lexically prior to the value of adhering to the tenets of a religious faith. What these examples point to is the complexity of saying anything uncontroversial about the universality of values, an issue we will return to again and again.

A related worry is that the interest view seems to be implicitly tied to an account of human nature. We might reasonably have expected this, given the historical connection between seventeenth- and eighteenth-century ideas about natural rights, very much grounded in conceptions of human nature, and contemporary human rights. However, just as there are widely divergent views about ultimate values, there are also many culturally, historically and religiously varied ways of meeting one's basic needs. These arguably point in the direction of variable, rather than universal human interests. Certainly, there are biophysical needs that are presumably universal – human beings need food, water, some degree of shelter and medical care when they are sick. But we typically think that these biophysical needs do not exhaust the range of human rights that can be properly so called and that legitimately give rise to duties. Indeed, it is often argued (and often accepted), that human beings have a human right not only to access basic goods like food, but to access these goods in culturally appropriate forms, hence the intuition that some moral wrong has occurred if a Muslim is only offered access to non-halal foods. Human rights, then, do not just signal an entitlement to survive at any price; they represent a set of claims to entitlement *to lead a life worth living*.

The interest-based approach does seem to capture some intuitions that it is difficult to deny. It is difficult to deny, for example, that all human beings have an interest in not being tortured. Surely no one would deny, then, that all human beings have a right to food and water, as well as to not be tortured? But in order to lead a life worth living, all human beings have an interest in being loved. All human beings have an interest in leading fulfilling lives. These interests may be more complex than the interests in food and shelter, they may be less immediate, but they do not seem less weighty or morally important.

This raises two sorts of concerns. One is a political worry about the credibility and potency of human rights claims. Does recognizing a human right to, say, periodic holidays with pay diminish the power of asserting human rights against torture, as Cranston (1967) suggests? Torture seems to be a *prima facie* moral wrong, and a particularly egregious one. Periodic holidays look like a plausible universal human interest (contrary to Cranston's famous scorn – see Chapter 5), but it is not obvious that it is as morally weighty an issue as the right not to be tortured.

The other concern is conceptual: what sorts of interests can be and should be defended via the mechanism of rights? There is no reason to assume that all interests (or all values) are best defended in this way. The fundamental human interest in being loved does not look likely to be well served by an ethical structure that seeks to enshrine in some agents a right to be loved while imposing on others duties to love. Such a structure would seem to reflect a misunderstanding of the character of the good of love. Thus, a plausible restriction on the rights that can be justified via the interest view is not just the moral weightiness of the interest that is sufficient to ground a duty, but also whether it is the sort of interest that can or should be well served by the moral architecture of rights and duties. This raises quite profound questions about our approach to ethics. One reason to be cautious about the interest view, then, is that it struggles to demarcate what is, and is not, the object of a human right. Or rather, it may fail to answer the justificatory question in a way that allows us to explain why X is, and Y is not, the object of a human right, whilst maintaining the position that human rights are strong action-guiding principles. We should note that Raz (2007) is aware of this difficulty, and thus adopts a structure broadly sympathetic to the political view (see next chapter), which serves to curtail the defensible scope of human rights claims.

Another worry is that the interest view does not fully capture the quality of the claim that is being made when an agent claims entitlement to protection for a human right. To say that a human right has been violated is not coterminous with saying that an interest has not been fulfilled. An interest, even a morally weighty and universally held interest, could fail to be realized for a number of reasons. Human rights are violated when an interest is frustrated in some way by some purposive human agent. Indeed, the standard view is that a human right is violated when an important interest is frustrated or serious harm is inflicted by a government or authoritative agent. For example, a person's interest in shelter and bodily integrity is compromised by an earthquake that causes injury. But it would be odd to say that the earthquake *violated* her human rights. However, if a government or relevant authority behaved negligently towards its citizens or some particular group of its citizens in the aftermath of a natural disaster, then it would be appropriate to speak of a violation of fundamental rights, a claim that was often raised in the aftermath of Hurricane Katrina in the USA in 2005.

Insofar as the interest view of human rights signals the responsibilities of agents, this theory justifies our blaming or condemning particular agents when human rights are violated. One might reject this blame-based approach altogether and say that a strength of the interest view is that it can ground a duty in some relevant agent in the absence of causal responsibility. This is an important advantage, to which we will return in later chapters. That said, amongst the many points of controversy as to what justifies a human right is the question of whether a theory of human rights can successfully and adequately identify *which* agents to blame or hold responsible for (in)action (see O'Neill, 1996, 2005, for an account of ethics which *begins* from duties, rather than rights).

Tasioulas (2011) criticizes the interest view on the grounds that it fails to tell us anything specific about human *rights*; it is dependent upon a story about human interests, and rights, in the end, look like a spare wheel. If what grounds the duty is the interest or the value, then what work is the concept of a right actually doing? And if the concept of a right is doing no philosophical work, then how, precisely, can the interest view serve as a justification for human rights? Tasioulas' answer is that it cannot: in order to offer a philosophical foundation of human rights one is obliged to say something substantive about the good of human beings, in other words, to return to a much richer account of what is and is not good for human beings.

If that is true, then the interest view is at best an incomplete philosophical foundation for human rights. Another element that we should pay attention to is brought forward by Thomas Nagel: 'I believe it is most accurate to think of rights as aspects of status – part of what is involved in being a member of the moral community' (Nagel, 1995, p. 85). The approaches to providing philosophical foundations for human rights that we will look at in the next sections – dignity and personhood – both speak to this notion that the moral status of human beings (indeed, of *all* human beings *individually*) is at the heart of the normativity of human rights, and both engage substantively with questions of what is good for human beings. They will each prove to be as complex and contested as the interest view, and both overlap with elements of the interest view in certain ways (as well as with each other), so we should not draw lines of demarcation too strongly between them. What is fruitful here is to notice the resources each of the three approaches offer and the challenges that each confronts.

Human dignity

Article 1 of the Universal Declaration of Human Rights asserts that 'All human beings are born free and equal in dignity and rights.' Being able to offer a philosophical foundation for human rights grounded in human dignity would have practical significance for an account of human rights. Human dignity is widely invoked in human rights documents and is often drawn upon as an explanation for the much-stated claim that 'human rights are rights held by all human beings, simply in virtue of their humanity'. Several scholars have drawn attention to the various ambiguities in this statement (for example, Gardner, 2008; Hope, 2011; Tasioulas, 2011). For example, does it imply a definite claim about the content of humanity (that is, about human nature) that somehow qualifies human beings for rights? Is the 'in virtue of' descriptive or stipulative?

Implicitly, the validity of claims about human rights depends upon there being something morally significant about *being human*, which moral significance entails certain rights. But what explains, justifies or even defines that moral significance is, to many observers, ambiguous, not to say mysterious. Many, many scholars reach for the concept of human dignity when trying to elucidate this puzzle (see, for example, Nussbaum, 2011; Kaufmann et al., 2010; Arieli, 2002; cf. Rosen, 2012).

Human rights texts often refer to the 'inherent dignity of the human person'. Christopher McCrudden explains the persistence of these references to human dignity thus:

[W]e can see that the significance of human dignity, at the time of the drafting of the UN Charter and the UDHR (and since then in the drafting of other human rights instruments), was that it supplied a theoretical basis for the human rights movement, in the absence of any other basis for consensus. (2008, p. 27)

He goes on, 'Dignity was included in that part of any discussion or text where the absence of a theory of human rights would have been embarrassing' (2008, p. 28). Accounts of the drafting of the UDHR also attest to the malleability of understandings of human dignity and this accounting for its presence as a foundational concept that could be accepted from diverse and even conflicting philosophical, ideological and theological perspectives (Maritain, 1948; Morsink, 2009; cf. Sharma, 2003).

As a normative foundation, however, some doubt the value of dignity, given the multiple ways in which it might be interpreted and understood. Indeed, the bioethicist Ruth Macklin (2003) famously calls dignity a 'useless concept'. (We should note that equality of dignity is historically a relatively recent idea – dignity used to connote status; to treat people with dignity was precisely to treat them unequally, because the dignity of the lord is distinct from the dignity of the peasant (Waldron, 2009). The evolution of the idea of equal and inherent human dignity is something else that stands in need of explanation.) Theorists of human rights, as well as legal scholars and bioethicists, have thus gone to some trouble to try to understand what human dignity might mean, and why a unique dignity that is said to inhere in human beings might entail human rights.

One promising strategy is pursued by Joel Feinberg (1970). Feinberg uses the concept of dignity to indicate the specialness of rights (as with Raz, above, Feinberg talks about rights rather than human rights, though both have been enormously influential in the literature specifically focused on human rights). For Feinberg, then, understanding the concept of dignity is helpful in illuminating the distinctiveness of rights vis-à-vis other moral concepts, such as duties, interests, or the good.

Feinberg approaches the concept of dignity negatively, by inviting us to imagine a world, Nowheresville, in which people do not have rights. He proceeds to draw out the ways in which human dignity would be compromised by the absence of individual rights, even in the presence of fully functioning virtues such as benevolence and compassion. For example, there is no such thing as a right to free speech. It may be that people are so tolerant of one another that no one is prohibited or inhibited from saying what they wish, but they do not have a *right* to do so. What do we make of this situation? Feinberg's thought is that a person so situated would inevitably find their dignity compromised. There is a sense in which the status of humans *qua* humans rests on their entitlement to assert the right to free speech – the entitlement to the right is more telling for the status of the person than is the question of whether or not they actually avail themselves of the right. The crucial point here is that the act of claiming rights functions as an expression of dignity, without which mechanism there are multiple ways in which dignity would be compromised (and of course we tend not to find ourselves in situations of perfect tolerance, harmony, and justice).

This arguably tells us why rights are important for the preservation of human dignity, but it cannot tell us what dignity is, or why dignity matters. And indeed, as Meyer (1989) notes, there are instances where the claiming of rights looks to be expressive of characteristics that are distinctly at odds with dignity if we understand dignity descriptively. Think, for example, of the 'bumptious man' who is continually claiming his rights (even his fundamental human rights) when they are not under threat, but when he perceives them to be under threat, and makes a noisy nuisance of himself to demand that they be respected. Clearly, the claiming of rights in this instance does not look at all like the expression of dignity (Meyer, 1989, pp. 525–7).

One thing this example might suggest is that something more is implied in the quality of human dignity than the descriptively valid state of being dignified. To have inherent human dignity, if it is to serve as a foundation of human rights, must mean something distinct from behaving in ways that cohere with what a society considers to be outwardly dignified (something that is in any case culturally and historically variable). We might get around this objection by saying that it is the capacity to act with dignity, rather than the proper use of that capacity, that is being referred to in the preamble to the UDHR and other documents that speak of humans' inherent dignity as something by virtue of which we have rights.

I will say more about capacity later on, but we can note at this stage that the so-called 'argument from marginal cases', wherein persons whose mental and physical capacities are severely constrained, leads this argument into very difficult territory, where, if one is consistent, one might have to say that such persons do not have human dignity (thus, they do not have human rights). Peter Singer rightly notes that this argument is tactlessly named. The thought here is that there are cases where descriptively, there is little difference between the capabilities of some human beings (both very young children and some severely disabled adults) and some animals. If the possession of certain capabilities is the benchmark for having certain rights, then it is not obvious why some animals should be denied the same rights, or why some humans should be protected from treatments considered acceptable with respect to animals. Singer's claim is that what explains such inconsistent treatment is humans' 'speciesism', a kind of prejudice akin to racism and sexism (Singer, 1975; Pluhar, 1987; cf. Frey, 1988). (Of course, these sorts of doubts are not unique to the justification of human rights – any ethical claims that presuppose the moral equality of human beings will face these issues.)

If we are inclined to reject this move, then presumably this is because when we appeal to human dignity, we mean to appeal to a metaphysical property of human beings, rather than make a descriptive claim about the conduct of human beings (Kaufmann et al., 2010). As Michael Rosen (2012) has put it, there is nothing less dignified than a human two-year-old (a variant of Meyer's 'bumptious man'). Nevertheless, we typically think that there is something morally special about a human two-year-old such that he ought not to be treated in particular ways and ought to be provided with conditions that allow him to flourish. Indeed, there seem to be strong and widely held intuitions that individual human beings do matter morally in a distinct way that marks them out from other beings. If we did not have these intuitions, we could not make sense of the moral outrage that greets particularly egregious cases of child abuse and neglect.

Whether or not this intuition is structurally dependent on a system of rights is another matter, but taking seriously the implications of this intuition potentially offers a route to justifying rights negatively, or inductively, by identifying those harms that seem intuitively to be such egregious wrongs that they compromise human dignity. Advocates of this approach (for example, Stoecker, 2010; Dershowitz, 2004; Morsink, 2009) proceed by reflection on wrongs that seem especially bad. As Ralf Stoecker explains, 'there are numerous instances of vile and reprehensible behaviour that could not be morally accounted for at all, or at least not adequately, except as violations of dignity' (2010, p. 11). If we think, for example, of the now notorious mistreatment of prisoners at Abu Ghraib, then we might notice that, bad as the physical mistreatment of prisoners was, still it is the wilful humiliation of prisoners, through particular kinds of insults and sexual abuse, which most strongly provokes a reaction of moral indignation.

Similarly, the public reaction to scandals surrounding the mistreatment of care home residents speaks to there being a sense in which what outrages us is the lack of respect for the special moral value of the individual human being that is expressed in various forms of mistreatment. The thought here is that there are intuitions about moral wrongness for which we cannot account without the concept of inherent human dignity. Thus, there must be such a thing as inherent human dignity, a metaphysical property that both explains and justifies the moral status of individual human beings. (Note, also, that in particular consensual contexts the very same physical treatment that is here considered a human rights abuse would not be a human rights abuse at all. The context, the participants and the perceptions of those involved all make a crucial difference to a judgement as to what constitutes 'cruel, inhuman and degrading treatment', which is prohibited in Article 5 of the UDHR (see Asad, 1997).

Intuitions, though, are fickle foundations for moral claims (see, *inter alia*, Singer, 2005; MacIntyre, 1994). Alan Dershowitz (2004) finds it intuitively 'obvious' that slavery is wrong, and from this obviousness we can be certain that slavery violates human rights. There is, undoubtedly, something in the thought that philosophers often pursue 'one thought too many' (and then a few more). Following Dershowitz, one need not let the fact of deep disagreement over, say, rights to gay marriage deter us from acting on issues where there is deep agreement, for example, on rights not to be tortured. This suggests a common-sense type approach that many could be expected to approve. Indeed, if everyone can see that slavery violates human rights then the important task seems to be the eradication of slavery; philosophizing about the nature of the wrongness of something universally agreed to be wrong looks not just to be intellectual navel-gazing, but wilfully misapplying one's energy.

But the difficulty is that it has not always been obvious to all that slavery is wrong, nor is it unequivocally the case today that such agreement is universal. If it were, then organizations like Anti-Slavery International would have nothing to do, which is clearly not the case (see www.antislavery.org). Relying on intuitions ultimately hamstrings the project of giving justifying reasons. If you do not share my intuition about the wrongness of something that I hold to be a human rights violation, further argument, if said argument relies on intuitions, would seem to be scuppered. For example, the International Bill of Rights is intentionally agnostic on the question of whether capital punishment is a cruel and inhuman punishment. This is an issue that is subject to debate in human rights circles and where opponents have deeply held and divergent intuitions.

It is no surprise, then, that some scholars profess dissatisfaction with a negative or inductive account of human dignity as a foundation for human rights. As Marcus Düwell concludes, 'a "negative approach" ... can only offer some heuristic tools and not an "approach" to human dignity' (2010, p. 217). Düwell further points out, rightly I think, that the

negative approach is apt to capture intuitions in cases of direct interper-
sonal violations of human rights, but is less useful when trying to
conceive of the wrongness of severe poverty, or the deprivation that
results from being denied access to basic education. Insofar as we hold
these also to be human rights issues, we will want a foundation for
human rights that is able to capture different sorts of wrongs. He therefore argues for the need for a positive account of human dignity that
captures the moral status of human dignity that can serve as a foundation
for human rights (cf. Kohen, 2007, who doubts the availability of such
an account).

It remains to be seen whether a clear concept of human dignity will
emerge from these ongoing philosophical debates, and whether such a
concept can do the normative work asked of it. I will return to some of
these questions about dignity in Chapter 5, for now, I move on to a third
approach to the project of providing philosophical foundations for
human rights.

Personhood

An alternative strategy that is in many respects closely related to the
dignity-based argument is the argument from personhood. At times,
personhood and dignity are used almost interchangeably (that is, to have
dignity is to exhibit the characteristics of personhood, and vice versa).
What I will refer to here are two important attempts to derive a philosophical defence of human rights from accounts of what it is to be a
person, or of what it is that is morally significant about being a person
that calls forth the special protections embodied in human rights.

The first of these two examples, Alan Gewirth's (1982) Principle of
Generic Consistency (PGC), has been described by the human rights
sceptic Alasdair MacIntyre (1994, p. 66) as the most careful attempt to
advance a philosophical foundation for human rights (for a fuller discussion see Singer, 1985; Beyleveld, 1991; Kohen, 2007; Raz, 2007; as well
as MacIntyre and indeed Griffin). The second, James Griffin's (2008)
pluralist personhood view, looks set to be similarly influential (for more
discussion see Raz, 2007; Tasioulas, 2007, 2011; Hope, 2011; Forst,
2012; and issue 120 of *Ethics*). They share an interest in autonomy, or in
Gewirth's term, purposive agency, as a defining feature of the moral
status of human beings.

Gewirth develops a 'dialectically necessary' method, which reveals
that

[I]t is possible and indeed logically necessary to infer, from the fact that certain objects are the proximate necessary conditions of human action that all rational agents logically must hold or claim, at least implicitly, that they have rights to such objects. (1982, p. 41)

The claim here is that it follows from an individual's conceptual need of certain conditions for action that there are human rights to which all persons are entitled, a claim which Gewirth argues cannot be denied without self-contradiction or logical error. Hence, if one accepts the principle of consistency, this yields a universal justification for human rights (Gewirth, 1982, p. 46). These are rights to freedom and well-being, which Gewirth holds to be the necessary conditions for action. From this basis, he argues (Gewirth, 1982), it would not be difficult to draw up a list of rights that largely coincided with that found in the International Bill of Rights.

The attraction here is the minimalism of the premises from which the argument is derived. Insofar as I act purposively, I implicitly affirm the value of my being able to do so, and thus implicitly affirm the value of having the necessary conditions of being able to do so. Note that the whole argument is conditional upon my understanding my own agency to imply entitlement to rights. In claiming rights for myself I am logically committed to recognizing them as held by those others against whom I claim them. The descriptive claim is very limited: human beings are creatures whose reason gives them the capacity to act purposively. This is constitutive of their personhood.

Given that the capacity for rational agency is central to his argument, it is plain that Gewirth's thesis cannot support full rights for children and the insane, a point he concedes himself (Gewirth, 1979, pp. 1157–8). This exclusion does not preclude persons having duties of care or respect towards children and the insane, but it does suggest that whatever their moral status is, it cannot be justified from the same grounds as that inhering in 'purposive agents', as Gewirth terms rights-bearers, and thus these excluded persons cannot be bearers of rights themselves. One might avoid these problems by thinking of rational agency as a range capacity, so that it could capture most human agents, but the problem is not entirely defused by this move. Nevertheless, advocates of Gewirth's approach conclude that agents have prudential reasons for understanding the range of purposive agency in very broad terms. In other words, it is in my interest, if I have reason to think I might want to say to some creature that they ought to respect my rights, to assume that they are themselves a purposive agent, and thus to commit myself to respecting their rights.

A further, deeper problem arises in the links between steps in his argument; from the logical necessity of the individual agent asserting that he has need of certain conditions for action to the agent having rights to freedom and well-being. Gewirth sums up his argument in seven steps (1982, pp. 50–1). The problem arises between his points (2) and (3). It only follows from 'I, as an actual or prospective agent, must have freedom and well-being' (point 2) that 'All others persons must at least refrain from removing or interfering with my freedom and well-being' (point 3) if there is something special about purposive agents (myself included) that means they are *entitled* to what they need for action. It may be that there is some special quality that so distinguishes purposive agents, but Gewirth has not specified what it may be. Argument is needed here, as MacIntyre (1994, pp. 66–70) has complained.

Gewirth has amplified his argument elsewhere:

> [T]he agent is saying that because freedom and basic well-being are necessary goods for him, other persons strictly ought to refrain from interfering with his having them. And this is equivalent to saying that he has a right to them, because the agent holds that this strict duty of noninterference by other persons is owed to him. (1976, p. 291)

However, this thesis remains unsatisfactory because the equivalence Gewirth asserts is not self-evident. Joseph Raz (2007, p. 4) has complained that Gewirth 'misconceives the relation between value and rights' here, in that he assumes that something that has crucial value for a person must be the subject of a right that that person holds. As we have seen, there may be necessary goods (like love) to which persons would not necessarily have rights. The underlying difficulty here has been summed up by Michael Freeman: 'the theory of human rights presupposes a moral ontology in which human persons not only exist but have special value. Such an ontology is not universal' (Freeman, 1994, p. 510). Nor is it self-evident. Philosophical proof remains wanting.

Raz also draws attention to slippage in Gewirth's use of the concept of freedom. Gewirth holds that freedom is necessary for action, and thus insofar as I act purposively, I implicitly claim this right for myself, and if I recognize others as agents at all, then I am logically committed to respecting their equally necessary right to freedom. But there is slippage here between what we might think of as the moral freedom that is necessary for humans to have free will, and the external freedom that is the conceptual opposite of slavery. Raz's claim is that it is simply false to say that humans cannot purposively act without freedom if that means that slaves cannot act purposively, since they evidently can (Raz, 2007, p. 4). It seems that Gewirth's defence of human rights is grounded in his commitment to moral freedom, but is structurally indebted to the idea of external freedom.

James Griffin (2008) bases his account of the philosophical foundations of human rights on an account of personhood that is fuller than Gewirth's, but is structurally similar insofar as it is intimately connected to the necessary conditions for normative agency. The fullness of the account reflects a commitment to the view that an account of human rights must be substantive, in the sense of giving some substance to the content of human rights, a view shared by Tasioulas (2004; 2011). Both are informed by sympathy for neo-Aristotelian naturalism, which commits them to some substantive views about what human flourishing consists in. Thus, this version of the moral view will be richer but also, potentially, more controversial than the thinner account offered by Gewirth.

Griffin (2008) has described human rights as 'an incomplete idea' as they exist in political practice, and in much political philosophy. The lack of a cogent and comprehensive answer to the question, 'what is a human right?', is, for Griffin, a challenge that philosophers ought to confront. His personhood account is his attempt to do just that. An account of personhood, together with reflection on practicalities, offers a way out of the unsatisfying indeterminateness of our concept of human rights, or, at any rate, this is Griffin's claim.

The necessary conditions for normative agency Griffin identifies are 'autonomy', 'minimum provision' and 'liberty' (2008, p. 81.4). These three parts of personhood entail that a minimally decent life is one in which a person has a range of valuable options, the minimal capabilities (provision in terms of education, welfare, etc.) to realize them, and is not obstructed in her choice to pursue one or other of them.

> Grounding human rights in personhood imposes an obvious constraint on their content: they are rights not to anything that promotes human *good* or *flourishing*, but merely to what is needed for human *status*. (Griffin, 2008, p. 34)

In other words, what we find in Griffin's account is a clear acceptance of the idea that human rights are not just about interests, the good, or even the conditions for living a decent life (though they are about all of these things), they are about the entitlements we have that connect to our moral status as creatures that command a special position in other agents' considerations, such that we hold them to be under a duty to respect certain of our claims.

Tasioulas presses a worry that the account Griffin offers may be less parsimonious than at first appears, or rather that the personhood approach gives rise to a list of rights that is, after all, indeterminate. Raz's worry about the capacity of the slave to engage in purposive action is again relevant here. Either it is the case that the personhood account is a thinly abstract account of minimum necessary conditions in which the slave is technically a person, because she has the capacity to pursue (limited) options, has the minimum provision necessary to do so, and is not impeded in doing so. If so, then the personhood account cannot say that slavery violates a human right. Or, it is not the case that the slave can meaningfully be said to enjoy the necessary conditions of personhood, because she does not have a meaningful array of choices. Thus slavery does violate her human rights. But then we face the indeterminacy of not knowing at what point the threshold of autonomy sufficient for the personhood conception of human rights to be met is satisfied. How many viable options, and with what extent of capability-generating provisions, are needed to meet the threshold?

Griffin does not so much answer this challenge as reject it:

> Is the threshold line sharp? Of course not. That is why it is not enough simply to object that the threshold I define is 'vague'. Most terms are vague, if only at the edges. The degree of vagueness is what is crucial. What matters here is whether the vagueness is so great that it cripples important thought. Will a society have to do work to make the threshold sharper? Yes. Will contingent matters such as the wealth of a society influence the placing of the line? They need not, but they might. Have societies dealt with comparable threshold problems before? Often. (Griffin, 2010, p. 748)

But if the point is to be able to say something about human status, then the question of thresholds of agency is only one puzzling factor here. There have been slaves who have had considerable wealth, who have lived in the same societies as free persons who have been so destitute as to command very few choices. The wrongness of slavery lies not just in its limiting external freedom but in it being a denial of (indeed, an affront to) the moral freedom of human beings.

Raz (2007, p. 5) compares Griffin's account favourably with Gewirth's in part because of the resources that Griffin has to meet this challenge. Griffin holds not merely that normative agency has value *for agents*, but that normative agency *is* valuable. Griffin defines human autonomy not as the logically necessary autonomy of an abstract agent, but as the 'functioning' autonomy of a human being in the world now. Functioning autonomy, is, Griffin claims, 'especially valuable' and is in essence a feature of human nature, not understood as a sparse set of facts of science (nor about practicalities), but understood phenomenologically as a rich ethical concept. Hence, he is able to claim: 'So my notions of "human nature" and "human autonomy" are already well within the normative circle, and there is no obvious fallacy involved in deriving rights from notions as evaluatively rich as they are' (Griffin, 2008, p. 35).

Should we be satisfied with this move? It seems to me that Griffin in the end presupposes what he purports to set out to demonstrate, namely, that human beings are creatures that have the special moral value (status) that entails the special protection of human rights. Tasioulas presses a further challenge: Griffin holds that all humans have a fundamental interest in autonomy, minimum provision and liberty (though the content of those interests will be historically variable). But, Tasioulas complains, Griffin does not provide a means of demarcating between rights and interests, nor does he explain how interests give rise to human rights specifically, which Tasioulas takes to be intrinsically related to categorical duties (Tasioulas, 2010; 2011). Griffin (2010) has responded to some of this criticism by underlining the fact that he does indeed differentiate between rights and interests – hence his insistence that his personhood account imposes constraints on those goods (or interests) that can be the object of a human right. But, Griffin (2010, p. 746) also acknowledges that he does not think a completely satisfactory account of when and how interests do and do not give rise to duties has yet been achieved, though, in his view, Raz comes closest to doing so.

The most that can be said on Griffin's analysis, it seems, is that especially important interests that connect directly to the capacity for normative agency (and thus status) give rise to rights, or call forth the protection of rights, because of their morally weighty character. This claim stands independently of whether the rights impose duties that cannot be enforced, or distributed, or realized. Tasioulas (2010), on the other hand, like Onora O'Neill (2005), worries about the indeterminacy of an account of rights that is disconnected from an account of duties. Indeed, O'Neill's position is that duties are in fact prior to rights (see Chapter 8 for more on this). For Tasioulas, an adequate account of human rights is one that can supply justifying reasons to duty-bearers, and thus is one that must speak to corresponding duties. We cannot, for Tasioulas (2011), adequately capture the individualistic justification of rights if we are unable to articulate this relation between rights-holder and duty-bearer (see also Cruft, 2005a, 2013).

But the Griffinesque route of deriving rights from interests in those goods necessary for normative agency cannot meet this challenge, and, further, can only offer a piecemeal, phenomenological answer, and not a systematic answer to the question of when interests give rise to human rights, and when they do not. Indeed, Griffin (2010) charges that a systematic answer is unavailable, and ultimately unnecessary to the task of understanding human rights. As his answer to the charge of vagueness implies, Griffin is comfortable with the thought that a coherent understanding of human rights is available without the systematic precision that Gewirth aimed for, and which Tasioulas and others demand.

Writing more than a decade earlier, Michael Freeman's sympathies are evidently on Griffin's side of this debate. Freeman (1994) attempts to synthesize philosophical foundations for human rights from resources found in work by a slew of theorists who have written on rights, equality, justice, and notions of the good. His conclusion is that respect for human rights cannot, ultimately, be derived from truths about human nature that would disclose the normative core from which the moral status attached to human beings may be derived. To that extent, respect for human rights is contingent, but, it is not arbitrary insofar as it reflects the realities of the world we inhabit now. He goes on:

> A theory of human rights that is contingent and not arbitrary should not be alarming. A conception of human rights should be flexible enough to allow space for the human creativity it seeks to defend and to address the changing conditions of the world that may threaten its values. (Freeman, 1994, p. 514)

The search for philosophical foundations for human rights appears, ultimately, to be incomplete, if not doomed to fail. If we insist on the need for robust philosophical *foundations*, then human rights may remain, in Griffin's phrase, 'an incomplete idea'. In the next section I consider two critics of human rights (or, at any rate, of human rights philosophizing), who would say we ought not to be surprised by this conclusion, one of whom says we need not even be troubled by it.

Sceptics: MacIntyre and Rorty

There are many, varied critiques of the project of offering philosophical foundation for human rights. Two of the most interesting and influential have been put forward by critics with quite divergent views about the proper task of moral and political philosophy, which inform the character of their views on human rights theory: Alasdair MacIntyre and Richard Rorty.

MacIntyre has a habit of puncturing the complacency of moral and political thought that proceeds from commonly accepted views, which makes his work both unsettling and insightful. He famously complains that the arguments advanced to defend belief in human rights could equally be advanced to defend belief in unicorns and witches (1994, p. 69). Of course, unicorns and witches are different types of things than human rights – one would seek to prove their existence (if at all) in rather different ways – but there is more to this than just rhetoric.

MacIntyre's favoured approach to ethics is to defend a teleological account of the good (that is, one in which the ultimate good or flourishing of man is the foundation upon which moral claims and judgements may be built), in contrast to a rights-based morality (where a person's rights or entitlements prescribe the demands of justice), though he has recently softened his hostility to rights and considered the possibility of an Aristotelian inflected account of rights (see MacIntyre, 1994, 2008; cf. Bowring, 2008; Tasioulas, 2011).

The underlying objection he raises against human rights relates to their purported universality. For MacIntyre, the institution of rights is historically specific. Morality itself is a thick, historically and contextually specific phenomenon, so to imagine that there are universal moral codes is to deny the importance of history and context in shaping and determining our understanding of moral concepts. Morality exists within a web of meanings that are historically, culturally and politically situated. If we remove moral concepts from that web, we remove them from the context that gives them meaning and potency. Thus, he argues that one reason why a Gewirthian defence of universal rights fails is because the means of recognizing rights to freedom and well-being have not been universally available:

> One reason why claims about goods necessary for rational agency are so different from claims to the possession of rights is that the latter in fact presuppose, as the former do not, the existence of a socially established set of rules ... (As a matter of historical fact such types of

social institution or practice have not existed universally in human societies.) Lacking any such social form, the making of a claim to a right would be like presenting a check for payment in a social order that lacked the institution of money. (MacIntyre, 1994, p. 67)

So, the claim of universal human rights runs aground on the fact that the institution of rights is a peculiarly modern and Western invention. Moreover, the historical moment at which these rights were invented – for MacIntyre, the European Enlightenment – was a moment when the foundations of moral thought moved from a story in which God and His vision of man's good was at the centre, to a story in which humans themselves were at the centre, asserting 'self-evident truths'. But this, for MacIntyre, entails a collapse into emotivism rather than a triumph of reason (Shrader-Frechette, 2001). (Emotivists hold that moral claims are akin to utterances of preference, and there is no sense in which they are objectively true (see Mackie, 1990)). On MacIntyre's view, contemporary human rights theorists presuppose what remains to be proven, namely, that there are (or can be) 'self-evident truths' about morality. As Susan Mendus observes:

> MacIntyre's criticism does indicate a genuine difficulty inherent in appeal to human rights. This is that such appeal is naturally interpreted as foundationalist either in the sense that it invokes rights as a basic category, or in the sense that it implies a background which is essentially theological ... Either way, theories of human rights purport to provide a foundation for moral and political thinking, but the foundation is elusive and precarious. (1995, pp. 11–12)

A teological account of human good is necessary, for MacIntyre, to ground moral claims, but he is not falsely optimistic about the prospects for this leading to moral harmony. On the contrary, in the context of pluralism, there is no reason to think that a teological account of the good could generate universally valid justifying reasons. But that difficulty should not lead us into the error of affirming universal moral claims expressed in an idiom, such as rights, that is historically and culturally situated.

In defence of MacIntyre's thesis, we should acknowledge that the idea that all humans everywhere are morally equal has not universally been endorsed throughout human history, indeed, it is historically quite peculiar. But to say that the existence of universal rights depends upon the existence of institutions to recognize those rights, as the 'presupposition argument' suggests, perhaps overstates the case. As Jack Donnelly (2003, p. 8) notes, rights are claimed not when they are protected by courts and other institutions, but precisely when they are denied. The concept of natural rights emerged from a discourse of natural *right*. Rights are claims about how societies should be organized, or more specifically about how individuals should be treated by those in authority in a society. There are likely to be alternative idioms for expressing this idea that will make the concept of a right to some degree comprehensible, even if the concept of *a right* itself is alien.

I will say more about this in Chapter 5, but for now we can note that what is at stake here is the strength of the claim that social forms are only comprehensible within a specific context. As Simon Hope (2011) points out in a discussion of the concept of common humanity, for us to be able to recognize that we disagree about the relevant social forms, or that we come from different historical contexts, itself presupposes some degree of intelligibility between different contexts. Disagreement about the purchase of claims about universal human rights discloses at least some degree of mutual understanding, if nothing else to the extent that both parties to the disagreement recognize that there *is* a disagreement about this.

So, whilst we must acknowledge the force of MacIntyre's general dissatisfaction with taking thick moral concepts from one particular context and applying them in other contexts, and expecting them to bear the same normative weight, it would be a mistake to condemn human rights as utterly unintelligible across cultural and political contexts, or to accept wholly the claim that support for human rights is of a piece with belief in unicorns and witches.

Richard Rorty's (1993) rejection of the search for philosophical foundations for human rights pursues a radically different line of attack. While MacIntyre gives us reason to doubt the principles that we take for granted in our search for philosophical foundations, Rorty argues that the search for philosophical foundations does no useful work. His anti-foundationalism is important, and is importantly different from MacIntyre's. For Rorty, it does not matter whether the project of finding philosophical foundations succeeds or fails. On pragmatic grounds, it would be best to ignore the question of philosophical foundations altogether. The moral view of human rights attempts to derive justifying reasons for human rights claims from moral facts, specifically moral facts about human beings. Rorty denies both that there are any important moral facts about human beings that significantly separate us from other animals, and that there are moral facts that bear on our behaviour *per se*.

If it seems that most of the work of changing moral intuitions is being done by manipulating our feelings rather than increasing our knowledge, that will be a reason to think that there is no knowledge of the sort which philosophers like Plato, Aquinas, and Kant hoped to acquire. (Rorty, 1993, p. 118)

Of course, the 'if' matters here. Rorty hangs a lot on the claim that what he calls a 'human rights culture' is entirely the product of the manipulation and development of sentiments of sympathy and compassion, and that 'no useful work seems to be done by insisting on a purportedly ahistorical human nature' (1993, p. 119). He is particularly insistent that the idea that human beings are uniquely rational, which informs accounts of human dignity and rights from Locke and Kant to Gewirth and Griffin, cannot effect the respect for rights that it aims to justify. This is because 'everything turns on who counts as a fellow human being, as a rational agent in the only relevant sense – the sense in which rational agency is synonymous with membership in *our* moral community' (1993, p. 124).

If this is right, then the task of the human rights theorist is neither to identify nor to invent philosophically robust foundations for human rights, but rather to expand the scope of the human rights community. Indeed, for Rorty (1989; 1999), the philosophical task is (almost) always to persuade rather than to discover. In other words, he has a distinctive understanding of what philosophy is and can do. Nagel (1995) is right that human rights are markers of status within a moral community, and if a given person is not recognized as belonging to that moral community, they will not be recognized as having the status of rights-bearers. This relationship between status and community explains how eighteenth-century advocates of natural rights could simultaneously affirm the natural and inalienable rights of man, and the non-personhood of slaves and women. Rorty's favourite example is Thomas Jefferson, principal author of the US Declaration of Independence, who both owned slaves and defended the idea of natural rights (Rorty, 1993, p. 112). Such inconsistencies are hardly a thing of the past.

As we saw in the previous chapter, debates about an ahistorical human nature certainly informed the emergence of the idea of natural rights as valid claims held by individuals. So to insist, as Rorty does, that theorizing on such rights and foundational concepts like human nature does no useful work may be a stronger claim than can be sustained. Certainly, Norman Geras' (1995) investigation of the reasons given by rescuers of Jews in the Second World War suggests that some people do reach for concepts like common humanity and rights when they seek to rationalize and justify moral demands, though, of course, that may not tell the full story of their motivations.

Nevertheless, there is much to be said for Rorty's rejection of an exclusively rationalist justification for human rights. Unless we side with Kant in holding that the only just motive is the motive from duty, we mis-calibrate the project of practical reason if we conceive of justifying reasons in exclusively rational and abstract terms. Human beings, if there is anything that can be said of their natures, are creatures of reason *and* sentiment. The key point for Rorty, though, is that the rationalist story that is most often told is one about philosophical foundations as a justificatory move. His point is that the most (and the best) that philosophers can do is not to provide bullet-proof justifications for actions, but rather to persuade people of the merits of a human rights culture, by enlarging their sympathies.

Though it is ultimately unsatisfactory as a response to the challenge of offering justifying reasons for human rights claims, the idea that human rights are best understood as a 'culture', that is, as a malleable phenomenon that can command diverse allegiance via the cultivation of sentiments as well as rationally defended argument, speaks to Freeman's thought at the head of this chapter. Freeman ultimately steps back from endorsing Rorty's sentiment-based defence of human rights: '[I]t is not enough, considering Rorty, to know that we support human rights. We need to know why we do so' (Freeman, 1994, p. 514). But he ultimately concedes that we face a 'nonrational decision'; regardless of the success or failure of the project of finding philosophical foundations for human rights, an important part of the success or failure of human rights *as a practice* will be the willingness of human beings to choose solidarity with one another. They may not.

Conclusion

This chapter starts from the assumption that human rights claims are intended to be action-guiding. If I say that Bob has violated Adam's human rights, then I am saying that Bob has committed a grave wrong and ought to stop, or be stopped, from acting in this way. Given the stringency of this implied duty, one might reasonably expect that the justifying reasons that are to be offered in support of respect for human rights will be strong ones. To meet this demand, the philosophical foundations of human rights need to explain what it is about human beings that means that they are possessors of special and inalienable moral value, which value gives rise to a legitimate demand for special protections. The debate about the most plausible and successful explanations available is rich and varied and very much alive in the early twenty-first century. Here I have canvassed three influential and overlapping approaches: the interest view, the human dignity approach and the personhood approach.

None of these is without its critics, and none, it seems to me, can provide a complete and bullet-proof argument in defence of the claim that human beings, and only human beings, have special moral value of the sort that entails human rights. Critics of the project of finding philosophical foundations point to the implausibility of the normative purchase of an exclusively rationalist story and the ineffectiveness of foundationalist normative thought, or to the incoherence of an historically constructed moral concept being universally and transhistorically applied. Yet, Rorty, at least, was a vocal human rights advocate, arguing that the job of philosophers is to promote a human rights culture.

Irrespective of the outcomes of these debates, human rights *practice* is a feature of the contemporary world, and though philosophers disagree deeply about the reasons why persons have human rights, few, if any, deny the idea of human rights altogether. The content of these debates matters, though, when we confront the task of giving justifying reasons for rights claims when particular rights, or particular claimants, are denied. Moreover, it matters, given the primacy of human rights claims as an important ethical language that dominates contemporary political practice, that we understand the nature of the claims we make when we claim human rights. In the next chapter we will look at the arguments of scholars who have taken human rights practice, rather than political philosophy, to be the starting point for the best answers to the questions: what are human rights and why are they action-guiding?

4 A Political Conception of Human Rights

'[H]uman rights are synchronically universal. They are rights which all people living today have, a feature that is a precondition of, and a result of, the fact that they set limits to state sovereignty and justify accountability across borders. Human rights function in the international arena to underline the worth of all human life.' (Raz, 2010, p. 31)

Introduction

The project of justifying human rights, considered from various philosophical perspectives canvassed in the previous chapter, might be thought to be characteristic of what is variously called the 'naturalistic', 'orthodox' or 'traditional' conception of human rights. These approaches typically hold that what grounds human rights is to be found in some kind of account of the nature of human beings or some facet of humanity. But how the moral rights so justified translate into political and legal realities remains somewhat mysterious, even if the project of justification itself is successful. In contrast to this approach, the political conception of human rights holds that the naturalistic conception is mistaken in important and fundamental ways.

For advocates of the political view – such as Joseph Raz (quoted above) – when answering the question 'what is a human right?' we must start from political and legal practice in the real world, rather than starting from abstract philosophical ideas or principles. A crucial part of the practice of human rights relates to the interaction between human rights and sovereignty. Thus, in the first part of this chapter we will reflect on the concept of sovereignty and its relation to the ways in which human rights emerge and function in international politics.

In the second part of the chapter we will explore the key arguments advanced by advocates of the political view. As in any field of human rights theory, there are diverse voices and perspectives within this group of scholars. But what they share is the conviction that one should resist thinking morally about human rights in ways that float free from political and legal practice. This need not commit human rights theorists to a strong positivist thesis – that is, they need not hold that human rights only exist insofar as they exist in law – but it does signal a substantial departure from the sorts of defences of human rights pursued in terms of dignity, personhood and so on discussed in the previous chapter. In the final part of this chapter we will look at some criticisms of the political view, namely, that it is problematically state-centric, and that it struggles to determine the proper content of human rights. First, though, we may turn our attention to the question of how ideas about human rights might become laws about human rights.

Human rights in international legal and political practice

In Chapter 2 we touched upon the history of the transformation of human rights ideas into human rights proclamations. In the eighteenth century, national assemblies in France and the USA commissioned prominent political leaders to draft declarations of rights, which were then debated in committees and assemblies before being ratified. The declarations that emerged – the *Declaration of the Rights of Man and the Citizen* in France, and the Bill of Rights in the USA – were notably inflected with the language and ideas of philosophers who had published defences of natural rights in the seventeenth and eighteenth centuries.

When the newly created United Nations turned to the project of creating a Universal Declaration of Human Rights in 1947, the process was in some ways similar, and in some ways radically different. As discussed in Chapter 2, leading scholars and politicians were assembled to develop a draft, under the stewardship of Eleanor Roosevelt, which was eventually presented to the General Assembly of the United Nations and approved by the Assembly in December 1948. Significantly, the UDHR was drafted and approved by an *international* cohort, which, arguably, lends some credibility to its claims to universality (though see Chapter 2 for more on this).

The other significant difference is the political and institutional context in which contemporary global human rights regimes are proposed, debated, rejected and adopted. Whereas eighteenth-century declarations of natural rights applied, legally if not rhetorically, to the national contexts from which they emerged, today's human rights regime has global reach. But the way in which the globe is politically organized has a telling influence on human rights practice today. The world is divided up into sovereign states, and it is against this backdrop of political and legal organization that we understand the complex practice of human rights.

As noted in Chapter 1, the concept of sovereignty plays an important role in contemporary political human rights practice, so it is worth understanding something of the complexity of sovereignty as both an institutional arrangement and a norm. The United Nations Charter recognizes and affirms the norm of sovereignty as a cornerstone of the organization of international politics. The world is divided into formal political units that we refer to as sovereign states. The governments of sovereign states have a unique authority within their own territories, and mutual recognition of that authority by other sovereign governments is a marker of the status of sovereign authorities compared to other actors in international politics, such as multinational corporations (MNCs) like BP, international organizations like the UN, or non-governmental organizations (NGOs) like the Red Cross.

International relations theorists trace the history of sovereignty to the Peace of Westphalia of 1648, a treaty that marked the end of the Thirty Years' War in Europe (Bull, 2002; Jackson, 2000). Just as eighteenth-century declarations of natural rights do not quite 'give birth' to human rights, nor does the Peace of Westphalia mark the sudden appearance of sovereignty as a recognized and functioning norm of international politics. But it is true to say that the contemporary understanding of sovereignty is significantly indebted to a set of ideas that first find concrete expression in the Westphalia treaty.

What the Peace of Westphalia established as a principle for international relations is the idea that the prince, or sovereign authority, of a given state, would have the right to determine the religious affiliation of a state (in fact this was first affirmed in the earlier Peace of Augsburg, 1555). This committed other sovereign authorities to respect the religious choices of a given state, and to reject the practice of taking religious disagreement to be a pretext for war:

> The principle *cujus regio ejus religio* was designed to prohibit religious imperialism with its inevitable destruction and instability, but it helped to nurture a much more general principle prohibiting intervention against sovereign states that has come to be a central tenet of

the international system that grew out of the Peace of Westphalia. (Buchanen, 2000, p. 703)

We should not overlook the influence of territorial ambition and other factors in the causal variables leading to the Thirty Years' War, but as Buchanen asserts, we can nevertheless say that in this element of the Peace of Westphalia we find the kernel of the contemporary idea of sovereignty as the expression of a state's right to self-determination. Respect for a political community's right to self-determination has been understood to be central to the preservation of peace in international affairs.

It is for this reason that sovereignty is recognized so centrally in the United Nations Charter, which may itself be thought of as the expression of the post-Second World War powers' determination to avoid world conflict on the scale seen in the 1930s and 1940s. The norm of sovereignty implies the right of a government to decide on the good for its people, and disables the authority of external agents to make such decisions. In other words, it is because of the principle of sovereignty that the government of France does not have the right to tell the government of the USA how it ought to organize its welfare programmes.

It is also for this reason that international law is produced by sovereign states. There is no higher authority than sovereign states in international politics. Organizations such as the UN, international legal regimes such as the International Bill of Rights, the International Criminal Court (ICC), and so on, are not, and in an important sense *cannot* be, imposed upon states; rather, they are the creation of states. Through their collective will, states can and do create powerful norms around compliance with international treaties, including but not limited to human rights treaties. Sovereign states have the power to choose to subject themselves to the authority of legal regimes, or not, by signing and ratifying the treaties establishing them. So, for example, the ICC, set up to prosecute war crimes, has jurisdiction over many countries in the world, but not the USA, because the USA has opted not to sign up to the ICC statutes.

Sovereign states have the right to choose to create and sustain international agreements to uphold norms of human rights, or to choose to exempt themselves from the collective will of states should other states pursue such practices. We should note that there are very good reasons for defending the right to political self-determination that sovereignty embodies. I might reasonably think that my own government, particularly if that government is democratically elected by me and my fellow citizens, has a better chance of knowing and understanding my best interests than some foreign agent. Certainly, the record of colonial powers in the sixteenth to twentieth centuries suggests that colonized peoples are vulnerable to exploitation. Thus, we look to sovereign states, not just to create international treaties that establish human rights (among other things), but also to protect and uphold our human rights. The contemporary international human rights regime is noticeably state-centric, in that the rights affirmed are principally the rights of citizens of a state. They are rights that *all* citizens of *all* states ought to have, but the primary responsibility for upholding these rights is assigned to the states themselves.

This is the 'sovereignty paradox' referred to in Chapter 1: the international political order, of which the norm of sovereignty acts as a cornerstone, both upholds the universal validity of human rights and assigns responsibility for those rights to sovereign states. Indeed, the universal legitimacy of human rights is, on one level at least, a product of the agreement of sovereign states to create international treaties recognizing universal human rights. We may well discern the influence of philosophical debates on the foundations and justifications for human rights in the language and substance of human rights treaties, we may even hold that the moral authority of human rights is independent of their existing in positive law, nonetheless, the reality is that human rights practice is, at one level at least, largely dependent on the will of sovereign states. Moreover, the norm of sovereignty both facilitates the legal authority of states to make international treaties and provides the moral and legal justification for states to assert their right not to be bound by international obligations that are not of their choosing. It is because of the principle of sovereignty that the USA is free to assert the validity of the International Covenant on Civil and Political Rights and to resist calls to submit to the authority of the International Criminal Court. Hence, An-Na'im argues, 'A realistic and appropriate objective, therefore, is to diminish the negative consequences of the paradox of self-regulation by infusing the ethos of human rights into the fabric of the state itself and the global context in which it operates' (2001, p. 97).

When a given state signs and ratifies an international treaty, for example one that upholds human rights, the state may then honour its newly acquired obligations by incorporating this into its domestic laws. So, for example, the European Convention on Human Rights (ECHR), established in 1953, obliges signatories to ensure that their national laws and constitutions are consistent with the principles of human rights enshrined in the convention. This process can take a long time. It was not until 1998 in Scotland and 2000 in the rest of the UK that the Human

Rights Act was passed into law, requiring the UK government and the devolved governments in Scotland, Wales and Northern Ireland to ensure that all legislation binding its citizens was consistent with human rights as set out in the ECHR. The ECHR establishes a European Court of Human Rights which is the ultimate arbiter in disputes between signatory governments and their citizens as to whether or not the governments have upheld their citizens' human rights. Thus, citizens have human rights recognized under European law, but these are rights against their governments. However, governments bound by the European Court of Human Rights have agreed to surrender a part of their sovereignty and to respect the authority of the Court to arbitrate in disputes between citizens and governments (though cases only reach the European Court after appeals to domestic courts have been exhausted). At the time of writing, a small but well publicized number of cases have ended in rulings against the UK government. This, amongst other things, has prompted the UK Conservative Party to propose withdrawing altogether from the ECHR and establishing its own Bill of Rights instead.

So, we can see that sovereignty both defines and limits the scope of human rights. But this is not the whole story, for international politics is not simply an arena of rules, it is also an arena of power, discourse, persuasion and (sometimes) manipulation. So there will be multiple factors that lead a sovereign state to decide whether or not to join an international treaty regime which establishes human rights in law, for example, the International Covenant on Civil and Political Rights (part of the International Bill of Rights; see Chapter 1). Human rights are asserted not just by governments, but also by people, both individually and collectively in social movements. Indeed, the contribution of social movements to the development of human rights is enormously significant (Stammers, 1999). Governments respond not just to 'hard power' – to military threats and economic sanctions – but also to 'soft power' – the power of attraction that cultural and political discourses and phenomena can exert. Moreover, international organizations, such as the UN, act as advocates of human rights, particularly through the activities of the Human Rights Council, which monitors human rights conditions around the globe and makes recommendations on issues of concern. In addition, NGOs at national and international levels put pressure on governments to protect human rights. Many have developed extensive and sophisticated media operations to mobilize individual citizens in support of their campaigns.

The recent 'Arab Spring' is illustrative here. Governments across the Arab world faced pressures not just from other governments, who may, as in the case of Libya, threaten military force in support of populist uprisings, but also from world opinion, from media censure, from individual citizens at home and abroad, from Amnesty International and Human Rights Watch. The Arab Spring unfolded in the context of a world in which the norms of human rights carry enormous moral authority. As noted earlier on, hardly anyone denies the validity of human rights. That has not, of course, led to spontaneous and complete respect for human rights everywhere in the Arab world, nor the wider world, but it is nonetheless part of the political reality.

This, then, is the political and legal context to which the political view of human rights theory responds. If we are to understand what human rights are, and if we are to say something about why they might be justified, we must begin with human rights as they are practised in the world. They exist as laws and treaties, they exist at the heart of the sovereignty paradox, they exist in national constitutions, but they also exist in the claims advanced by individuals and social movements, who simultaneously respond to and affirm the status of human rights as global norms.

The political view

Advocates of the political view take human rights *as a practice* as the starting point for theorizing about human rights (see , for example. Beitz, 2004, 2009; Cohen, 2004; Pogge, 2002; Rawls, 1993; Raz, 2007, 2010). In doing so, they avoid at least some of the pernicious philosophical doubts that plague the traditional view. The job of philosophy, with respect to theorizing human rights, is not, on this view, concerned with providing deep philosophical foundations. In the context of a plural world, there is little reason to expect such foundations to be available, or at any rate persuasive, to a potentially global domain of agents. However, a political, rather than a moral philosophical argument, is available that both justifies our commitment to human rights and offers a mechanism for understanding more precisely what human rights are and what work they can justly be invoked to do. (We will say more about the significance of moral pluralism for human rights in Chapter 6.)

The initial source for this political argument is John Rawls' (1993/1999) 'Law of Peoples', which is deeply influenced by his more general philosophical work on the nature and scope of political justification (see Rawls, 1999b, 2005; Wenar, 2008a). For Rawls, global justice is a two-stage project. Domestic justice – justice at the level of sovereign states – is independent of, and prior to, global justice. The norms that govern domestic justice, such as principles of fair cooperation and equality of opportunity, do not necessarily apply at the level of international justice. Just as cultural and religious diversity, and related value pluralism, is a fact of life at the domestic level, so too is pluralism a fact of life at the international level. Given this, we should not expect complete agreement on which principles of justice should govern our political institutions. On the contrary, disagreement is inevitable, but that does not preclude cooperation. At the domestic or national level cooperation can be sustained by an 'overlapping consensus' around principles of justice, which consensus depends upon our agreeing on constitutional rules even if we disagree on why those particular rules are the right ones. This is possible at the domestic level in part because our experience of cooperation allows us to move beyond a mere *modus vivendi*, where our agreeing on rules is contingent and provisional, to a genuine experience of solidarity which will underpin the overlapping consensus.

Some theorists, such as Jack Donnelly (2003), hail the UDHR as the product of an international overlapping consensus understood in Rawlsian terms – that is, the UDHR is the expression of an agreement about the basic rules of justice for international society: we agree on its content and that it is right, even though we disagree profoundly about the underlying values and thus the reasons why it is right. The point is that the device of the overlapping consensus facilitates agreement on principles that can be the subject of political cooperation, whilst remaining agnostic on *moral* agreement about fundamental values. This move rather ignores both the limiting conditions Rawls himself placed on the conditions necessary for an overlapping consensus, and arguably downplays aspects of the historical conditions in which the UDHR emerged (see Chapter 2).

Rawls himself is rather more cautious. He takes human rights to set the limits of legitimate toleration in the international domain. 'Human rights are a class of rights that play a special role in a reasonable Law of Peoples; they restrict the justifying reasons for war and its conduct, and they specify limits to a regime's internal autonomy' (Rawls, 1999b, p. 79). Only those states that exhibit respect for basic rights are entitled to international respect and to claim the right to self-determination, which implies sovereign authority and thus the non-interference of external forces: '[B]asic human rights express a minimum standard of well-ordered political institutions for all peoples who belong, as members in good standing, to a just political society of peoples' (Rawls, 1993, p. 68).

However, Rawls' account of basic rights is notably sparing, insofar as it includes only the right to life (which includes the means of subsistence and security), liberty (which includes freedom from slavery and 'a measure of liberty of conscience'), to personal property, and to formal equality (1993, p. 65), and a right to emigrate in some circumstances (1993, pp. 65–77). Basic rights do not include rights to democratic participation, rights to non-discrimination on grounds of gender, rights to education, nor several other rights included in the International Bill of Rights. For Tasioulas, among others, this counts as a reason to reject Rawls' account, though he is also critical of Raz for 'fetishizing' the content of the International Bill of Rights to the exclusion of abstract theorizing about the content of human rights (Tasioulas, 2011, pp. 51, 53).

Conceptualizing human rights as Rawls does avoids the need for recourse to deeply contested philosophical, religious and ideological views about the nature of human beings or the universal demands of morality. Instead, the argument for human rights can be 'politically neutral' in the sense of being justifiable from within multiple and deeply divergent philosophical perspectives (Rawls, 1993, p. 69). Thus understood, human rights function as a 'disabling mechanism' in regulating the behaviour of sovereign states. As Raz explains:

> Individual rights are human rights if they disable a certain argument against interference by outsiders or deny the legitimacy of the response: I, the state, may have acted wrongly, but you, the outsider, are not entitled to interfere ... Disabling the defence of 'none of your business' is definitive of the political conception of human rights. (Raz, 2007, p. 14)

This is exactly what Rawls' 'Law of Peoples' does – it establishes classes of states, dividing the world into those that respect basic rights and those that do not. Indeed, according to advocates of the political view, the most distinctive feature of human rights in practice is that they provide 'defeasible' (Raz, 2007) or 'pro tanto' (Beitz, 2009) reasons to set norms of sovereignty aside and pursue some form of humanitarian intervention, such as military action or economic sanctions.

Those states that respect basic human rights are entitled to claim the protections of the norms of sovereignty. This includes both liberal states and what Rawls calls 'well-ordered hierarchical societies' that respect basic rights. Those states that are hampered by lack of capacity, but are also basically decent, have a claim to international assistance. However, 'outlaw' states, those that fail to respect basic rights, may legitimately be subjected to military or economic sanctions by liberal states (see Rawls,

1993/1999b). (Note that Rawls does not intend 'peoples' and 'states' to be co-terminous, but in sketching the general outline of his theory we can understand the classes of states in this way – see Buchanen, 2000.) This vision of the operation of basic rights in international politics informs Donnelly's (1998) view of human rights as a 'standard of civilisation', whereby respect for human rights is the price that a state must pay if it is to expect the cooperation of other sovereign states on fair terms.

As Raz notes, however, Rawls' 'Law of Peoples' makes the protection of human rights contingent on the availability of honourable and capable international actors willing to police the international society. If this is true then something of the character of human rights claims as normative claims, that signals the moral status of individual human beings, has been lost. Rawls' 'Law of Peoples' looks to many critics to be some distance from our ordinary understanding of human rights, however vague and contested that ordinary understanding might be.

Moreover, Rawls' readiness to tolerate hierarchically ordered societies, provided they respect basic rights, is deeply controversial. Recall that basic rights do not include rights to equality, but much human rights practice that is bottom up, that is, driven by social movements, has been precisely concerned with claims to equality. To this extent, Rawls' theory departs from human rights practice. His stated aim, of course, is to work back from a 'realistic utopia' towards the political realities we find today. Rawls is aware that societies are treated deeply unequally and that this is inconsistent with liberal principles of justice: 'Rawls takes great pains to construct a law of peoples that affirms the equality of peoples. He is to be commended for emphasizing that interference in societies that differ from ours can be a repudiation of this equality' (Buchanen, 2000, p. 709). But, as Buchanen points out, Rawls' focus on peoples rather than individuals leaves individuals at the mercy of their leaders' views regarding equality in ways that will be unsatisfactory to many, if not most, advocates of human rights.

Raz's work on human rights has influenced at least some of those who advocate what he calls the traditional view of human rights, which is why we looked at his account of interest theory in the previous chapter. But Raz is clear that the traditional view offers a wrong-headed account of human rights, because it understands the purpose of human rights theorizing in unhelpful ways. As he explains:

> The ethical doctrine of human rights should articulate standards by which human rights practice can be judged, standards which will indi-

cate what human rights we have. In doing so it will elucidate what is at issue, what is the significance of a right's being a human right. (2007, p. 2)

For Raz, Rawls' account is flawed because it fails to adequately capture some rights which protect important human interests, but the philosophical project that Rawls is embarked upon, namely, to identify and set standards for the practice of human rights in international affairs, is essentially sound. Hence, Raz argues, '[m]oral rights that cannot be fairly and effectively protected through legal processes are not human rights' (2010, p. 31). Where Raz differs from Rawls is in ascribing obligations to other international actors besides states (for example, MNCs), and in his account of the limits of state sovereignty.

Another advocate of the political view who is sympathetic to these claims is Charles R. Beitz (2009). He develops and extends the Rawlsian approach in his practice-inspired account of human rights. On Beitz's view, however, human rights not only set the limits of legitimate sovereign authority, they also function as a guide to establishing the roles and responsibilities of other actors in international politics:

> [T]here is a broad range of non-coercive political and economic measures that states and international organizations can use to influence the internal affairs of societies where human rights are threatened, measures that are better classified as assistance than interference ... Beitz believes that from the perspective of a theory's attempting to explain the current international practice of human rights, it would be better to take a broader view of the international role of human rights than Rawls's narrower view. (Liao and Etinson, 2012, p. 5)

The thought here is that the purpose of theorizing about human rights is to identify what human rights and what the distribution of responsibilities for human rights should look like. According to Beitz, the answers that the traditional or naturalistic account can give to these questions 'tend to distort rather than illuminate international human rights practice' (2004, p. 198). Beitz thus advocates the political view because better understanding what human rights are will help to overcome some of the 'disabling scepticism' (2009, p. 2) surrounding contemporary human rights, and, again, the proper method by which to proceed is to theorize from contemporary practice, rather than expect practice to conform to theory. An account of human rights must begin with political and legal reality, then, but it is also Beitz's intention that his method will give scope for reflexive criticism of human rights practice. In effect, analysis of human rights practice gives individual agents as well as social movements justifying reasons for critiquing the practices of states where they fail to uphold human rights.

What emerges, then, is a 'two-level' model of human rights that divides responsibility for human rights between states, who are the primary duty-bearers, and individuals and non-government actors, whose responsibility is to raise concerns when states fail to do their job. Beitz writes approvingly of Thomas Pogge's (2002) 'institutional' model of human rights, which we will consider in more detail in Chapter 8. On an interactional model of human rights, a person has honoured their human rights obligations by not directly violating the rights of another person. On an institutional model, by contrast, individual responsibilities for human rights are mediated through their engagement with institutions, so whilst (political, economic) institutions have direct responsibility for the human rights of people affected by their activities, individuals have indirect responsibility to the extent that they are complicit in the activities of the institution. A fuller explanation of this is available in Chapter 8. The point to note here is that for Beitz, this two-level model 'is a distinctive feature, perhaps the most distinctive feature, of contemporary human rights practice' (2009, p. 115), yet detailed discussion of this sort of division of responsibility for human rights is largely absent from naturalistic accounts of human rights, such as those discussed in the previous chapter.

Another contrast with the naturalistic view is that it follows from the practice-based starting point that Beitz denies an ahistorical universality to human rights claims. Human rights are not logically or foundationally true, as the most determined advocates of the moral view hope to prove; they are facets of contemporary international politics that serve a particular function. That function is to protect the interests of individuals by regulating the conduct primarily of states, but also of other powerful actors, like MNCs.

The mistake of the traditional or naturalistic view, Beitz argues, is to focus on questions of human nature and the interests and duties that might be derived from it, which serves to 'deflect attention' from the more difficult and important questions of human rights, namely, 'the extent of failure or default at the domestic level required to trigger protective or remedial action by outside agents', as well as the distribution of responsibility for such action and the 'demandingness of the reasons for action' vis-à-vis other reasons (Beitz, 2009, p. 65). In contrast, the focus on the practice of human rights brings these issues to the fore. This is to be welcomed, as these are questions to which any theory of human rights must supply answers.

Criticisms of the political view

So far we have explored the views of advocates of the political view. Advocates of the political view contend that it is superior to the sorts of justifications for human rights that were considered in the previous chapter. But the political view is itself controversial. Here I will draw out two principal strands of critique: first, regarding the state-centrism of the political view, and second, the claim that the political view struggles to determine the content of human rights. Following on from this, we will look at a recent argument that suggests that the distance between the political view and the traditional view is rather shorter than adherents of each suggest.

John Tasioulas is amongst those who comprehensively reject the political view. He argues:

> [The political view] construes human rights as conceptually parasitic on the idea of some kind of political institution ... But the language of human rights is often employed by people who do not accept the desirability of states ... [and] they often appeal to human rights principles in order to defend their views about the state and the state system. (2011, p. 47)

This is an important point that can be pressed against a number of theorists who draw their inspiration from Rawls' 'Law of Peoples'. Certainly, Donnelly's (1998) vision of human rights as a 'standard of civilization' looks vulnerable to this attack. In fairness to Rawls, the principal question motivating his work on the 'Law of Peoples' concerns the foreign policy obligations of liberal states. Advocates of a somewhat thicker vision of human rights based upon the political view, such as Raz and Beitz, are not committed to saying that states are the only agents with responsibility for human rights. Thus, to the extent that they assign responsibilities for human rights more widely than Rawls does, they can be defended against the charge that their ideas are wholly dependent on states as agents.

But Tasioulas' point goes deeper than this. The political view rests on the premise that we understand human rights best by taking account of actual political practice. The contemporary human rights regime is undeniably state-centric. Individuals have rights against their own state first and foremost. Contemporary human rights practice presupposes a state-centric framework in law and politics for the operation of human rights at all (and indeed for the organization of political communities). This fact explains Hannah Arendt's (1971) critique of human rights as not human rights at all, but rather *civic* rights, rights whose protection and expression presuppose a political community. As Arendt is aware, amongst the most dangerous conditions for a human being is to be without membership of a political community. Hence, she thinks of the most fundamental kind of rights as a 'right to have rights' (Arendt, 1971; cf. Parekh, 2004).

It is not inevitable that we would think of human rights, and of the organization of political communities, in this state-based way. Beitz begins his theorizing of human rights from one manifestation of human rights practice, but largely ignores others. He is deeply critical of the legacy of natural rights theorizing in terms of its impact on contemporary accounts of the philosophical justifications for human rights (2009, ch2), but he begins his account of human rights *practice* with the post-Second World War United Nations system, and ignores the legacy of eighteenth-, nineteenth- and twentieth-century international campaigns against slavery, for feminism, for labour rights, and so on. This leads him to ignore the impact of these global movements in shaping human rights practice (see Chapter 2). There is in fact a long tradition in campaigning that may be plausibly called human rights oriented that asserts alternatives to the statist global order, from cosmopolitanism to anarchism. It is one thing to avoid debates about the purported ahistoricity of human rights that the claimed universalism of human rights seems to demand. But it is quite another to pretend that human rights emerged, fully formed, in the 1948 UDHR, and that if we are to understand human rights as a practice, that is where we should begin our researches.

Moreover it is deeply problematic, if we are to be informed by the reality of human rights practice in our thinking about human rights, to privilege the state-centric structure of contemporary human rights practice, over, say, the advancing of human rights as moral claims by campaigners and activists, as deterministic of the nature of human rights. On the contrary, doing so leads us to miss important aspects of the contemporary *and historical* practice of human rights. Whilst philosophers certainly do not have a monopoly over the definitions of concepts, it is simply not true that there has not been a long-standing and significant discourse of internationalism that has sought to undermine the privileging of the state as the primary political unit.

The state-centrism of contemporary human rights is particularly criticized from post-colonial perspectives by a number of scholars who call attention to the practical imprudence of assigning primary responsibility for human rights to agents who are formally equal but not functionally equal (Clapham, 1999; An-Na'im, 2001; O'Neill, 2004, 2005). The sovereignty-based international order formally recognizes sovereign governments as having equal standing in international affairs to the extent that they comply with the norms of international politics. But it is simply not the case that states are equal in terms of economic, military or other forms of power (Buchanen, 2000). Relatively poor developing countries, such as Mali, do not have capacities to protect the human rights of their citizens equal to the capacities of rich, developed countries, such as France. Indeed, as Abdullahi A. An-Na'im (2001) points out, the underfulfilment of human rights is the norm, not the exception, in the world's poorest states. In the context of such divergent capabilities, it is foolish, on this view, to expect success from a system that assigns responsibilities equally to sovereign governments *qua* governments. Of course, as noted above, there are nevertheless very good reasons to respect the norms of self-determination, and post-colonial states are often amongst those most vocal in defence of national sovereignty, and most critical of global human rights norms. We will return to these issues in Chapter 8.

For now I want to pursue the second concern, namely, that the political view struggles to establish the content of human rights. Again, this problem follows from the method of taking political and legal practice as the starting point for our analyses of human rights. What is the status of the rights that are recognized in existing human rights conventions? What is the status of calls for new rights, for example, environmental human rights, to be enshrined in human rights laws? Pablo Gilabert sets out the difficulty here:

> Now, most defenders of the political approach are not crude conventionalists. They say that although we should start with practices as they are, we may come to criticize aspects of them, demanding that beliefs involved in them be changed. This is certainly Beitz's view. But how do we come to criticize the contemporary practice of human rights? If we look at it, we find a myriad of often opposing views ... How are we to settle such disputes? Beitz suggests that we critically arbitrate these disagreements by considering how the different claims

fit the 'aims' or 'role' of the existing human rights practice. But, as Beitz acknowledges, contention exists not only regarding the content of the Declaration but also about the aims and role of human rights discourse itself. (2011, p. 447)

Having accepted the political view's claim that we should take human rights practice as our starting point for theorizing about human rights, we are left wondering how to arbitrate between conflicting and competing claims that arise. Human rights practice is not a singular phenomenon, unless one takes human rights practice to be co-termi-nous with one set of agents (for example, states), though even then it would hardly be without conflict. One of the appealing features of the ways in which contemporary theorists such as Beitz and Raz have moved forward from the narrowly statist vision in Rawls' 'Law of Peoples' is that there is room in their accounts for the contribution to human rights practice made by non-state actors. But this very richness opens up more sites of conflict about the practice of human rights. It is unclear how the political view can resolve questions of what the content of human rights, and what the function of human rights, should be, if the method for addressing these questions is to reflect on human rights practice alone.

    This issue leads two critics to suggest that there is less separating the political view from the traditional view than it first appears. Liao and Etinson (2012) claim that the political view can only give a formal answer to the question: what is a human right? That is, the political view can point to practices in the world, and can do so to build an analytical framework that allows us to differentiate between those rights that are properly to be called human rights, and those that are not. Recall Raz's claim, above, that '[m]oral rights that cannot be fairly and effectively protected though legal processes are not human rights' (2010, p. 31). Moreover, he sees it as part of the purpose of an ethics of human rights to accurately account for the significance of a right being a human right. But these two functions do not add up to what Liao and Etinson call a 'substantive' account of human rights: 'A substantive account ... provides criteria for generating the content of human rights' (2012, p. 26). Beitz resists providing a list of human rights, instead proposing a 'model' of the criteria that human rights must meet in order to be consid-ered human rights. These criteria reflect the dynamic between human interests, standard institutional threats to those interests, and the capaci-ties and interactions of institutions in contemporary international politics (see Beitz, 2009, pp. 105–6).

The preference for formal criteria for rights, rather than a substantive account of what rights we have, is consistent with the rejection of traditional or naturalistic accounts of human rights that attempt to provide philosophical foundations for their justification. But this also neglects an important practical role that philosophizing about human rights in fact plays in human rights practice: 'philosophical notions such as human dignity and worth are found in many prominent declarations as well as national constitutions and have been central to the reception of human rights across cultures' (Liao and Etinson, 2012, p. 11). Liao and Etinson conclude that the political view is in an important sense incomplete, and that it is dependent upon elements of the naturalistic or traditional accounts of human rights which we discussed in the previous chapter in order to fully answer the question, 'what is a human right?', as well as in order to fully capture contemporary human rights practice.

Conclusion

In this chapter we have considered the political conception of human rights, which stands in opposition to the traditional view of human rights, examples of which we discussed in the previous chapter. The political view takes as its point of departure not abstract philosophical accounts of the human being, her inherent interests, dignity or personhood, but rather, human rights practice as it exists in law and politics in the real world. As such, the political view casts light on important dimensions of the reality of human rights, and prompts us to make sense of the concept of sovereignty, which stands as a foundational norm in contemporary international politics.

Yet, from this brief overview we can see that the political view of human rights is as contentious as the traditional or naturalistic account its advocates aim to supersede. The greatest strength of the political view is that it accurately captures something of how human rights might operate as a normative demand in international politics. Its weakness, though, is that it cannot entirely overcome what it takes to be the mistaken enterprise of giving moral, rather than political, reasons for acting in support of human rights. The traditional view may be ultimately unable to supply such reasons in the terms that its adherents find desirable. However, the political conception of human rights also appears to be incomplete.

Once again, human rights activists may find frustrating and dissatisfying the persistence of philosophical doubts that apparently plague the efforts of human rights theorists to answer such basic yet urgent questions as 'what is a human right, why do we have them, what obligations do they entail?' But if we take seriously the thought that the demand that individuals respect human rights is a demand made to morally free agents, who each have equal entitlement to pursue their own conception of the good and who have diverse conceptions of the good, then we should not be surprised to find that these questions are in fact extremely difficult. In the next chapters, we will delve deeper into the reasons why cultural, religious and moral pluralism makes the project of justifying human rights a complex one.

5 Religion and Human Rights

'[T]he very secular foundation of the Declaration is deemed episte-
mologically insufficient to account for the derivation of inherent and
inalienable human rights.' (Sachedina, 2009, p. 6)

Introduction

Declarations of natural rights in the eighteenth century referred to men
and their rights as 'sacred'. Contemporary human rights make no reference to a religious foundation. Abdulaziz Sachedina, quoted above, is
amongst those who wonder whence derives the moral authority for the
special status of human beings if we subscribe to a secular account of
human rights. Other critics are sceptical of the capacity of purportedly
secular human rights to command the allegiance of religious believers in
a deeply diverse world. The UDHR protects both the right to freedom of
conscience and the right to freedom of religion in the same article (18).
The right to freedom of conscience protects the right to hold beliefs
consistent with atheism or agnosticism. The right to freedom of religion
as detailed in the UDHR also includes the right to change one's religion.
Freedom of conscience, then, implies the right to hold any religious
beliefs or none. This appears to be incompatible with religious traditions,
such as Islam, that prohibit apostasy.

However, for the framers of the UDHR it was important that religious
freedom be included in the text and be broadly construed: Charles Malik,
the Lebanese Christian who was involved in the drafting of the UDHR,
argued staunchly for the need to protect rights of citizens to 'develop
ultimate loyalties' (above loyalties to the state), otherwise there would be
no real freedom (quoted in Perry, 2005, p. 385). Indeed, some contemporary defenders of the right to freedom of conscience (particularly in

85

the USA) see it as a particularly important right that has privileged status within the pantheon of fundamental rights (Nussbaum, 2008; cf. Mendus, 2011).

This chapter explores two sets of questions around religion and human rights. The first concerns this issue of secularism and whether, given the fact that two-thirds of the world's inhabitants profess a religious faith, a secular account of human rights is an obstacle to commitment to human rights for adherents of religious faiths. Against this view, some stress the Judeo-Christian influence on the development of human rights, and find in this reason to think that human rights embody a particular religious tradition that is problematic for both secular people and adherents of other faiths. Others still argue that the concept of human dignity, which we first met in Chapter 3, can serve as a bridge between secular and religious conceptions of human rights.

The second set of questions to be addressed in this chapter concerns the ethics of understanding human rights within a particular religious framework, where some generally recognized element of human rights seems to be at odds with the teachings of a particular faith. In this context we will pay particular attention to Islam, but conflicts between these religious values and what might be called the values of human rights are not unique to Islam. First, though, it is helpful to get a sense of the difference it might make to a claim about human rights whether one takes secular or religious ideas as being the appropriate starting point for normative claims, so let us begin with that.

A secular or religious source for moral authority?

Critics from various perspectives advance the view that human rights are inherently secular, and that this undermines the claimed universality of human rights. On the other hand, a smaller number of scholars hold that human rights are inherently religious, and that they cannot be adequately understood and justified from within a secular world view.

We should be careful to consider what the term 'secular' actually means. As Talal Asad (2003) points out, it is impossible to make sense of the term secular in isolation from its perceived antonyms, sacred, religious, and from concepts of private and public reason. Secular, within Christian theology, has been understood in some contexts as signalling that which is not sacred, and so could include much which is understood to be 'religious'. On the other hand, within contemporary liberal political thought we routinely encounter a conception of secularism that is tied to the notion of (Rawlsian) public reason, where reason is a practice of giving sharable justifications within a political community (cf. Taylor, 2007). In popular media debates we sometimes find secular construed as 'anti-religious'. In the present discussion we will use secular simply to mean 'non-religious', but of course this definition is not perfect.

Another point we should note is that, in some respects, the conflicts animating this chapter reflect a deeper metaethical debate about whether or not morality can be commanding in the absence of God. While ancient philosophers were concerned with questions of what it is to lead a good and flourishing life, the concepts of ought and duty, corollaries of the concept of a right, arise from the Abrahamic faiths and the notion that human morality consists in obeying the commands of God (Loobuyck, 2010; cf. Williams, 1972). In a theistic worldview, morality has normative force – that is, it is action-guiding, indeed, action-demanding – because it is connected to God's Law. The rise of secularism in the organization of law and politics in the West (in particular) has disestablished the authority of God for morality whilst retaining the conception of morality as a set of commands and demands (Korsgaard, 1996).

Immanuel Kant's systematization of moral philosophy as a set of 'categorical imperatives' is amongst the most influential examples of attempts to retain the normative structure of moral philosophy without relying on the normative authority of God. His thought is especially important for human rights theory because he gives an account of the relationship between human dignity and morality that significantly informs secular accounts of human dignity (Arieli, 2002). In his *Fundamental Principles of the Metaphysics of Morals*, Kant (2004) tells us: 'Morality, and humanity as capable of it, is that which alone has dignity'. Moral freedom, for Kant, consists in following that law which the agent has willed for herself. Humans are uniquely capable of this freedom on earth (the other animals are not), thus, humans occupy a place of unique value: 'Autonomy then is the basis of the dignity of human and of every rational nature' (Kant, 2004).

Thus, the quality that gives humanity the special moral character that constitutes its value, is the capacity to act morally. Because the capacity to act morally is a function of rationality, for many interpreters of Kant, rationality is implicitly the source of value. Quite how and why this should be the case is a difficult question to answer, and we spent some time addressing it in Chapter 3. Schopenhauer famously derided Kant's conception of dignity and its use by subsequent moral theorists:

That expression, *dignity of man*, once uttered by Kant, afterward became the shibboleth of all the perplexed and empty-headed moralists who concealed behind that imposing expression their lack of any real basis of morals, or, at any rate, of one that had any meaning. (Quoted in Rosen, 2012, p. 1)

Nevertheless, Kant's conception of dignity as related to morality and reason is important for the present discussion both because it is the most consistently invoked basis of a secular understanding of the source of human moral value, and because it reflects a vision of morality in which moral authority and moral value exist independently of God.

In contrast, Michael J. Perry, the most prominent advocate of the view that human rights are ineliminably religious, bases his argument around the claim that only a religious worldview can supply an adequate framework for comprehending the claim that human beings are morally valuable in a special way, and give force to the normative injunctions that rights claims are intended to invoke (Perry, 1992, 2000). In Perry's thought the inherent dignity of the human person is a necessary prior assumption for the concept of human rights (Elshtain, 1999).

Responding to Perry's challenge, Ronald Dworkin proposes a secular account of human dignity that is equivalent to the religious view of the sacredness of human life based on two 'principles' of dignity: The first is the principle of intrinsic value, which holds that human life has objective value, and which, it is argued, matters not just to the individual but to all humans, in the sense that, '[t]he success or failure of any human life is important in itself, something we all have *reason* to want or to deplore' (Dworkin, 2006, pp. 9–10). The second is the principle of personal responsibility, whereby each person is responsible for his own potentiality (Dworkin, 2006, p. 10). These two principles of dignity are informed by the values of equality (the first principle) and liberty (the second principle).

The difficulty with these principles as a secular explanation of human dignity is that Dworkin does not explain, so much as assert as fact, the claim that human life has objective value, which dignity is itself invoked in human rights documents to explain. Perry argues that something more is inferred in the quality of human dignity than can be supplied in a secular cosmology because a secular view would have to assert that there is meaning and worth in humanity in the context of a view of the universe as meaningless, or at least a view that is agnostic about the possibility of meaning. Humanity, then, is the only solid reference point.

Dworkin seems to be using 'sacred' in what we can call a weak, or 'subjective', sense – something (such as a human life) is sacred *because*, or *in the sense that*, it inspires awe in us and we attach great value to it – rather than in the strong, or 'objective', sense – something is sacred and *therefore* it inspires awe in us and we attach great value to it (Perry, 1998, p. 28).

A religious explanation of the inherent dignity of the human person can be derived from claims about the divine that connects human beings to ultimate value. In Christian theology, which is Perry's focus, we find the position that man is sacred, and has dignity, because man is made in the image of God. But while Perry's argument is developed through a discussion of Christianity, it is not intended to be tied exclusively to a Christian ontology. Christ's injunction to love one another gives a universalistic command to respect one another as persons, which is not so dissimilar to Kant's vision of the universal demands of morality.

Others have doubted the feasibility of Perry's purported ecumenicalism in his religious defence of rights. For example, Jean Bethke Elshtain, in a Catholic-inflected reading of Perry's account, doubts the cogency of Perry's argument: 'too much of the deep background and justification for rights has been jettisoned along the way in order to maximize the palatability of rights in cultures in which rights are not an outgrowth of the dominant order of things' (Elshtain, 1999, pp. 55–6). Leaving this concern to one side, the crucial factor is the availability of an account of ultimate value, of the divine. Many philosophers who have attempted to find ways of grounding human rights in non-Western traditions have found the secularism of the philosophical foundations reviewed in Chapter 3 to be especially problematic, and have, against this, affirmed the ways in which human personhood is connected to the divine to explain and justify the normativity of human rights. For example, Sachedina writes: 'Islamic doctrines speak about equal creation of human beings, sharing the parentage and endowed with honor and dignity as the "children of Adam"' (2009, p. 12), while Seyyed H. Nasr (1980) justifies human rights in terms of duties owed to God (Allah). This connection between the human and the divine serving as a foundation for normative claims is not unique to those committed to the Abrahamic faiths. Kwasi Wiredu, in an interpretation of human rights grounded in an Akan perspective, explains whence the special moral value of persons arises:

> By virtue of possessing an *okra*, a divine element, every person has
> an intrinsic value, the same in each, which he does not owe to any
> earthly circumstance. Associated with this value is a concept of
> human dignity, which implies that every human being is entitled to an
> equal measure of basic respect. (Wiredu, 1990, p. 244)

To draw attention to these similarities is not to deny the deep and important differences between specific religious faiths, but it is to affirm that
many religious ontologies share access to a source of normativity that
the secular perspective cannot call upon. Perry's concern is that this
leaves the human rights advocate grounded in the secular perspective to
assert meaningless claims, because the justificatory story that she can
tell can only go so far. She can explain why it is that human beings ought
not to be tortured because it harms their interests or undermines their
autonomy, but she cannot explain why these properties of human beings
are morally important, what meaning or value there is to human life that
entails that it ought to be protected. Only a religious explanation, it
seems, can adequately answer the question of why we ought to respect
Christ's injunction to love the least of men as we love him, which Perry
takes to be instantiated in the practice of human rights.

The challenge that Friedrich Nietzsche's (1844–1900) thought poses
to modern moral philosophy becomes apparent in this debate.
Nietzsche's (1982, p. 95) famous claim, 'God is dead', speaks to exactly
the problem of the source of normativity in the absence of divine
command. If God is dead it is because human beings, with their search
for rational proofs of his existence, have killed him; they killed the possibility of being guided by stories about ultimate meaning in the universe.
For Nietzsche, of course, this is an emancipatory development in moral
thinking. The relevance of this for human rights is that it displaces
reasons to accept universal moral claims, and leaves nothing in their
place, as Ari Kohen explains: 'the lack of faith in a god necessitates the
acceptance of the total absence of foundations for individual values,
beliefs, and thoughts' (Kohen, 2007, p. 29).

The fundamental question that Nietzsche poses, then, is what will
become of morality when both religious truth and morality itself are
exposed not as eternal and immutable truths, but as human constructs.
The strongest amongst us can create a morality that suits our purposes,
Nietzsche thinks, but as Rorty (1993) is acutely aware, the Nietzschean
superman has no reason to adopt the morality of human rights; notions
of equal concern and respect will not serve his purposes. Only the weak
have interests in this sort of moral code, but the strong ought to be able

to suppress the weak. If that is right, then it casts doubt on the whole idea of the social contract, beginning with Hobbes' (1984) claim that the weakest of men has the capacity (either through cunning or combining with others) to kill the strongest, which makes it rational for them to bind together to create a commonwealth to protect their natural rights.

Though others have not followed in the nihilistic direction in which Nietzsche is sometimes read as having pointed, there is widespread conviction that the rationalism of Western moral philosophy necessarily yields an account of morality that is secular in its understanding of the world and indeed the universe, and that this secularism is a problem for human rights universalism in the context of a world where significant numbers of people profess a religious faith. There are two sorts of claims to be unpacked here: one that human rights *are* secular, and the other that this inhibits or renders impossible the affirmation of human rights by those who are religious. We will unpack each of these claims in the next section.

Religious freedom and secular liberalism

The purported secular character of human rights is typically held to be a consequence of their emerging from a liberal tradition in political thought. Liberalism, like any political theory, encompasses a range of positions, but many, if not all, accept the natural rights theorist John Locke as the 'father' of liberalism. The Lockean account of natural rights is justified with reference to God – men are sent into the world 'about his [God's] business', moreover:

> Every one, as he is bound to preserve himself, and not to quit his station wilfully, so by the like reason, when his own preservation comes not in competition, ought he, as much as he can, to preserve the rest of mankind, and may not, unless it be to do justice on an offender, take away, or impair the life, or what tends to the preservation of the life, the liberty, health, limb, or goods of another. (Locke, 1988, II.6)

The authority of God and man's connection to God is clearly important to early justifications of natural rights, though we should not misread Locke as a proto-human rights theorist: Lockean rights are properly by-products of duties owed to God. This is a way of understanding rights that makes eminent sense from various religious viewpoints, but is rather different from the relatively foundationless assertion of universal rights in the UDHR. Nevertheless, Locke's seminal argument for freedom of conscience (limited to those within the Protestant faith: neither Catholics nor atheists are, on Locke's view, suitable candidates for this freedom), and for the separation of political authority and spiritual demands, are important markers on a path of increasing secularization in law and politics.

Writing after the religious wars that had devastated Europe in the seventeenth century, and which exerted a profound influence on the development of liberal thought in general (see McClelland, 1996, pt IV), Locke's position is that governments should respect the rights of citizens to practise their faith according their own conscience. The rationale for this is simple – the alternative, trying to force citizens to respect a particular religion, is not truly possible. Coercing *external* compliance with the commands of religious authority does not achieve the intended goal, because it is the compliance of the soul, and not the body, that matters. (Locke also sees that coercing compliance with a particular faith is unlikely to produce peace, but the *religious* justification for religious tolerance is most important.) But all that any government or other authority could achieve would be external compliance. Because coerced faith is not true faith at all, it has no value. Therefore, governments ought rather to leave matters of conscience up to citizens (Mendus, 1989). Political authority should concern itself, then, with those matters where it is actually (or potentially) competent, namely respect for natural rights, which will entail a concern for order and security and the protection of property. The state cannot and should not concern itself with the souls of its citizens. Locke is also alert to the fact that this strategy protects the church *from* the state.

In contemporary liberal democracies this separation between the spiritual and the political is taken for granted. Neutrality on the part of the state with respect to the religious convictions of citizens is deeply engrained within the liberal tradition as a proper limit of legitimate state power. What this means is that the state ought not to confer particular benefits or disadvantages on citizens on the basis of religious belief or membership. Contemporary liberal thought, particularly as influenced by the work of John Rawls (1999a), is typically characterized by what has been called the 'privatisation of religion' (Ahdar and Leigh, 2005, p. 46), wherein professing a religious faith is something that one does as private individual, a role that is distinct from one's role as publicly reasoning citizen. This does not imply, in Rawls' eyes, that religious adherents must practise their faith 'in private', but rather that when the individual acts as a citizen, and when the state acts towards the citizen, religious justifications cannot be publicly adduced in support of actions or policies. This does not suggest that religion is unimportant; on the contrary, it reflects recognition of the profound importance of religion from the perspectives of its adherents.

The issue of the place of religion in contemporary societies is particularly evident in debates about the French Republican doctrine of *laïcité*, or secularism, which can be seen as deeply indebted to the legacy of the French Revolution and its at times vigorously anti-clerical approach to freedom and equality (Jennings, 2011; cf. van Kley, 1997). Much discussion of *laïcité* in recent years has focused on the so-called 'headscarf affair' in France, a controversy that generated an enormous amount of discussion and tension. French law, based on the notion of Republican unity, prohibits the wearing of religious symbols in public institutions in France. This has been interpreted in some schools in some instances as entailing a ban on the wearing of the Islamic veil (or 'headscarf') by schoolgirls (for a detailed and careful discussion of the initial series of incidents and the subsequent furore, see Laborde, 2005). More recently the French state has banned the wearing of the *burqa* in any public place.

These moves are seen as virulently secular in the sense of being anti-religious by some critics, but the justification offered by defenders of the practice refer to notions of civic equality and the public–private divide. *Laïcité*, it is argued, underwrites the formal equality of citizens in the public sphere. Indeed, historically liberals and republicans have drawn attention to the repressive and coercive practices of the world's major religions as an obstacle to the freedoms that human rights are invoked to protect. Michael Ignatieff (2000) insists on the oppressive character of this legacy in a determinedly secular account of human rights. In contrast, Irene Oh (2007) is distrustful of the ways in which this vision of religious experience, wherein religious practice can and should be confined to the private sphere, overlooks the motivating power of faith as a foundation for human rights, and more generally the authenticity that religious belief gives to the life of believers. There are echoes, in this debate, of the individualism, rationalism and abstraction of natural rights theorizing attacked by Burke in the late eighteenth century. These points of conflict are equally the locus of critical scrutiny advanced by those concerned with the secularism of human rights in the twenty-first century (Adhar and Leigh, 2005).

The right to freedom of religion is regarded as a classic liberal right, which has made its way into the International Bill of Rights. Article 18 of the UDHR proclaims: 'Everyone has the right to freedom of thought, conscience and religion; this includes the right to change his religion or belief, either alone or in community with others and in public or private, to manifest his religion or belief in teaching, practice, worship or observance.' Article 18 of the ICCPR makes similar provision, with the addition, 'No one shall be subject to coercion which would impair his freedom to have or to adopt a religion or belief of his choice', and a provision protecting 'the liberty of parents and, when applicable, legal guardians to ensure the religious and moral education of their children in conformity with their own convictions'.

It is the affinity between liberal conceptions of the relationship between the state and the citizen, and the conception of this relationship that can be discerned in human rights documents, including the International Bill of Rights, that lead some to regard human rights as an attempt to impose liberal values on the rest of the world. The international relations scholar Chris Brown, for example, claims: 'The contemporary human rights regime is in general, and, for the most part, in detail, simply a contemporary, internationalised and universalised, version of the liberal position on rights' (Brown, 1997, p. 43).

The liberal position affirms a view that ascribes distinct domains to religious authority and political authority, both within the state and at the global level, since human rights are understood to be fundamental moral norms that cannot legitimately be violated. There are two objections to this: one is conceptual – for (many, if not most?) religious believers, there is no higher truth than the word of God, but human rights assert final claims within the temporal realm. The second problem follows from this in practical terms – which set of claims should prevail when particular iterations of religious values and the values of human rights appear to conflict? Michael Freeman is clear about the problem here: 'If there is a conflict between international human rights law and what a believer holds is necessary for eternal salvation, it would be both irrational and impious to accord priority to the law' (2004, p. 386). If we reflect on, say, debates about abortion in the USA and Ireland, or conflicting views on girls' education in conservative parts of Pakistan, we can see that these are live issues.

The separation between the political and the spiritual is precisely what offends some religious commentators on human rights. It is particularly problematic from the point of view of political Islam, a precept of which is the fundamental unity of the temporal and the spiritual realms. But we should never assume homogeneity within a political or religious community: while An-Na'im (1990, p. 21) notes that '[t]o the overwhelming majority of Muslims today, Shari'a is the sole valid interpretation of Islam, and as such *ought* to prevail over any human law or policy' (emphasis in original), Sen (2002) notes historical antecedents of an Islamic policy of observing a distinction between the temporal and the spiritual on the part of governments.

I will say more about this below. At this juncture, we should note that this is not a subject of controversy only in non-Western contexts. Evangelical Christianity is a strong political force in the USA in the late twentieth and early twenty-first centuries. In more distant history the Catholic Church opposed the idea of natural rights, which posed rather a challenge to the hierarchical authority of the Universal Church (Ishay, 2004), though today the leaders of most world religions profess a strong support for (most) human rights. That the liberal position on rights is secular can hardly be denied; that this indicates a division between 'the rest and the West' is far from evident.

A strong critic of precisely this idea is Amartya Sen, who traces a history of secular foundations for moral thought in both the East and the West going back several centuries (2002):

> Different cultures are thus interpreted in ways that reinforce the political conviction that Western civilization is somehow the main, perhaps the only, source of rationalistic and liberal ideas, among them analytical scrutiny, open debate, political tolerance, and agreement to differ ... Sanskrit and Pali have a larger atheistic and agnostic literature than exists in any other classical tradition. There is a similar neglect of Indian writings on nonreligious subjects, from mathematics, epistemology, and natural science to economics and linguistics. (The exception, I suppose, is the Kama Sutra, in which Western readers have managed to cultivate an interest.) (2002, p. 35)

On Sen's reading, then, we should resist the correlation of West/rational(secular), East/religious. Moreover, on Sen's view, we should expect people with deeply divergent worldviews to be able to endorse *the same* conception of human rights. But this does not quite speak to the challenge that has been posed in the debate about the inherently religious character of the claim that human beings are special, have inherent dignity, etc. – it is perfectly open to Perry and those who agree with him to say that those who affirm human rights from a secular perspective are conceptually confused, even if fully committed. Nor does it fully speak to the claim that secular human rights, insofar as they deny (or are unmoved by) an ultimate authority that stands beyond a human constructed morality, are at odds with particular religious conceptions of the good.

Most attempts to address the first of these challenges adopt some variant of pragmatism. So, for example, we have already discussed, in Chapter 3, Rorty's claim that human rights are best understood as a culture, and that the best thing to do with regard to the debate between Nietzsche and Kant about the foundations for morality is to ignore them. We can do without an answer to the question as to why humans have value so long as enough of us affirm that they do.

Few philosophers find this a satisfactory answer (cf. Hiskes, 2009; Sweet, 2003), but the alternatives that have been advanced do not seem to me to be much more persuasive, though the philosophical 'fudge' is perhaps itself a reflection of the drafting of the UDHR:

> A proposal to include a reference to God was made during the drafting of the Universal Declaration, but rejected because it was not universally acceptable. The Universal Declaration grounded human rights in the secularized, neo-Kantian formula of 'the dignity and worth of the human person' rather than on any particular religious doctrine. This formula is not itself very controversial, but its implications still are. (Freeman, 2004, p. 391)

Arvind Sharma (2003) seizes on the use of the term dignity here to argue that because both rationalists (such as Gewirth) and religious theorists (such as Perry) affirm the inherent dignity of the human person, they can agree on dignity as a foundation for human rights. But this ignores the fact that various theorists mean quite different things by the term dignity (as we have seen); indeed, Perry's point is that secular theorists cannot coherently say anything meaningful about dignity at all. Sharma's thought seems to ask us to just 'have faith' in the idea that man has dignity, to 'suspend our disbelief', as it were. On the other hand, critics such as Kohen (2007) and Elshtain (1999) doubt the cogency of Perry's translation of the term 'dignity' into 'sacred'.

Doubts about the translatability of moral concepts and moral vocabulary are a persistent feature of this debate (Panikkar and Panikkar, 1982): can concepts that make sense within a web of meanings that presuppose an ontology that is 'religious', in the sense of affirming the existence of the divine and of ultimate values, be translated into terms that make sense within a web of meanings that deny such an ontology? Similarly, Nazila Ghanea-Hercock registers a significant vein of scepticism about the promise of dignity as a unifying concept:

By trading in the foundation of 'God' for the humanist alternative of 'human dignity' it could be argued that 'depth' of commitment to human rights has been replaced by an elusive 'breadth' of appeal that has not been entirely successful. It is not clear that such problematic foundations will ever lead to genuine and wholehearted participation by the masses, thus putting the entire project of a universal culture of human rights in jeopardy. (2000, p. 218)

Perhaps this is over-stating things. There is evidently widespread support for human rights, including strong support from within all the world's major religious communities. We should also note that a strong part of the rationale for a secular framing of human rights is surely rooted in the fact that a religious justification for human rights is likely to inhibit, rather than foster, pluralist support for human rights. A cogent religious justification for human rights must come from within a particular religious tradition. To that extent, it must invoke the web of meanings that have salience for adherents of that faith, but this will be distinct from, and potentially (likely?) in conflict with those of adherents of other faiths. The point remains that there are real theological and philosophical issues that call into question the foundations of secular support for human rights, but as we have already seen, there are many who argue that these deeper questions can and should be circumvented. What matters for the present discussion is that some religiously informed critics of human rights see in that 'political' response (see Chapter 4) not neutrality, nor even pluralism, but an inherently secular *and Western* set of beliefs and practices.

The most sustained attempts to address some of these questions within the context of a specific religious tradition have come from scholars working on the relationship between Islam and human rights. To further explore this issue, then, let us turn to this literature.

Islam and human rights

The rise of political Islam over the past 30 to 40 years has coincided with the ascendancy of human rights as a political *lingua franca*. Since at least the publication of Samuel Huntington's (1993) somewhat notorious *Clash of Civilisations*, and more intensely since the al-Qaeda-orchestrated attacks of 11 September 2001, there has been much (at times intemperate and ill-informed) public debate about the compatibility of Islam and human rights. Huntington argued that the world is divided into culturally distinct civilizations, which would inevitably clash with the collapse of Cold War stability (see Edward Said's (2001) excellent riposte 'The Clash of Ignorance'). Human rights theorists have not been immune to contributing to this debate: Jack Donnelly (1999; 2003) appears at times to think that Islam is inevitably in conflict with human rights and defends the universal applicability of 'Western values'. On the other hand, governments of some Islamic countries, such as Iran, who have repudiated the UDHR on account of its Judeo-Christian and secular heritage and supported a specifically Islamic account of human rights, have also been guilty of misrepresenting and exaggerating the degree and terms of conflict.

Human rights and Islam (like Christianity) have been seen as competing universalist ethical systems. There is certainly hostility within many Muslim communities (both in Western and non-Western states) to some aspects of liberal political practice, though much of this is a response to perceived (and indeed, actual) double standards in the political practice of Western states that profess a commitment to human rights but do not always honour that commitment in their own endeavours, both at home, and more often abroad (Brown, 1997; Hussein, 2001; Donnelly, 2003). Again, the aftermath of 11 September 2001 and the advent of the 'war on terror' has intensified these criticisms in recent years, but the charge of double standards against Western governments in their approach to human rights is in fact of long standing.

Nevertheless, we should be careful not to overstate the degree of opposition or contestation between human rights and Islam. Abdulaziz Sachedina argues, 'even the staunchest opponents of the Universal Declaration of Human Rights, who regard the document as being morally imperialistic and culturally ethnocentric, concede the fact that human beings have rights that accrue to them as humans' (2009, p. 6). Sachedina might be over-stating his case here – it is far from clear that those who identify with the aims of al-Qaeda for the supremacy of a traditionalist reading of Islamic law would endorse this claim. Yet the broader point stands; commitment to Islam and commitment to human rights are by no means mutually exclusive and a variety of positions are held amongst Muslim leaders (Bielefeldt, 1995).

There is also irrefutable evidence of Islamic leaders' interests in the idea of human rights in the Universal Islamic Declaration of Human Rights of 1981 and the Cairo Declaration of Human Rights in Islam in 1990. The former was presented to UNESCO following a meeting organized by the London-based Islamic Council for Europe (two years after the Iranian Revolution, when the Iranian leadership had repudiated the 'Western' UDHR); the latter was adopted by the Islamic Council of Foreign Ministers at a meeting in Cairo. While the former is a product of NGO activity, the latter was agreed by government ministers and thus arguably carries more political weight. Both have been politically controversial because they affirm the Qur'an as foundational, and thus are at odds with the 'foundationless' character (or, at any rate, the foundational agnosticism) of the International Bill of Rights. Both also reflect conservative readings of a Qur'anic-inspired human rights (Bielefeldt, 1995). What they undoubtedly signal is the political power of the rhetoric of human rights – even critics of the International Bill of Rights draw on the concept of human rights to make their case. In doing so, they lend credibility to the claim that human rights have universal, cross-religious appeal. Moreover, at the grassroots level, the Arab Spring of 2011 can be seen as an affirmation of many freedoms that are protected under the UDHR. Certainly, much was made in the Western press of Arab revolutionaries' clamour for 'Western-style' freedom and democracy. In predominantly Muslim South-east Asian countries such as Malaysia and Indonesia there are substantial grassroots movements acting in support of human rights (Othman, 1999; Langlois, 2001). Governments of these states have also affirmed their commitment to human rights (Hussain, 2001).

That said, there are genuine questions to be asked not just about the claims of those who argue that human rights are an imperialist project cloaked in universalist language, but also, perhaps more importantly, about whether allegiance to human rights within Islam is allegiance to an idea of human rights that can be described independently of Islam, or whether an Islamic interpretation and justification for human rights is (a) philosophically sound, and (b) politically necessary. An answer to this set of questions will encounter two particular points of tension; the rights of women, and rights to religious freedom.

The secularism of human rights can be defended as valuable to the project of human rights on the grounds that it is neutral between competing religious traditions and views. However, this presupposes that the idea of secularism itself can be seen as neutral, but the reverse can also be argued, namely, that secularism itself is at odds with religious conceptions of value. This view informs the approach of those who defend the interpretation of human rights values from *within* a given religious tradition, such as Islam, as the best, perhaps the only, legitimate means of endorsing human rights for adherents of that faith (Othman, 1999; Freeman, 2004; Oh, 2007; Sachedina, 2009).

The primary focus of Muslim scholars who have pursued this object is the (re-)interpretation of Shari'a as providing foundational authority for the rights protected in contemporary human rights documents (such as the International Bill of Rights). Sachedina (2009) notes the persistence of conflict between 'traditionalists' who insist on the antipathy between the values inscribed in Shari'a and the values enshrined in human rights, but he also draws attention to the absence of meaningful dialogue between traditionalists and the majority of Muslim scholars who have written Islamic-informed defences of human rights. For example, much of the literature in this field written in Western languages is not translated into Persian and Arabic, and vice versa.

Nevertheless, there are a number of Muslim scholars committed to the claim that Islam offers fruitful grounds for a justification of human rights (see, for example, Nasr, 1980, An-Na'im, 1990; 1996, Hassan, 1996, Oh, 2007, Othman, 1999, Sachedina, 2009, Shah, 2006). Indeed, Hassan describes the Qur'an as the 'Magna Carta of human rights' (1996: 85). A complementary argument is advanced by Norani Othman, a leading member of the campaign and support group Sisters In Islam:

> Consideration of the position of any special category or subset of human beings can only follow from, and exist within the parameters of, an acceptance of the rights of humans simply by being human. This awareness is by no means alien to Islam. It is grounded in the *Qur'an*ic notion of a common human ontology (*fitna*) and couched in an Islamic idiom of moral universalism that predates much of the Western discourses about human rights. (1999, p. 173)

However, Abdullahi A. An-Na'im points out that 'Many rights are given under Shari'a in accordance with a strict classification based on faith and gender, and are not given to human beings as such' (1990, p. 22). He draws attention to verses of the Qur'an which justify slavery, which make apostasy a capital crime, and which justify the unequal treatment of women, as particularly problematic for the advocate of human rights. The rationale for his doing so is not to assert a fundamental incompatibility between human rights and Islam, but rather to be clear about the distance to be travelled in any project of interpretation that would find affinities or foundations for human rights in Shari'a: 'Significant possibilities exist for reform, but to undertake such reforms effectively, we must be clear on what Shari'a *is*, rather than what it can or ought to be' (An-Na'im, 1990, p. 40).

A central justification for the unequal treatment of women and men is found in the principle of responsibility or guardianship and authority of men over women (An-Na'im, 1990; Othman, 1999; Sachedina, 2009). Verse 4:34 of the Qur'an states:

> Men have *qawama* [guardianship or authority] over women because of the advantage they [men] have over them [women] and because they [men] spend their property in supporting them [women]' (in An-Na'im, 1990, p. 37). [Othman (1999, p. 181) translates '*qawwamun*' as 'have responsibility [for]'.]

The Qur'an is credited with guaranteeing certain rights for women, including the right to marry and to divorce, and property rights, but also with limiting inheritance rights of sisters compared to brothers, and legitimizing the practice of polygamy by men (Othman, 1999, pp. 178–9). Shari'a is also invoked as a justification of the restriction of women's freedom of association, the rights of women to certain occupations and to education. Insofar as the International Bill of Rights prohibits discrimination on the grounds of gender, and is supplemented by the 1979 Convention on the Elimination of All Forms of Discrimination Against Women (CEDAW), there is clearly a conflict between the rights of women as protected in Shari'a and the rights of women as protected in human rights.

The proper response to this conflict, and the correct interpretation of the principle of responsibility/guardianship of men over women, is a matter of sustained dispute. An-Na'im argues that this principle should be acknowledged as a legitimate interpretation of the Qur'an in past historical contexts, but should be re-interpreted for contemporary times. So, An-Na'im's (1990) reading of this holds that the physical advantage that men have over women in terms of strength is no longer important in contemporary societies where the rule of law proceeds from a principle of equality, and that the financial responsibility of men over women is similarly redundant, given the advent of modern financial practices. On the other hand, Niaz Shah (2006) argues, via an historical contextual analysis, that the original intention of the passage should be read as protecting the status and interests of women, and that the appropriate contemporary interpretation should reflect contemporary means of doing that.

Another approach again is advanced by Othman (1999), who rejects the idea of accepting as valid the position that the Qur'an recognizes the moral priority of men over women, on the grounds that other verses clearly do not differentiate between the spiritual status of men and women, and it is this status that is important to their being moral beings, and thus having rights. The Muslim advocates of human rights can thus draw on justification from the Qur'an to defend both human rights standards in general and many aspects of CEDAW. Moreover, Othman draws attention to the process of Qur'anic (re)interpretation and moral change as a practice that is authoritatively embedded within Islamic traditions.

But others are less optimistic about this practice of interpreting human rights from within Islam (for example, Arkoun, 1993; Mayer, 1993). Oh (2007) draws on the hermeneutic approach of Gadamer and Habermas' ideas about communication ethics to describe the conditions for a process of internal dialogue about the affinity of Islam with universal human rights, but it is not obvious why the resources offered by Western theorists of cultural and textual interpretation and debate should be accepted as useful or appropriate guides to the practice of interpretation by those who are sceptical of the project of elaborating Islamic human rights. Nor, indeed, is it obvious that all examples of conflicts between Shari'a and human rights can be resolved in this way: there seems less scope for an understanding of the Shari'a position apostasy – the repudiation of Islam by a person known to have been a Muslim – in ways that cohere with the UDHR vision of the right to freedom of religion, which explicitly includes the right to change one's religion. Interpreting the right to freedom of religion within Islamic communities as the right to practise one's religion, thus as rights against interference by the state (as is sometimes suggested), does not protect the same substance of right (see Langlois, 2001). There is quite an important difference between the freedom to practise a given religion, the freedom to practise any religion, the freedom to change one's religion, and the freedom to assert atheistic or agnostic views. Thus we confront the question of whether the practice of interpretation of human rights from within a given religious tradition yields the same or substantially similar content of the right as is found in the 'universal' conception of the right. We will return to this question in the next chapter.

Conclusion

What we have covered in this chapter offers an introduction to some of the ways in which religion and religious beliefs influence and pose challenges for thinking about human rights. Essentially we have explored two questions: why it might be problematic if human rights are understood to be either inherently secular or religious, and whether a practice of interpreting human rights from within a given religious tradition can overcome perceived tensions and conflicts between human rights and religious values.

Perry holds that a religious ontology is needed to make sense of the claim that human beings have the special moral status that calls forth the protection of rights. Only a vision of the world in which there is ultimate meaning can supply an account of ultimate value that could connect to human beings. Though his account is Christian, adherents of other faiths who express commitment to human rights have often sought to explain the inherent dignity of human beings in terms that connect morality to the divine. In contrast, the historical development of accounts of human and natural rights in the West took place against a backdrop of increasing secularism in moral and political life and thought. This, too, is taken to pose a challenge for the universality of human rights. Contemporary liberalism certainly does appear to presuppose the separation of religious authority from political practice, and arguably presupposes the 'privatization of religion', which, from a religious point of view, there may be good reasons to reject.

On the other hand, there may not. Leaders of every major religion frequently express support for human rights, though, there are also frequent disputes about what is, and is not, properly, the object of a human right. The project of arriving at an elaboration and justification of human rights from within Islam, currently being pursued by an array of scholars, illustrates the widespread appeal of human rights. Islam and human rights are both examples of universalist ethics. The conviction of Muslim defenders of human rights that they need not be in conflict, and that the former can serve as a foundation for the latter, is promising for the idea of a global human rights culture. Nevertheless, as was evident, there remain difficult questions about the completeness and depth of that purported harmony.

6 Universalism and Relativism

'The universalism/relativism debate essentializes both culture and rights.' (Merry, 2001, p. 32)

'Western liberalism with its prescription of human rights has had a worth-while effect not only on Westerners but on many peoples of this world. It is, however, by no means the only rational way of living human life.' (Cobbah, 1987, p. 328)

Introduction

In the last chapter we considered human rights and religions as competing universalist moral visions. The idea of universalist ethics has itself been attacked by various defenders of some form of cultural or ethical relativism. We should be careful, however, not to overstate these challenges and their salience for human rights. The points raised by Sally Engle Merry and Josiah A.M. Cobbah, above, both herald potential pitfalls for a serious discussion of the issues of universalism and relativism in the context of human rights: there is the risk of essentializing nuanced and complex aspects of the debate, and there is also the risk of failing to grasp the precise sites of disagreement. The fact that a critic of human rights raises doubts about their universality does not entail that they affirm relativism. Outside of university seminars, full-blown relativists are fairly rare: few people actively deny the validity of any universal precept. But both the idea of relativism at a philosophical level, and the persistence of conflicts between what are taken to be cultural values and the freedoms and values protected in human rights, present challenges for a defence of human rights that merit careful consideration.

In the first part of this chapter I separate out different sorts of relativist claims and reflect on the validity of each sort of claim. I then discuss the so-called 'Asian values' debate, in the course of which claims about the relativity of certain values to particular cultures played an important role. This is one of many examples of a debate in human rights theory where philosophical issues take on political significance. The second part of the chapter reflects further on universalism. Important in this context is the vision of the self, or the conception of human nature, that is found in liberal and communitarian thought, and the extent to which these competing visions are reflected in universal human rights. In this section I will also discuss the possibility of 'moral minimalism' – the idea that there is, or can be, a minimum universal account of the necessary conditions for a good life. Such an account will be necessarily thin.

The final section of the chapter draws on feminist theory as well as human rights theory to consider some conflicts between defenders of particular 'cultural' practices that are held to contravene human rights and others who uphold universal norms. These debates also invite reflection on whether rights, as a cultural practice, are themselves the best or the only means to promote the individual protections envisaged in human rights documents.

Types of relativism and the 'Asian values' debate

In very general terms, relativists deny the validity of universal values. They contend that values are locally, culturally, or historically specific, and doubt the possibility of finding meaningful the demands of a universalist moral claim such as those advanced in human rights declarations. Beyond this general description, to get to grips with relativists' arguments it is important to distinguish the different types of claims that a cultural relativist might make.

First, a relativist might make a *descriptive* or empirical claim; she might assert that there just are no universally held moral values, and argue from this fact to the conclusion that anyone who advances a moral claim in terms of a universal ethical language is simply making a mistake. Some anthropologically informed commentaries on human rights appear to proceed on this basis, though many anthropologists also reject a straightforward descriptive relativism (see Wilson, 1998; Cowan et al., 2001; cf. Merry, 2005, pp. 8–10). The fact that there are no universally held values does not seem in itself to tell us anything about the

validity of universal human rights, as opposed to their appeal. The fact
that a set of values is or is not affirmed by a group of people does not tell
us whether the value should be affirmed at all. So while the descriptive
claim may be true, it does not, in itself, entail the normative conclusion
that universal human rights should therefore be rejected. Moreover, the
descriptive claim seems to posit a view of culture that is static and fixed,
which is distinctly at odds with the lived realities of cultural practices
and values (Merry, 2001).

Second, a relativist might make a *metaethical* claim based on her
scepticism about the status of moral utterances. She might, for example,
hold to some variant of subjectivism. Subjectivists are sceptical of the
idea that there is such a thing as moral truth, or ultimate right and wrong.
Thus, to say that killing a child is bad is to do no more than to express a
dislike of the practice of killing a child. Others may share my dislike, or
they may not, but the fact of consensus on a particular moral claim does
not give that moral claim the status of a truth claim (Mackie, 1990). The
difficulty with this approach is that it seems to get the direction of moral
intuitions the wrong way round. On this view, killing a child is wrong
because I dislike it, but the conventional thought would be that I dislike
the practice of killing a child because it is wrong, and even if I were,
perversely, to assert that I liked the practice, I would be saying something that is objectively morally wrong. The subjectivist, however,
wonders what the source for this objectivity is where moral claims are
concerned. In debates about human rights, subjectivists are mostly to be
found working in Western universities; those who press relativist claims
on cultural grounds rarely embrace radical subjectivism.

Alternatively the metaethical relativist might make a claim about the
scope of moral judgements and the extent to which these depend upon a
deeper web of meanings and concepts for their coherence (cf. MacIntyre,
1994). The thought here is that moral concepts are rich phenomena with
limited translatability across cultural and historical contexts. This
approach need not accept the radical conclusion that there is nothing that
one can say to the subjectivist who asserts a preference for killing children, but it does suggest that the use of thick moral concepts such as
'human rights' will have limited use in contexts where human rights do
not exist as part of the moral landscape. I will say more about this below.

Third, a relativist might make a *normative* claim; she might say that
people ought to affirm and be guided by different values that reflect their
different cultural traditions. There could be a number of premises for this
argument. One route would proceed from the descriptive position above,
with the addition of a second premise that different ways of life are in

themselves morally valuable. (John Stuart Mill's (1985) account of the value of 'experiments in living' is sometimes trivially taken to imply this, though Mill himself was hardly a relativist.) Or the normative claim could be informed by some variant of the metaethical claim just discussed (the two foundations are logically independent). The central point is that the normative position denies the possibility of there being any values that are good for all humans everywhere.

This sort of argument can be rejected at a trivial level by pointing out the contradiction inherent in it. The claim is that moral values are relative to each group or culture that affirms them, and should not be exported beyond the confines of that group or culture. But, insofar as this is a claim about the proper scope of moral rules everywhere, this is itself a universalist claim (Williams, 1985). The normative relativist performs a logical contradiction here: everyone (universally!) should be a relativist because only relative values are valid.

No doubt this fails as an argument, but the seriousness of the challenge posed by relativism demands a more thorough response than this (see Williams, 1985, pp. 156–73). The normative relativist informed by the weaker metaethical claim about translatability may hold that the authenticity of a flourishing life is compromised by externally imposed universal values, and for this reason, people ought to affirm the values that are relative to their culture and history, and repudiate external claims that purport to be universal. As I noted in Chapter 3, the business of moral disagreement (say, about the proper scope of moral claims) itself presupposes at least the possibility of recognizing that there is some substantive element that is the subject of the disagreement, so the problem of translatability cannot go all the way down, but it may still raise some important concerns about the both the content and the concept of universal human rights.

To explore this further, it will be helpful to fill out some of this abstract discussion with some specific examples. The first obvious example to turn to is the Asian values debate, as it has generated a lot of attention both politically and philosophically.

The Asian values debate emerged in the 1990s on the wave of the East Asian financial boom. In the Bangkok Declaration of 1993, released immediately prior to the Vienna World Conference on Human Rights, a number of East Asian political leaders, particularly from Singapore, Malaysia, and China, publicly and vocally rejected the applicability of 'Western' civil and political human rights to Asian societies, and asserted that the values of human rights are not universal because there are specifically Asian values. Broadly speaking, these were claimed to be the priority of social and economic rights over political and civil rights, the priority of duties to family, community and the state over the rights of individuals (and more generally the priority of duties as an ethical concept in comparison to rights), and the priority of respect for, and obedience to, elders and figures of authority in the community over individual freedom of belief and expression (Bauer and Bell, 1999; Føllesdal, 2005). The former Singaporean Prime Minister Lee Kuan Yew remarked that Asians have 'little doubt that a society with communitarian values where the interests of society take precedence over that of the individual suits them better than the individualism of America' (in Bauer and Bell, 1999, p. 6).

Many responses, from both Asian and Western commentators, have viewed the assertion of Asian values in the Bangkok Declaration as a cynical move on the part of Asian leaders. The Kenyan legal scholar Yash Ghai cogently glosses the general view: '"Asian values" were asserted for domestic reasons as an attempt to legitimise authoritarianism' (2009, p. 110). Nevertheless, there are principled rejections of human rights, both within Asia and beyond, that give us reasons to take seriously the issues raised. Cobbah is quite scathing about human rights as a universal practice, rejecting in particularthe individualism of human rights as being unable to capture human dignity as it is understood in the Akan worldview: 'African societies are communitarian. It is only when we see these communities for what they are that we can understand their concepts of human dignity and further enhance or even modify these concepts' (Cobbah, 1987 p. 320).

One issue to be unpacked here is whether there are distinctly 'Asian' values; many commentators reject the claim that there are (for example, Sen, 1997; Inoue, 1999) on the grounds that this denies both the enormous diversity of values, cultures and traditions within the Asian geographical region, and the resonances with values associated with human rights, such as the fundamental moral importance of the human person, found in multiple Asian cultures. It is certainly the case that those who came together to proclaim Asian values included representatives of Buddhist, Confucian and Islamic traditions, capitalist and communist systems of economic governance, with distinct systems and traditions of political organization, and also varied languages and cultural heritages. One might, then, find implausible the thought that such diversity could be encompassed in one coherent set of values that one could identify and describe as 'Asian'.

Yet, for all that, the same is true of the group of states and peoples referred to as 'the West'; if it is accepted that there are Western values, then there seems no reason to deny that there are some broadly Asian values, even if one rejects the view that these are universally assented to. It seems to me one must either deny that there are broadly Western values *and* broadly Asian values (*and* broadly African values, and so on), or one must accept the existence of all. Accepting that broadly Asian values do or may exist need not entail the claim that they are cohesive and completely affirmed throughout Asia any more than a claim about the existence of Western values would imply that everyone in the USA, Canada, Europe and Australasia are committed to exactly the same moral principles.

But this fact of internal diversity yields another point against the claim that the existence of Asian values tells us something concrete about the validity of universal human rights. Amongst those aspects of human rights that are most criticized by advocates of the idea of Asian values are the abstraction, individualism, and rationalism of the vision of human nature that lies at the heart of human rights, and the claim that it is duties, not rights, that are ethically most important. Recall that Edmund Burke advanced remarkably similar complaints about the idea of natural rights in the eighteenth century (see Chapter 2). Moreover, the idea that 'Western' civil and political rights offer an illusory sort of freedom, and that social and economic rights are what matter most to the well-being of people, could easily be endorsed by Marxist-inspired Western critics of human rights as well as by Asians.

That said, it should be acknowledged that there is politics as well as philosophy in all of this. The particular historical moment of the Bangkok Declaration – shortly after the end of the Cold War and the collapse of a bipolar international struggle that had largely been played out through satellite states, and at the end of the process of decolonization that had proceeded fairly rapidly and somewhat haphazardly since the Second World War (Clapham, 1999) – sheds light on the Declaration as an affirmation of independence and self-determination as fundamental rights.

Moreover, it is quite obviously the case that universal human rights as instantiated in the UDHR and the UN system assert limits to state sovereignty, even as they affirm the sovereign state as the authoritative political unit. The question, then, is whether the interests and freedoms that human rights protect reflect interests and freedoms that are valued in diverse Asian societies, *and* whether other interests or important values are compromised or eroded by the promotion of human rights.

The defence of human rights offered by some Western theorists rather neglects the second part of this question. Jack Donnelly, for instance, argues that human rights evolved in the West as a necessary response to the overbearing power of markets and centralized states, and that since these means of economic and political organization have 'spread, in very similar forms, throughout the globe' (Donnelly, 2003, p. 59), the need for human rights can be taken to be universal. Michael Freeman takes a slightly more nuanced line:

> All human societies have power structures, and many of them have throughout history had some conception of the abuse of power. The concepts of *natural rights* and *human rights* are particular ways of expressing this concern about the abuse of power. (Freeman, 2002, pp. 167–8)

Donnelly (2003; 2007) proposes an oft-endorsed principle of accepting the *relative* universality of human rights, characterized by agreement at the level of concept (rights to religious freedom), but differentiation at the level of conception or interpretation (religious freedom understood in a particular way). This may be a plausible way forward in terms of political compromise, though it arguably deflects rather than addresses what is at issue – if the 'Asian' account of religious freedom denies the right to proselytize for an 'alien' religion, then it is not clear that the conception defended in that context coheres with the concept held in other contexts. Note, also, evidence from anthropologists such as Merry (2005), who both rejects the static vision of culture implied in the idea of Asian values, and finds there to be genuine costs in specific local contexts of advancing moral and political claims in terms of human rights (her particular focus is on women's human rights).What matters for the present discussion is whether human rights as *a* particular way of expressing concerns about threats to dignity, freedom and well-being, and mobilizing necessary protections, should be accepted as *the* best or only way in all social and political contexts. To get closer to an answer, it will be helpful to look at this debate from the other end – what sort of universalism can be justified?

Universalism and the self

The charge of abstraction at the heart of universal human rights relates to the vision of human nature implied therein. The idea of a universal ethics is made possible by an account of the human being that is stripped of particularities. An example of this approach can be found in John

Rawls' liberalism. We should note that Rawls (1999b) himself held that it would be wrong to apply this sort of liberal reasoning internationally, hence he is careful to distinguish liberal rights from the basic rights that are to be respected globally in his account of the 'Law of Peoples' (see Chapter 4). Conversely, some Rawlsian thinkers, such as Thomas Pogge, defend much more extensive and demanding accounts of human rights (see Chapter 8). Another point to bear in mind is the influence of those, like Donnelly, who have taken Rawlsian ideas (such as Rawls' account of an overlapping consensus) and applied them directly to the concept of human rights, a move Rawls' own writings does not endorse.

For our purposes in this chapter it is worth understanding some facets of Rawls' thought, and the debate between him and communitarian thinkers, in order to get to grips with the validity of communitarian-based doubts about universal human rights. Rawls claims that 'the self is prior to the ends which are affirmed by it' (1999a, p. 560). If that is true, then the self is independent of his community, his goals, his cultural traditions, and so on, and the self has value and substance independently of these things. That said, Rawls originally conceptualized the self as the head of a family (cf. Okin, 2005), so the individual is not entirely an atomistic creature. Nor does Rawls suggest that the community has no value for the self; on the contrary, the social character of human beings is recognized in the value he accords to the social bases of self-respect, which he takes to be an important 'primary good' (that is, a good with which a theory of distributive justice should be concerned – see Rawls, 1999a; or Wolff, 1996). But this priority and independence entails a Kantian claim about the necessary condition of freedom, namely, that to be free the self must be able to stand back from social roles and practices and judge them for himself. One way of guaranteeing that freedom would be to accord particular rights to the individual (and not to the community, group or state). Thus, the individual, not the family or other group, is the unit of moral concern in this ethical system. Moreover, the relationship between the individual and his social and cultural context is largely contingent.

Michael Sandel has glossed this as follows:

[R]ights-based liberalism begins with the claim we are separate, individual persons, each with our own aims, interests and conceptions of the good, and seeks a framework of rights that will enable us to realize our capacity as free moral agents, consistent with a similar liberty for others … The priority of the self over its ends means I am never defined by my aims and attachments, but always capable of standing back to survey and assess and possibly to revise them. This is what it means to be a free and independent self, capable of choice. (1984, pp. 4–5)

Practical reason, then, is a process of deliberation about choices and values, a continual process of judgement, in which the individual stands apart from his social and cultural context.

Communitarian critics of the liberal position, like Sandel (1982), find this vision of the 'unencumbered self' to be fundamentally wrong-headed (cf. also MacIntyre, 1994; Taylor, 1989). In contrast, Sandel posits the necessary existence of a 'situated self' (the historical cue for this notion is Hegel's thought). The situated self is not prior to its ends but constituted by them. As a human being, I have no identity prior to the social and cultural context in which I live and develop. Indeed, in order to develop moral concepts, like a sense of justice, I must necessarily reflect on and be informed by the concepts in which I am socially, cultur- ally, historically embedded. If that is so, then practical reason is not a process of judgement at a distance and in a vacuum, rather, it 'is always one of comparing one "encumbered" potential self with another "encum- bered" potential self' (Kymlicka, 2002, p. 225; cf. Feltham, 2003). Judgement about the social and cultural norms of one's community is not thereby rendered impossible, but it is the case that the communitarian position explains the value that cultural traditions have for individuals far more readily than the liberal position can. If I judge the values and practices in which I am embedded to be morally wrong in some way, then there will be associated (psychological and social) costs.

The relevance of this for human rights lies in the extent to which the communitarian account presents problems for a universalist ethics. How should we understand the relationship between an individual and the values of her community? On the liberal view, those values are to be approved, or not, by that individual. On the communitarian view, the individual is embedded in the community to the extent that her identity is constituted by it. To put the point simply, how can I learn anything about what it is to make judgements and have values if not through a community of judgements and values?

Sandel, however, does not want to say that the individual has no rights against her community. On the contrary, he is broadly committed to liberal principles of justice. But his argument does give us grounds for taking seriously the metaethical relativist claim about the extent to which universalist claims can command the allegiance of diverse peoples or indeed be accepted as action-guiding for those to whom they are alien.

To accept the relativist thesis as going all the way down would be to imply that cultural and social traditions are sealed and fixed and that the self is totally constituted by them. One need not accept either of these extreme positions: it is quite obviously the case that almost no human society is completely isolated from interactions with other groups, and that social and cultural practices will therefore have a natural fluidity to at least some minimal degree, because external influence is inevitable. If that is right, then it also undermines the claim that the self is totally constituted by the social and cultural traditions in which it is embedded, because this deterministic view would be unable to account for the fluidity of social and cultural life. Bhikhu Parekh (1999) reminds us that, if the caricature version of the communitarian claim were true, then slaves or members of the lower echelons of a caste system would be simply unable to look critically on the socio-legal systems that justified their oppression, but historical and contemporary experience suggests that people in such disadvantaged positions are able to do so (and, in contemporary times at least, they often articulate their resistance in the language of rights).

More than that, however, the extreme positions would seem to deny the individual capacity for interpretation of, or reflection and judgement on, those practices that shape our communities. The resources that individuals can draw on to inform their judgement and practical reason may be constituted by the community, but the history of human creativity demonstrates the human capacity to develop new ideas from existing resources.

At this point it begins to look as though the distinction between the two views – the liberal and the communitarian – is collapsing. But rather than thinking of them as entirely discrete positions, we might more usefully think of them as points on a scale. The further we move towards the communitarian end, the easier it is to see why a universalist set of values that have been externally defined may not seem importantly action-guiding when they conflict with indigenous values. As we move towards the other end of the scale, we find universal values easier to accept to the extent that they reflect our rational judgements. But Sandel seems right to me to stress the extent to which the judgements we make are deeply embedded in the social and cultural practices that constitute our communities, and ultimately, ourselves.

Communitarian critics of human rights find fault with both the abstraction and atomism that underpins the liberal conception of rights, and the vision of the relationship between the individual and the community as antagonistic. Pursuing that path, rather than (say) stressing an ethic of duty, leads to social disintegration, which undermines, rather than fosters, individual flourishing. Again, this dispute is a matter of difference in degree, not kind:

> [I]nsistence on human rights does not prevent the acknowledgement of human duties and patriotism in general. Rather, the concern is to make clear when governments' claims to such duties and ties are morally binding on citizens, and when they are not. (Føllesdal, 2005, p. 276)

Of course, if it were the case that human rights are in fact universal values, not just in the sense of being universally valid, but in the empirical sense of being universally affirmed, and embedded (or at least traceable) in all major traditions, then some of these debates could be dismissed. So, I now consider whether there is, as some have suggested, a universal moral minimum.

A quite remarkable range of commentators, from scholars to peace activists to politicians to journalists (and probably some celebrities) have affirmed that there are universally held values. Peter Jones raises serious doubts about this:

> Even if we could find values that have been endorsed by everyone everywhere, these are likely to be so meagre, so denuded of content, that they will provide a set of human rights that is hardly worth having. (2000, p. 35)

And yet, many human rights scholars pursue this goal. One version of the claim points to the near-universal assent, at a political level, that can be observed with respect to the International Bill of Rights. There is, so the story goes, a global overlapping consensus on universal human rights. But, as Alison Renteln points out, the widespread ratification of human rights treaties tells us less than this thesis suggests – political consensus may or may not reflect a genuine consensus about values: 'First of all, those who ratify are the elites whose views may not correspond to those of the rest of the citizenry in a given state. Secondly, ratification may simply serve political and not humanitarian interests' (1985, p. 519). Incentivizing compliance with human rights and other international treaties through bilateral and multilateral trade and aid deals is common practice in international politics. Criticizing this, the former Malaysian Prime Minister Tun Hussein complains that 'the entire issue [of compliance with human rights norms] is reduced to a question of political might and *realpolitik*' (2001, p. 77). Note, however, that there is room for doubt as to whether respect for human rights in practice (rather than in proclamation) actually makes a significant difference to aid donors' choices (Neumeyer, 2003). At the level of state elites, then, there is reason to distrust any claims about a global consensus. But at the level of grassroots protest, there is also reason to distrust the motives of political leaders who reject the universality of human rights when defending the denial of such rights.

Another version of the universal moral minimum hypothesis begins at the grassroots level, and rests on claims about ordinary individuals:

> [T]here is a common normative principle shared by all major cultural traditions which, if construed in an enlightened manner, is capable of sustaining universal standards of human rights. That is the principle that one should treat other people as he or she wishes to be treated by them. This golden rule ... is shared by all major religious traditions of the world. Moreover, the moral and logical force of this proposition can easily be appreciated by all human beings of whatever cultural tradition or philosophical persuasion. (An-Na'im, 1996, pp. 162–3)

It is not obvious, to me, that this is really the case. The Hindu tradition is an obvious case in point. Hindu defences of the caste system do not imply that one ought to treat others as one would wish to be treated by them. An-Na'im himself concedes that traditional Islam does not readily recommend this principle to Muslims with respect to non-Muslims, nor Muslim men towards Muslim women. A traditional reading of Christianity does not necessarily yield this principle as a guide for relations between men and women. Kant and rationalist liberals would certainly find this principle intelligible, but, as Richard Rorty (1993) points out, accepting the theoretical force of this proposition is not at all incompatible with acting contrary to the principle; it all depends on who counts as 'one of us'. It makes sense to treat others whom I recognize to be my equals in a way that I wish to be treated by them; the difficulty lies in persuading people to look on the other whom they perceive to be different from themselves, or 'other' in some sense, as moral equals (see Chapter 3).

Let us consider another approach. In a widely cited paper, Bhikhu Parekh argues for a 'minimum core' of values that can be discerned in or from all religious and cultural traditions. On his account this need not be accessed through the medium of human rights *per se*. These minimum values constitute a 'non-ethnocentric universalism' that *can* support universalist ethics such as human rights, but the institutional forms that norms should take are those that will be most effective, and these are most likely to be relative to the institutional structures of norms indigenous to, or at any rate widely understood within, a given societal context (1999a, p. 152).

Universalism about ethics need not imply universalism about human *rights*. Charles Taylor (1999) also expresses agnosticism about the prospects for unforced consensus around *rights* as the vehicle for realizing universal values. Indeed, the African Charter on Human and Peoples' Rights includes a parallel list of Duties. Flexibility about the ethical framework, but universalism about the values it protects, is an approach that could be expected to find favour with many non-Western critics of human rights, who reject as alien the legalism of human rights and the implications of a rights-based rather than a duty-based ethic. It might also find favour with advocates of the capabilities approach (Nussbaum, 1997; cf. Sen, 2005).

But the lines of debate are not clear-cut here. For example, An-Na'im (2001) points out that the legalistic model of human rights presupposes that the violation of human rights is the exception, not the norm, and that insofar as this is the paradigmatic conception of human rights, it suggests that human rights are implicitly modelled on Western states, with well resourced legal systems, and designed primarily to protect civil and political rights, rather than social and economic rights. On the other hand, Ghai (2009) argues, with specific reference to Asian political leaders' defence of a duty-based ethics, that this may be more open to abuse and exploitation by powerful elites, since corresponding rights are then in the gift of the duty-bearers. This speaks to Feinberg's (1970) parable of Nowheresville, in the context of which Feinberg defends the fundamental value of rights to human dignity (see Chapter 3).

Parekh's minimum core of universal values is also interesting because he is alert to the problems that beset many competing attempts: either the account offered is so thick as to be culturally specific, or it is, as Jones feared, so thin and vague as to yield very limited protections for individuals. That said, it is not always clear whether he intends to say that the minimum universal values exist in the sense that they can be found, latent, in all cultures, or whether a consensus around these values can be constructed, along the lines of a Rorty-esque human rights culture:

> If universal values are to enjoy widespread support and democratic validation and be free of ethnocentric biases, they should arise out of

an open and uncoerced cross-cultural dialogue. Such a dialogue should include every culture with a point of view to express. In doing so we show respect for them, and give them a motive to comply with the principle of holding a cross-cultural dialogue. (Parekh 1999a, p. 39)

The dialogue is to take place at large-scale government and NGO meetings, and small-scale meetings of academics and intellectuals. Merry (2005) is critical of human rights practices that are divorced from ordinary citizens as well as such elites, and this seems an important consideration. The purpose of such dialogue seems to oscillate in Parekh's account between approving values that are found to be in all cultures and agreeing upon values that are universally valid irrespective of their provenance. Precisely what would constitute the conditions of an 'uncoerced cross-cultural dialogue' is a matter of ongoing debate amongst human rights theorists (cf. Taylor, 1999; Donnelly, 2003). Rawlsian ideas about an overlapping consensus permeate much of this literature, while critics of liberalism who see politics as inevitably a domain of power struggles and contestations will reject the goal of pursuing an uncoerced consensus as fatally misconceived (Foucault, 1984; cf. Manokha, 2009).

Parekh (1999a, p. 138) seems to be aware of the danger of idealizing away the 'deep cultural differences', as arguments beginning from an abstract account of human nature do, but he maintains that a minimal universalism is achievable. These are informed by features that Parekh finds to be present in all cultures, but it is difficult to see that these do not themselves amount to an account of human nature: 'the following features characterise human beings in all societies and form part of human identity' (1999a, p. 145). These are: a capacity for social interaction; capacities that distinguish human beings from animals; the capacity for creativity; and the need of certain conditions to thrive and flourish. What differentiates this from an argument derived from a thin liberal account of human nature is that this is not an unencumbered self; on the contrary, the self is fairly richly conceived within Parekh's account and thickly encumbered selves can, or perhaps should, realize these features.

A discussion of the implications of these characteristics yields five 'universal moral values'; 'human unity, human dignity, human worth, promotion of human well-being or fundamental human interests, and equality' (Parekh, 1999a, pp. 149–50), which can be variously interpreted and respected in distinct institutional ways, and thus function as a universal minimum moral standard.

There are two questions to consider here. One is whether this universal moral minimum is universally valid. If the claim is that these values could be discovered to exist in all cultures, then the obvious sticking point is 'equality'; as with the response to An-Na'im's account, it is simply not clear that the moral equality of all human beings is a value affirmed by all traditions and cultures (including Western culture – see Okin, 2005). (Parekh claims that the values can be 'shown to be worthy of universal allegiance, and are in that sense universally valid': 1999a, p. 150.) Perhaps, then, we should seek to affirm these values as a product of cross-cultural dialogue, assuming that uncoerced cross-cultural dialogue is itself a possibility.

Taylor (1999) is more cautious than Parekh on this point. But whether that dialogue is possible or not, again, it is not clear what the dialogue is *for*, if the values it should yield are determined in advance. This strikes me as being a question that can be directed in general towards those who insist on the need for dialogue to generate consensus, but have pretty clear ideas as to on what that consensus should be. The second question is whether the flexibility with respect to means and content that Parekh finds necessary to avoid the charge of ethnocentricity can deliver enough substance to protect important values or interests that are, or are taken to be, the object of a human right. One interesting thought is that the thinness that Parekh needs to maintain would be more likely to be achieved by a negative account that focuses on 'wrongs' rather than values (Baaz, n.d., though cf. the discussion in Chapter 3 for the justificatory limitations of this approach). These are difficult questions to pursue in the abstract, so I will explore the issue further by considering some practical issues in the next section.

Feminist and flexible universalisms

The freedom and well-being of women is very often a site of debates about the purported conflict between human rights and culture. Women experience discrimination and oppression in many cultures and states. Oppressive practices are sometimes justified as 'cultural' practices, valued either by the community or by the women themselves (or both), whereas the values of human rights (such as equality) that would condemn the practice are said to be alien to the cultural context, not universal, and therefore worthy of rejection. CEDAW, the UN convention prohibiting discrimination against women, has been ratified by over 190 countries worldwide, but these ratifications have been accompanied by more substantial reservations than any other international treaty (Bunch, 1997, p. 44).

There is a genuine dilemma confronting feminists in their analysis of human rights. On the one hand, there is a long history of feminist criticism of the concepts of natural rights and human rights – the rights that have been proclaimed to be universal, feminists contend, have too often been the rights of men, not humans: 'Human rights principles are based on experience, but not that of women' (MacKinnon, 1993, p. 84; see also Binnion, 1995; Peach, 2001). For example, MacKinnon draws attention to the widespread practice of sexual violence against women, which constitutes a common threat to women's dignity, freedom and well-being, but is not explicitly the object of a human right. Recognition of rape as a war crime in the 1998 Statute of the International Criminal Court is a significant step forward.

Feminists, then, have grounds to be suspicious of the validity of claims about universalism. Indeed, within feminism there is considerable debate and tension around the universalist claims advanced by liberal feminists that are rejected by second- and third-wave feminists as reflecting white, Western biases (see Beasley, 1999 for an introduction to this). Yet, Western feminists' criticisms of non-Western cultural practices can have invidious tendencies, both practically in terms of the adverse reaction to feminist principles it may generate in non-Western contexts, and in terms of the reification and denigration of other cultures that it reinforces in Western contexts, thereby compounding the problem of intersecting issues of injustice (Okin, 1998a). Western feminists, and indeed many others concerned with the condition and status of women in developing countries, certainly do criticize 'cultural' practices and values that restrict the freedoms and opportunities of women and girls (see Nussbaum, 2001, as an important exemplar). In an excellent essay, Alison Jaggar (2005) calls attention to the ways in which these critiques downplay the significance of broader economic injustices in fostering the context for women's oppression.

On the other hand, to invoke cultural defences as grounds for denying the validity of human rights standards that would protect women's equality itself offends feminist principles of gender equality. That the self is situated in a web of meanings that happen to deny the equal status of women and men is grounds for critically rejecting the web of meanings. As above, at issue here is the extent to which 'internal' versus 'external' resources for such critique are (a) conceptually accessible, and (b) effective as tools of communication. It is no surprise, then, to find some ambivalence about the status of human rights as a universal norm, specifically with respect to women, reflected in the discourses employed to promote women's equality. Merry (2001, pp. 31–2) reflects on the struggle of women activists campaigning for equality (in the Solomon Islands, in this case) to articulate their concerns in terms that can simultaneously signal their opposition to externally defined visions of what justice should be and the value they attach to indigenous cultural practices and values, and their opposition to men in their own culture who reject their claims to equality.

More complex, from the point of view of the feminist dilemma, is the case of women who affirm the value of practices that are at odds with international human rights norms, such as the practice of clitoridectomy/female circumcision. One's choice of terminology is contentious here – many feminists and other critics of the practice would call this female genital mutilation (FGM). For defenders of this practice it is an expression of deep-seated cultural values that demand respect because the situated self is constituted by such values. Opponents reject the very idea that a practice that intentionally limits a woman's capacity to experience sexual enjoyment, and may often threaten her sexual and general health, can be in any sense 'good' for the woman. But feminists are in bit of a bind here. Typically feminists will want to reject patriarchal accounts of what is in a woman's best interests, and will want to affirm that women themselves can and should articulate their own good. But logically this also limits the scope for feminists to say that a woman who affirms the value of a human rights-contravening practice is wrong to do so. There is also a very strong current of feminist thought that, for good reason, rejects the essentializing category 'woman' (Spelman, 1990).

One way of responding to this sort of dilemma (proposed from within human rights theory, rather than feminist theory) is to think that human rights are 'individualistically justified' (Cruft, 2005a). Taking a cue from Parekh's work, the thought here is that there is in fact a disjunct between individualism and universalism, and that cultural diversity and individualism entail one another. Particular human rights are justified according to the needs or interests of a given individual, and are not justified by reference to an abstract story about rational freedom or universal human nature. Moreover, the individual is presumed to be social, so the individualism on which the justification hangs is avowedly anti-liberal in the sense of rejecting a vision of the individual that is pre-social. On this model, though there may be some interests that are widely shared, there is nevertheless reason to doubt perfect universality:

[It] seems highly unlikely that the interests that are of *individualistic right-justifying importance* will be the same for every person; people's well-being comes in too many differing forms for this to be likely. (Cruft 2005a, emphasis in original)

The set of human rights held by one person may, then, vary from those held by another. Thus, for the woman for whom clitoridectomy is an important interest, this will serve as a human rights-based justification for not being prevented from undergoing the practice. (Parekh (1999b) says that clitoridectomy is sometimes voluntarily practised by (educated) adult women after the birth of their last child 'as a way of regulating their sexuality and reminding themselves that from now onwards they are primarily mothers rather than wives'.) This argument accepts the communitarian thought that social and cultural contexts in an important sense determine, or, if that is too strong, significantly shape, the interests that a person will have, and that especially important interests will be the object of rights. On the other hand, for a woman for whom sexual freedom is an interest of rights-justifying importance, then that will count as a justificatory reason to protect her from practices of female genital cutting.

In a sense Cruft's thesis is simply a reflection of actual human rights practice: neither culture nor rights – even rights inscribed in positive law – are fixed and determinate. Cultures change over time. Indeed, what 'culture' is is not easily defined, but it is presumably a set of practices and values recognized and affirmed by multiple actors simultaneously and overlappingly. As such, it could hardly be one single, fixed and static thing. Rights are subject to interpretation and contestation, and unless one holds that human rights to be conceptually valid must be fully compossible, rights will be the subject of negotiation (cf. Steiner, 1994). For example, the right to freedom of speech may justly be curtailed to the extent that it prohibits defamation. The political practice of human rights advocacy typically involves public discussion of whether and when notions of human dignity justify the suppression or the respect of given practices. Concluding her discussion of a number of cases of such contestation in Botswana, the anthropologist Anne Griffiths argues:

These cases should not be interpreted as exemplifying a conflict between cultures in terms of universalist or relativist positions with respect to human rights … disagreement and conflict form part of culture which is ongoing. (Griffiths, 2001, p. 119)

I find this picture of culture persuasive, but I also find the picture of human rights that is emerging unsettling. Cruft himself does not discuss the example of female genital cutting – I am extrapolating from his argument. But I have taken female genital cutting as a case with which to do so to illustrate just how controversial this idea has the potential to be. The idea that human rights are individualistically justified realizes and perhaps extends the flexibility that Parekh hoped for. It might meet the approval of a feminist who is deeply sceptical of a Western woman's claims to know what is best for a non-Western woman, say. The authenticity of the situated self's claims to know her own good demands respect. Susan Moller Okin treads a careful middle ground here:

> [T]he kind of intellectual and political support from Western feminists, and from the international community, [is one] that does not assault other cultures, but takes care to acknowledge their many valuable or neutral aspects while it criticizes those aspects that are harmful to women and girls. (1998, p. 48)

On the other hand, this approach seems to undercut the critical purchase of normative universalism and indeed the very idea of human rights, even if we accept that universal norms are themselves as constructed, and thus as fluid, as cultural practices. Jones gets it rights when he says:

> the doctrine of human rights is meant to be a fighting doctrine. Its purpose is not to leave the world as we find it, but to transform it into a better, more just world. A doctrine of human rights should challenge other ways of thinking; it should confront and seek to displace cultures and ideologies that fail to recognise human rights. (2000, p. 28)

Conclusion

In this chapter I have tried to move the debate beyond a static and binary reading of universalism and relativism. The first part of the chapter distinguished different types of claims that a relativist might make. The validity of normative relativism, informed by the weaker variant of metaethical relativism, was then explored in relation to the Asian values debate. The Bangkok Declaration of 1993 was undoubtedly a significant moment that called attention to the question of the validity of universal claims about value, even if the politics behind the Declaration can cast doubt on the motives of those most vocal in its support. In the second section of the chapter, reflection on the debate between liberal and communitarian thinkers gave us grounds for accepting some part of the critique of the individualism and abstraction of human rights, but also gave us grounds for rejecting the opposition between universalism and relativism as fixed extremes.

The idea that there is, or could be, a universal moral minimum commands widespread support, even amongst some who accept broadly communitarian views of the self as necessarily situated. Bhikhu Parekh's particular version of the moral minimum claim is of particular interest because he separates the idea of a moral minimum with respect to *values* from an account of *human rights*. Human rights as a means of realizing the universal moral minimum may not be able to meet the challenge of diversity.

Finally, in the third section of the chapter I looked at one example of a theory that takes Parekh's thought further, and used this as a means of reflecting on feminist dilemmas that arise with respect to the idea and the practice of universal human rights. But this does not exhaust all that we might say, either about feminism or about debates surrounding culture and human rights, so we will return to these themes in the next chapter.

7 Minority Groups and Minority Rights

'Traditional human rights standards are simply unable to resolve some of the most important and controversial questions relating to cultural minorities.' (Kymlicka, 1996, p. 4)

'Woe betide anyone who has the misfortune to be a member of a minority whose behaviour contravenes the norms of an intolerant minority!' (Barry, 2001, p. 308)

Introduction

The previous chapter continued the discussion, begun in Chapter 5 in relation to religious ethics, of the implications of diverse thick cultural, religious and moral values for the idea of universal human rights. This is not a simple debate between universalism and relativism. Though moral particularism and the concept of the self are important elements of this discussion, it is often a debate between competing universalisms, and sometimes a debate about the sorts of goods that universal norms ought to promote or protect.

This chapter considers another area of this broad field, namely, the claim that justice within liberal societies that respect human rights cannot be realized through the implementation of universal principles such as human rights alone. This is Will Kymlicka's claim in the quote above. He asserts that respect for human rights must be supplemented by multicultural rights that afford recognition to the particular injustices that arise in plural societies to which only minorities are subject. The central claim is that human rights, though important and valuable, cannot deliver comprehensive justice for cultural or religious minority groups within liberal democracies.

In the first section of the chapter I look at the arguments that have been advanced for multiculturalism, principally by Kymlicka, who has played a leading role in this field, highlighting the problems resulting from the 'difference-blindness' of liberal universalism. I will then turn to three types of criticism that have been levelled at liberal multiculturalism. First, Brian Barry's egalitarian critique of multiculturalism, which rejects many of Kymlicka's central claims. The quote from Barry, above, alludes to another important line of attack on the multiculturalist thesis, that is, the problem of 'minorities within minorities'. Much of the debate about multiculturalism is inflected with ambiguity about the types of minority groups that may claim special rights – cultural, religious, and ethnic minorities, women, disabled persons, and lesbian, gay, bisexual and transgender (LGBT) minorities all seem to crop up in the literature. The positions in this debate are themselves contested by scholars who problematize the very notion of culture and accuse both liberals and liberal multiculturalists of essentializing groups.

In the final part of the chapter we will return to the notion of difference-blindness and its significance within human rights. Advocates of both women's human rights and LGBT rights express frustration with the limitations of difference-blind universalism, but they tend to respond by arguing not for minority rights, as the multiculturalist does, but rather for the critical enlargement and reshaping of human rights. So there is a shared diagnosis of the problem confronting different minority groups, but a different view of the appropriate solution.

Liberal multiculturalism

Multiculturalism is a term that covers both an empirical phenomenon and a normative concept. It is a fact that pretty much every liberal democracy is now multicultural, in the sense of having multiple cultural communities living within its borders. But there are different ways that governments might respond to the challenges that are raised by this diversity. One response can be called 'multicultural', as opposed to, say, an 'assimilationist' or 'integrationist' approach. The (normative) multicultural approach to the (empirical) phenomenon of multiculturalism will, broadly speaking, hold that cultural minorities within the liberal state ought to be afforded some special considerations or rights that are not generally available to the majority as a means of fostering what we might call functional (rather than simply formal) equality.

Even though multiculturalists are typically somewhat critical of the difference-blindness of human rights, this should not lead us to expect them to reject the validity of human rights *per se*. Nor, if we accept the multicultural thesis, should we imagine that human rights impose a uniform mode of life on people. On the contrary, human rights set out the freedoms and resources to which people are entitled, and which are held to be the minimum goods necessary for a decent life. But a decent life is not narrowly defined or determined by human rights. Notwithstanding the concerns registered in the previous chapter, it is true that human rights allow for diverse ways of living. As we shall see, the claim of multiculturalists is that they nevertheless fail to correct for some forms of disadvantage because they are not sufficiently difference-sensitive.

As Kymlicka observes (1996, pp. 2–3), the problem of how best to protect and accommodate minorities in plural societies is a very old one. Prior to the Second World War, this was mostly achieved in Europe (not always effectively) by international treaties, in which 'kin' states essentially protected their minority in a neighbouring state by using their military weight to guarantee minority rights within the neighbouring state. This is just one dimension of the bilateral treaty system that regulated European international relations throughout the nineteenth century and into the twentieth. The failure of this system to prevent the First World War led to the creation of the League of Nations, which itself failed to protect minorities (and to prevent war) in its short existence.

Hence, after the Second World War, it was realized that an alternative and more effective system for protecting minority rights would be needed, and the framers of the UDHR intended that a set of universal rights would perform that function. The logic of this is simple: if universal rights protect all from injustice and oppression, there should be no need for any special protections for minorities. Simply by virtue of being human, members of minorities will be protected from standard threats to their inherent dignity, along with everyone else. On this model, the state is effectively blind to the particularities of its citizens. Whether they be men or women, Christian or Jewish, native born or foreign born, black or white, able-bodied or disabled, the state sees only a citizen, who is to be treated with the same dignity and respect as any other citizen.

The issue of minority rights began to appear more urgently in public and political consciousness in Europe after the collapse of communism unleashed a wave of what was described as ethno-religious conflict in the former Yugoslavia. We find evidence of this resurgence of attention at the international level in the developments in human rights treaties at this time: European bodies adopted declarations recognizing the rights of national minorities and of minority languages in the early 1990s, the UN began discussions of the Universal Declaration of Indigenous Peoples' Rights in the late 1980s (it was adopted in 2007) and adopted a Declaration on the Rights of Persons Belonging to National or Ethnic, Religious and Linguistic Minorities in 1992. However in Canada, the USA, Australia and New Zealand, there were debates of longer standing about the best way of accommodating cultural diversity.

Contemporary liberal democracies are generally pluralistic in multiple directions: they have cultural, ethnic, religious and linguistic minorities as a result of the coexistence of long-standing colonial immigrants and indigenous populations in new-world countries, long-standing patterns of pluralism within old-world countries, the massive waves of forced migration associated with the transatlantic slave trade of the seventeenth to nineteenth centuries, and from more recent waves of immigration in the wake of the collapse of colonialism, and, in Europe, the advent of free movement within the European Union. There are, thus, multiple types of minorities, facing different types of challenges, within every liberal democracy.

Liberal multiculturalism covers quite a spectrum of opinion. What unites the diverse positions within it is a view about the limitations of liberal neutrality and the importance of recognition for substantive rather than formal equality (Loobuyck, 2005). Charles Taylor is credited with having drawn attention to the importance of 'recognition' for contemporary social justice. There is a long tradition of thinking that the recognition of equal respect, the affirmation of one's peers, is a necessary condition for a flourishing life. What Taylor finds particularly salient for contemporary societies is that in conditions of pluralism, where there are dominant groups and minority groups, the condition of mutual equal respect may be systematically unfulfilled for members of the minority, and the formal equality of liberal rights cannot redress this imbalance:

> There is a form of the politics of equal respect, as enshrined in a liberalism of rights, that is inhospitable to difference, because (a) it insists on uniform application of the rules defining these rights, without exception, and (b) it is suspicious of collective goals. (Taylor, 1994, p. 60)

The uniform application of rules defining rights is not a necessary corollary of human rights, but it is a part of the structure of human rights that they are often rooted in justificatory stories that deny, or rather do not acknowledge, difference. Suspicion of collective goals proceeds from the sorts of protections that universal rights offer. These are protections for the individual abstracted from social and cultural contexts. As we saw in the previous chapter, one motivating concern here is that universal conceptions of rights seem to presuppose an unencumbered self. Insofar as the protection of equal human dignity is understood to consist in maintaining the formal equality between agents, then the self remains unencumbered. But Taylor's thought is that the dignity of members of minorities may in fact be compromised by conditions of formal equality. The key point here is that there are two ways we might foster equality in society: (i) show equal respect through *uniform* treatment; and(ii) show equal respect through *differential* treatment.

The lived experience of many people who are members of minority groups is that there is a gap between formal equality and substantive equality; members of minorities often experience both overt and subtle forms of discrimination and exclusion. Kymlicka's argument is that the individualistic rights guaranteed under conventional human rights instruments and in the basic rights-type constitutional guarantees (such as the US Bill of Rights) are not enough to protect minorities from discrimination and potential oppression. The multicultural context common to all contemporary liberal democracies requires an additional set of rights to protect minority groups. As he argues:

> [I]t has become increasingly clear that minority rights cannot be subsumed under the category of human rights. Traditional human rights standards are simply unable to resolve some of the most important and controversial questions relating to cultural minorities: which languages should be recognized in the parliaments, bureaucracies, and courts? Should each ethnic or national group have publicly funded education in its mother tongue? ... Should political offices be distributed in accordance with a principle of national or ethnic proportionality? Should the traditional homelands of indigenous peoples be reserved for their benefit, and so protected from encroachment by settlers and resource developers? What are the responsibilities of minorities to integrate? What degree of cultural integration can be required of immigrants and refugees before they acquire citizenship? (Kymlicka, 1996, pp. 4–5)

The worry here is not that human rights instruments give the wrong answer to these questions, but rather 'they often give no answer at all' (1996, p. 5). But these questions reflect important issues if we take seriously the communitarian view of the self as one whose identity is (at least partly) constituted by the social and cultural values and practices in which it is embedded (see Chapter 5). That said, Kymlicka does not see the multicultural debate as one between liberals and communitarians: 'the overwhelming majority of debates about multiculturalism are not debates between a liberal majority and communitarian minorities, but are amongst liberals about the meaning of liberalism' (2002, p. 338). In short, liberals are agreed that minority rights ought to be protected; the site of the debate is on how that is to be achieved.

Human rights protect individuals against standard threats to their inherent dignity. They are difference-blind in the sense that they conceive of the self in neutral terms, thus they are blind to the particularities of selves. The inherent dignity of members of minorities is undermined not simply through the violation of rights, but also by the subtle denigration of their collective goals, values, and aspirations. These issues are simply not experienced by the majority, and thus will not register in the lexicon of standard threats protected against by universal human rights.

Humans do not exist in isolation, and while some threats to humans are threats to individuals alone, in addition to our individualistic rights, we need recognition of the fundamental interests we all have in certain goods that can only be realized in the contexts of *groups* – things like the practice of our particular languages, the practice of the constitutive elements of our culture. Although these can be understood as rights held by individuals, they are rights that can only be exercised in the context of groups of people who also affirm the same right; thus Kymlicka refers to these as 'group-differentiated rights' (1996, p. 26). A totally different view is defended by Chandran Kukathas (1992), who argues that liberal rights should not be reinterpreted as Kymlicka proposes, and instead stresses the liberal right to freedom of association, which enables individuals to form groups of their choosing, which may (or may not) reflect particular cultural values.

Kymlicka once confidently declared that all the major debates about multiculturalism are settled; however, multiculturalism as a political project has been less enthusiastically supported in recent years than it once was. Particularly after the al-Qaeda-inspired terrorist attacks in Madrid in 2004 and London in 2005, European leaders have seemed increasingly disenchanted with the idea of multiculturalism and have said much about the importance of Muslims' integration (Modood, 2005). German Chancellor Angela Merkel declared in 2010 that 'multiculturalism has failed'. British Prime Minister David Cameron made similar remarks in 2011. Multiculturalism has been spoken of as undermining social cohesion (see Miller, 2006), though both Kymlicka and Taylor explicitly envisage a multicultural project that is consistent with, and indeed conducive to, solidarity with fellow citizens and the state on the part of cultural minorities. Again, these issues are difficult to grasp in the abstract, so let us briefly reflect on three examples.

(i) Language rights

It seems unlikely that there is any country in the world in which only one language is spoken. In some European countries, like Britain, Spain and France, there is both a national language and several indigenous minority languages, and further minority languages spoken by immigrant groups. Other European countries, such as Belgium and Switzerland, do not have a single national language. In the USA almost 1 in 5 people speak a language other than English in their homes (Patten, 2009).

These circumstances raise questions for the language(s) in which institutions operate. Should public education be available in one language only, or should speakers of minority languages be educated in their own languages? Should doctors and parliaments and courts be obliged to offer their services in multiple languages, or should speakers of minority languages be obliged to learn a national language? Should the status of immigrant minority languages be judged differently from the status of indigenous minority languages?

Taylor's discussion of French as a protected language in Canada is instructive here:

> One could consider the French language, for instance, as a collective resource that individuals might want to make use of, and act for its preservation, just as one does for clean air or green spaces. But this can't capture the full thrust of policies designed for cultural survival. It is not just a matter of having the French language available for those who might choose it … it also involves making sure that there is a community of people here in the future that will want to avail itself of the opportunity to use the French language. Policies aimed at survival actively seek to *create* members of the community … There is no way that these policies could be seen as just providing a facility to already existing people. (Taylor, 1994, pp. 58–9)

The point of multicultural policies, then, is not just to create options for minorities, rather it is to create and foster the conditions in which the minority can realize its vision of what it is to lead a good life, and that implies the conditions for sustaining itself. Educating children in the language of their family and community is thus an expression of the value of community as a good. It is also a means of the majority, via the state, affording recognition to the minority.

On the other hand, opponents of multiculturalism sometimes argue that integration and assimilation are essential to equality, not just in a formal sense, but in a material sense as well: 'A common language may well be essential if all citizens are to have an equal opportunity to work in the modern economy' (Patten, 2008, p. 105). Advocates of the integration approach to cultural diversity also are keen to stress the implications for state solidarity that a common language may have (Jennings, 2000). It is argued that democracy is better served by a shared language, indeed, this is particularly important if, as is increasingly suggested, deliberative forms of democracy are seen to be crucial to resolving multicultural dilemmas and tensions (Phillips, 2007). There are also legitimate questions of practicality to be considered here, given that there are literally scores if not hundreds of languages spoken in most countries.

(ii) Representation

Liberal democracies recognize the formal equality of all citizens by giving one vote to each citizen. The principle of one member one vote seems to many to be axiomatic of democracy (though in practice many electoral systems do not work like this). However, if citizens tend to prefer to elect representatives who understand and care about their interests, then it may turn out that a minority group will be continuously and predictably disadvantaged in the electoral process. On the other hand, members of minorities who are elected to public office, for example as MPs, may well resist attempts (from both within and outwith their ethnocultural communities) to designate them spokespersons for their group.

Still, if it is true that minority citizens' interests are better understood and better served by elected representatives who share those interests – and there are certainly reasons for believing that might be true – and if a minority group is a permanent numerical minority, then there is an argument to be made for having guaranteed representation for minorities in parliaments. For example, some small and geographically dispersed minorities in the USA – namely native Hawaiians, native Alaskans, and some native American tribes – have guaranteed representation on some local bodies that have authority over public services (Kymlicka, 1996). Similarly, New Zealand Maoris have reserved seats in parliament. But this sort of practice seems to create an inequality, in that it privileges the position and the voice of the minority relative to the majority. On the other hand, if the minority is not protected via special representation, then it may be difficult for the minority voice to be heard at all.

This can happen entirely without malice. Elected representatives may fully intend to represent the interests of all their constituents, but fail to be aware of the extent to which their own unconscious biases are reflected in their discharge of their duties. Certainly, when the 1997 intake of the British Parliament included more women as a proportion of MPs than any previous Parliament – largely a product of all-women shortlists for candidate selections (a practice later ruled to have been unlawful) – there was a notable upsurge in 'women-friendly' and 'family-friendly' policies being tabled for legislation, and being passed.

As a matter of fact many groups of people are under-represented in most democratic parliaments, and able-bodied middle-class white men tend to be quite significantly over-represented. Kymlicka has particularly discussed guaranteed seats in parliaments for members of minority groups, particularly indigenous and national minority groups (such as the Québécois) as a corollary of the right of self-government, implied in the right to self-determination. In contrast, strategies such as all-minority shortlists have a different aim, which accept the basic structure of the democratic institutions, but aims to address a contingent imbalance within them.

(iii) Exemptions

Amongst the most widely practised multicultural policies, and amongst the most contentious, are policies allowing minority groups exemptions from some generally applied rules or legislation. Examples include legislative exemptions for Sikhs in Britain that allow them to ride motorcycles without a helmet and entitle them to wear the *kirpan* in public. Muslim and Jewish butchers are exempt from certain animal cruelty laws in a number of European countries to allow for ritual slaughter of animals in ways consistent with their faiths. Some native Americans are able to restrict the commercial uses of their traditional lands by exemption from general competition laws.

Brian Barry (2001, p. 297) is probably correct to suggest that these exemptions are typically approved on an ad hoc basis, in response to cases brought by individuals or small groups who challenge the legitimacy of laws in the courts. What these cases reflect, in Barry's view, is the recognition of rights of *individuals*, based on their membership of particular groups, rather than rights of groups *per se*. Barry's particular claim is about Britain – he raises questions about the democratic legitimacy of ad hoc policy-making of this kind – but his point about the piecemeal practice of multiculturalism has wider validity. Contrary to the vision of multiculturalists like Kymlicka, accommodations of this kind are more the product of particular struggles and settlements and have in some contexts (like Britain) been resolved in ways that continue to prioritize individual rights; they are not really the product of an overarching multicultural programme that accords rights to groups.

Education policy is, again, a site of particular interest, with many claims for exemptions based on religious grounds, either to have children in non-denominational schools exempted from particular lessons (such as religious education), or to publicly fund schools that deliver education in accordance with a particular faith. What makes debates about multiculturalism particularly difficult in the context of state-school education is that there are potentially conflicting sets of rights-holders involved: the rights of the child and the rights of the parents may each weigh in the balance of judgement. There is also the question of the role of education *per se*; to what extent the creation of future citizens is a proper function of school education (Macedo, 2000).

Critics of liberal multiculturalism: egalitarianism, exit and essentialism

No sooner had Kymlicka declared the triumph of multiculturalism than a host of critics began to articulate their principled objections. Three strands of criticism are particularly worth considering. Firstly, there is the charge that multicultural critics are mistaken about the cause of the social disadvantage and oppression that they seek to remedy. On this view, the problem is not difference-blindness and a lack of cultural recognition, rather the problem is (often) economic disadvantage. Multiculturalists, if they care about basic rights, should be egalitarians. A second line of criticism is concerned with the problem of minorities within minorities. Here the charge is that multiculturalism does not offer protection for the fundamental rights of groups within minorities. The third line of critique suggests that the terms in which these debates have proceeded have generated more heat than light. Both friends and opponents of multiculturalism have been guilty of essentializing groups.

(i) Egalitarianism

Brian Barry is particularly scathing about liberal multiculturalism. In his view, it represents 'not so much a case of reinventing the wheel as forgetting why the wheel was invented' (Barry, 2001, p. 11). He criticizes Kymlicka and Young, as exemplars of multicultural thinkers, for misconceiving the problem to which they propose multiculturalism as a solution. The mistake, on Barry's view, is to attribute to all disadvantaged groups a trait called 'culture', the misrecognition of which is then taken to be the cause of their oppression. But Barry suggests multiple alternatives are in fact likely to be in play:

> [T]he members of a group may suffer not because they have distinctive culturally derived goals but because they do poorly in achieving generally shared objectives such as a good education, desirable and well-paid jobs (or perhaps any job at all), a safe and salubrious neighbourhood in which to live and enough income to enable them to be adequately housed, clothed and fed and to participate in the social, economic and political life of their society. (Barry, 2001, pp. 305–6)

For Barry, it is the job of the liberal state to protect the rights of its citizens by addressing arbitrary unfairnesses. Without doubt, some disadvantages experienced by members of minority groups are the result of direct and indirect discrimination. That the state should address this is not denied by Barry, but he does not accept that multicultural policies are the only or the best means to achieve this, not least because they have the effect of distorting the visibility of disadvantages that would be better redressed by redistribution of resources.

But the pursuit of multicultural policies renders the more important pursuit of liberal egalitarian policies more difficult, Barry argues, because of the divisiveness of asserting 'special claims'. Rather than supporting a redistribution of resources necessary to create excellent schools for all, the multiculturalist argues that a portion of resources should be reserved for the education of a minority in a particular way. On liberal egalitarian grounds, citizens should not be made to bear the costs of unchosen disadvantage, but it is perfectly permissible for costs that are the products of choice to be borne by the individual. As Barry puts it, '[a]ny disadvantage for which the victim is not responsible establishes the *prima facie* claim to remedy or compensation' (2001, p. 114). In this instance, then, if a parent has a preference that their child be educated in a particular cultural tradition, rather than in a state education system that is open to all children, the question arises, is the state obliged to bear the additional cost?

One concern here is that Barry's argument assumes that people who experience disadvantage all want the same things, and thus the answer is to eliminate the barriers to the same core goods. Again, the liberal universalist argument presupposes a basic human nature, which communitarians like Sandel, and difference theorists like Young, have found insufficient. Susan Mendus (2002) points out another sort of worry about Barry's argument from choice, namely, that it is not clear that the situated self really does 'choose' the goods to which she has allegiance.

In a reply to Mendus, Barry (2002) recognizes that choice is never fully unencumbered by cultural and community-based values, but defends his use of choice as a measure of when egalitarian commitments trump exemptions or justify special treatment. This problem also speaks to a more general concern about the costs and opportunities for exit from cultural groups. If we recall the notion of the encumbered self discussed in the previous chapter, we can see the tension here – do any of us fully choose our values?

(ii) Exit

Exit refers to the entitlement or ability of a person to leave a group. The motivating assumption here is that if a person remains within a group then they consent to its practices. Feminists have been particularly concerned to expose the complexity of the situation masked by this simple thought. In a remarkably influential article, Susan Moller Okin (1999) posed the question 'Is Multiculturalism Bad for Women?' Her answer is generally taken to be yes, though in a less polemical article (1998b) she is careful to distinguish between those types of multicultural policies that she finds benign or indeed positive – such as those that promote recognition through challenging the idea of a dead white male canon in education – and those that she finds to be in conflict with the principles of feminism – such as policies that recognize the leaders of cultural groups as authoritative with respect to their members.

The central claim of her argument is that insofar as the leaders of minority groups tend to be older men, it is plausible to assume that they may not, in fact, genuinely represent the interests of women within the group:

> Most cultures are suffused with practices and ideologies concerning gender. Suppose, then, that a culture endorses and facilitates the

control of men over women in various ways (even if informally, in the private sphere of domestic life). Suppose, too, that there are fairly clear disparities of power between the sexes, such that the more powerful, male members are those who are generally in a position to determine and articulate the group's beliefs, practices, and interests. Under such conditions, group rights are potentially, and in many cases actually, antifeminist. (Okin 1999)

Kymlicka (1999) has attempted to insulate his argument from this objection by differentiating between group rights that promote the well-being of the group against external interference ('external protections'), and group rights that permit the leadership of the group to practice internal oppression ('internal restrictions'). Whereas Okin finds that multiculturalism and feminism are in tension with one another, Kymlicka insists they are allies in addressing the complacencies of liberal universalism.

In practice, it is not obvious how policies that would facilitate internal restrictions could always be differentiated from those that would generate external protections. For example, Article 16 of the UDHR states that men and women have the right to marry and found a family, and, (16.2) 'Marriage shall be entered into only with the free and full consent of the intending spouses'. The UDHR may be read as prohibiting arranged marriages. If a minority group asserts that arranged marriages are a part of their culture, and that they should be entitled to practise them, is this an example of an external protection or an internal restriction?

Many feminists (and possibly many liberals) would judge it to be the latter, and that this is specifically a restriction that impedes the freedom of women. But it is also the case that there are women who endorse the practice of arranged marriages on religious and cultural grounds. Where is the dividing line between an 'arranged' marriage, and a 'forced' marriage? Okin's work draws attention to the fact that patriarchal norms are effective, and oppressive, when subtly endorsed and pervasively accepted. So, while there are undoubtedly women who enter into arranged marriages freely and happily, there are also women who are coerced into marriage. There need not be overt violence for there to be genuine oppression. Anne Phillips is alert to the complexities here:

> The question, rather, is at what point do the familial and social pressures that make arranged marriage a norm turn into coercion, and how, short of banning all arranged marriages, can public agencies act to protect young people from ones that are forced? (Phillips, 2009, p. 41)

Banning all arranged marriages would surely infringe the rights of the minority group who value the practice. But it will not always be easy to see when allowing a practice like arranged marriage constitutes an external protection for the cultural and religious integrity of a community, and when doing so facilitates the internal restriction of some members of the community. It is plausible that the same policy could be genuinely experienced as a restriction by some members and a protection by others.

Chandran Kukathas (1998; 2003) argues that states should pursue neither a policy of promoting cultural group rights, nor a policy of integrationism, but rather should practise 'benign indifference' to cultural groups. The rationale for this is that on Kukathas' view there are no minority *group* rights, only *individual* rights, including the right to dissociate, which is a logical corollary of the right to freedom of association. It follows from this that if a person remains within a group then they can be understood to consent to the norms and practices of the group. The state, then, has no business interfering in the freely chosen pursuits of its citizens. If that is right, then the state, on liberty-respecting grounds, should tolerate 'communities which bring up children unschooled and illiterate; which enforce arranged marriages; which deny conventional medical care to their members (including children); and which inflict cruel and "unusual" punishment' (Kukathas, 2003, p. 134).

The rights of children is a particularly complex issue that I shall leave aside here, and focus instead on the issues that come up in relation to adults (though see Okin, 2002; Van Der Ploeg, 2002). Kukathas' position is amongst the most extreme on what a liberal state ought to tolerate. Much of the weight of his argument hangs on the right of exit, and in this respect, the issues he raises have wider applicability to multicultural theories. For it seems that if a person is free to leave a group then they might justly be expected to bear some of the costs should they choose not to do so.

Feminist critics have forcefully rejected this line of reasoning. For example, Anne Phillips argues:

> [p]erceptions of what is desirable are formed against a backdrop of what seems possible, and choices are made from what appears to be the available range. Given these constraints, it may sometimes be outsiders rather than insiders who are better able to recognise the injustice of a particular practice or belief. Evidence of internal support cannot be taken as decisive, for it may reflect the poverty of aspirations rather than 'genuine' belief. (2007, p. 39)

Similarly, Okin (2002) argues that the costs of exit, particularly for women, are higher than the 'exit' view suggests. These costs include both the psychological costs of rejecting the way of life valued by one's family and friends, which may, in turn, lead to ostracism and rejection by one's social group, and the economic costs, which, again, may be especially punitive for women, particularly if they lack skills and qualifications that are valued in the economy, as many women will do if they come from conservative cultural groups that encourage women to occupy domestic roles.

Of course, there are always costs in choosing to exit a group, but the question is about the extent to which particularly disadvantaged minorities within minorities may reasonably be able to bear such costs. This is a concern not just about the genuine exit options of women, but about any vulnerable person within minority groups. Children, gay people, disabled people, religious minorities, racial minorities and others may have reason to fear the protections of group rights that serve to entrench the authority of group norms and group leaders.

(iii) Essentialism

However, to accept this point and leave the argument there is to neglect a significant strand of essentialism that runs through much of this debate. There are both strategic and philosophical considerations here. Amongst the strategic considerations are the practical implications of talking about 'cultural' rights at all. As Phillips points out, 'the failure to problematise culture has contributed to a radical otherness that represents people as profoundly different in their practices, values, and beliefs' (2007, p. 24). The rhetoric of cultural difference informs citizens' perceptions of their fellow citizens (Modood, 1998).

This is not to deny the depth and richness of cultural and religious and historical differences, but it is to call into question not just, as Barry does, the idea of culture as all-encompassing explanatory variable, but the very idea of culture at all. It is striking that in much of the literature about multiculturalism, the terms 'culture' and 'religion' are often used in ways that suggest that the two are interchangeable. It is not clear, in the literature, what this thing called culture really is. And yet culture has become a powerful concept in society – of particular concern to feminists is the (successful) use of 'cultural' defences in cases of male violence against women (Okin, 1999; Benhabib, 2002; Phillips, 2007).

Seyla Benhabib is among those who have criticized Okin for failing to be sufficiently careful in her use of the term 'culture': 'Although she recognizes gender as a cleavage, Okin writes as if cultures are unified structures of meaning in other respects' (2002, p. 103). Okin is not unusual in this – both conservatives and progressives seem to assume that 'culture' is a thing that each group of human beings has, and the preservation of cultures is valuable, from the conservative point of view, because they are rooted in tradition and authenticity, and from the progressives' point of view, because doing so rectifies past patterns of domination and oppression (Benhabib, 2002, pp. 3–5).

There is a genuine bind here, one that feminists have encountered in the context of arguments for women's rights: In order to protect a group of disadvantaged people from being marginalized, in order to assert the value and worth of their capabilities and endeavours, it is necessary to reject an essentialist reading of their identity. Yet, it is also necessary to assert that collective identity to facilitate one's claims. Thus, feminists both sought to reject traditional expectations of 'women', and to deny that there is an essential or natural way of being a woman, and, at the same time, they made claims on behalf of 'women' about what 'women' are, what they want, and so on (Scott, 1997).

Also relevant in the criticism of essentialism about feminism is the concept of intersectionality: second- and third-wave feminists have drawn attention to the ways in which sites of difference intersect, making it impossible to understand individuals' experience in terms of blanket categories such as 'woman', 'black woman', 'lesbian woman' and so on. Reflecting on the intersecting nature of factors implicated in social disadvantage, Fraser and Honneth (2003) argue for both a 'politics of recognition' and a 'politics of redistribution', rejecting the opposition between them as found in theorists such as Barry.

Rather than embracing the idea of 'strategic essentialism', adopted from feminism, Modood (1998, 2007) insists that it is both true that cultural identities are not signifiers of fixed and complete cultural phenomena, but that there is substance and coherence to cultural minorities as groups, and that these have value for their members. If he is right, then what is needed is a multiculturalism that can balance the tasks of affording recognition to minority group identities, yet avoid being oppressive of minorities within minorities.

More difference-blindness: LGBT rights

The analysis of liberal universalism that leads to the demand for multicultural rights begins from the premise that the difference-blindness of liberal universalism is not, as it purports to be, neutral with respect to difference, but rather, oppressive of difference. Human rights, this story says, are the rights of men rather than women, white people rather than black, Latino or Asian people, able-bodied rather than disabled people, and straight people rather than gay people. Advocates of women's human rights and of LGBT rights also critique the difference-blindness of liberal universalism, but women's rights and gay rights are not group-differentiated rights of the sort that Kymlicka describes: the exercise of them is not conceptually dependent on the simultaneous exercise of the same right by others.

Feminist theorists have long debated the content and indeed the usefulness of the idea of 'women's human rights' (Bunch, 1990; Charlesworth, 1995; Fraser, 1999; Peach, 2001). The call for recognition of LGBT rights is a relative newcomer to the pantheon of rights claims, and it is among the most contentious. Indeed, it is one of the cases where arguments proceeding from a purported global consensus on human rights, or a shared moral minimum, *pace* Parekh, are of little help (see Chapter 5). Amnesty International may have decided that 'love is a human right', but homosexuality remains illegal in many African states and several predominantly Muslim states in Asia. In a handful of these, sodomy (assumed to be a homosexual practice) is punishable by death. Discrimination and harassment are common experiences for gay people in many countries where homosexuality is legal, including some countries that have recognised same-sex marriage. South Africa, for example, is the first African country to have recognised same-sex marriage in law. However, 'corrective rape' and other forms of violence are experienced by significant numbers of black lesbians in particular. There simply is not a consensus on LGBT rights, either between states or within them. In the USA there has been state-level legislative action both to legalize and to prohibit gay marriage (Ball, 2002). Only recently has the Obama administration repealed 'Don't Ask, Don't Tell', a policy which prevented openly gay people from serving in the military. In Europe, many countries now formally recognize same-sex partnerships and some recognize same-sex marriage (and adoption and parenting rights), but these issues remain controversial at present.

What is of particular interest here is that within liberal democracies, proponents of both sides of the debate have drawn on the language of human rights to advance their claims. Liberal theorists, such as Martha Nussbaum (1995, 2009), essentially make an argument in favour of LGBT rights from consistency: the restriction of marriage rights, family rights, the right to serve in the military, protections from discrimination in employment, housing, and so on, on the grounds of sexual orientation, is arbitrary and unjust. It is a reflection of a long-standing prejudice, the continuation of which in the twenty-first century is an anachronism at best. Conservatives, however, have also drawn on the language of human rights to defend their positions. Here it is the right to religious freedom, or the rights of cultural minorities, that is invoked. For example, Catholic adoption agencies in the UK unsuccessfully sought an exemption from laws prohibiting discrimination on the grounds of sexual orientation in the provision of goods and services, as they objected on religious grounds to being forced to consider gay couples as prospective adoptive parents. On the other hand, the Catholic Church in Scotland has attacked what it sees as the manipulation of morality that the human rights framework affords to proponents of same-sex marriage:

> [T]hose who hold to this ideology rely on the modern preoccupation with human rights to press for a change in the concept and definition of marriage to cover what any group in society might want it to be. It provides same sex advocates with a philosophical tool to seek a change in our law and our definition, to serve their own purposes. (Conti, 2011)

To focus on only one aspect of this, the debate about gay marriage, it is useful to return to Article 16 of the UDHR, which states that men and women have the right to marry and found a family. The wording of the right was widely taken to imply that men have the right to marry women, and vice versa. The inclusion of this right speaks to a vision of family life as being the natural condition for human beings, with heterosexual marriage as the foundation of that, a vision widely endorsed by opponents of same-sex marriage.

But to posit a naturalness with respect to human sexual relationships is deeply contentious. John Finnis (1997) makes some odd claims in defence of an argument about the naturalness of heterosexuality and the unnaturalness of homosexuality. Marriage, he argues, is a fundamental good that recognizes the procreative potential of committed heterosexual relationships. Insofar as homosexuals cannot naturally procreate, they cannot fully express the good of such a relationship, thus even committed homosexual relationships are only corruptions of genuine unions.

On the other hand, some queer theorists have also been reluctant to endorse calls for same-sex marriage on the grounds that the normativity of marriage is itself problematic (Card, 1999; Ferguson, 2007). Extending marriage rights to LGBT couples does nothing to displace or disrupt the normative affirmation that marriage rights accord to long-term monogamous relationships, and, so it is argued, assimilate gay lifestyles to a heteronormative way of living. Seen in these terms, the capacity for human rights to imply a moderately specific vision of what it is to be a human being is once again contentious. These debates lead us to reflect on the limitations of liberal universalism as an ethical framework.

And yet, it would be a mistake to overstate the case here. The concerns raised in these discussions are genuine worries, but the very fact that diverse groups of people who fundamentally disagree with each other can and do draw on the language of human rights to advance their claims itself speaks to the critical power of human rights as a universal doctrine. For critics of human rights, however, it may also signal their vulnerability to ideological co-option.

Conclusion

This chapter considered issues arising from the critique of difference-blind universalism, of which human rights may be taken as an example. A significant body of philosophical work in this area has focussed on debates about multiculturalism and the call for recognition of minority group rights. Liberal multiculturalists, like Kymlicka, hold that human rights are an inadequate framework for delivering minority rights; additional rights are needed to protect the interests of minority communities.

Critics of multiculturalism call attention to the problems of exit and essentialism. Feminist theorists have been particularly prominent in these debates, both in calling attention to the ways in which multiculturalism seems to ignore the problems faced by minorities within minorities, including, but not only, women, and in calling attention to the ways in which culture as a concept reifies minority groups and values.

The final section of the chapter briefly touched on a more recently emerging area of debate that proceeds from the same foundational critique of difference-blindness, but yields a different conclusion – to protect the interests of LGBT people what is needed is not a specific set of minority rights, but the recognition of LGBT people's entitlement to universal human rights.

8 Global Poverty and Human Rights

'Despite the undisputed great importance of such basic necessities for human life, there is no agreement on whether human beings have a *right*, or *human right*, to the necessities of life.' (Pogge, 2004, p. 2)

'[N]otions of poverty and wealth are only meaningful within a given cultural context ... while the poverty of the continent is taken for granted, there are voices throughout Africa that resist this blanket classification, invoking the wealth of the continent in untapped natural resources, vibrant indigenous cultures and dynamic human potential.' (Deng, 2009, p. 30)

Introduction

There has been an explosion of philosophical interest in global poverty and human rights in recent years. It was not always so: almost as soon as the UDHR was proclaimed, sceptics of social and economic rights denounced them as mere 'manifesto rights', of little political value, and expressive of conceptual confusion about the very idea of human rights.

However, a generation later, Henry Shue's (1980) seminal work demonstrated that support for what he calls 'security rights', or traditional civil and political rights, implies support for what he calls 'subsistence rights', or minimal welfare rights included in social and economic rights. Another generation later, Thomas Pogge (2002) moved the debate on by developing an account of the duties that people in rich countries have in relation to the human rights of the global poor. Pogge's innovative work has undoubtedly set the tone for much contemporary theorizing about global justice. His critics draw attention to the ways in which he conceptualizes poverty, harm and agency, but many remain broadly supportive of his central claims.

143

In this chapter we will look at the arguments advanced in support of rights against poverty and in support of framing the issue of poverty this way, that is, in terms of human rights. We will also touch on the points raised by critics of this approach, and in doing so return to the issue of the relationship between rights and duties first raised in Chapter 1. Pogge is right (above) to say that there is substantial disagreement about the extent to which people have rights against severe poverty, yet there are many, including Pogge, who find the persistence of severe poverty in the world today so weighty a moral blight that they see an obvious correlation between the moral authority of human rights and the moral urgency of global poverty. But we should also be wary of using the term 'poverty' indiscriminately. As Francis M. Deng (above) suggests, we might understand poverty in different ways in different contexts. This raises not only practical questions about the content of rights, but also deeper questions about the ways in which discourses of human rights and of global poverty shape and inform political practice.

Manifesto rights, subsistence and security

As we saw in Chapter 2, early advocates of natural rights, including Locke and Paine, understood natural rights to include rights to a minimum standard of subsistence. Nevertheless, the concept of natural rights was widely understood to privilege civil and political rights (cf. MacPherson, 1962). Human rights, as conceptualized in the International Bill of Rights, explicitly include provisions for welfare rights: Article 22 of the UDHR states that everyone has the right to 'social security ... through national effort and international co-operation and in accordance with the organization and resources of each State'. Article 23 proclaims a right to work; Article 26 proclaims a right to education. Article 25 defends the right of all to a 'standard of living adequate for the health and well-being of himself and his family', and makes specific mention of food, clothing, housing, medical care, security against contingencies such as sickness and disability, and special assistance for childhood and motherhood. Article 24, famously, proclaims the rights of all 'to rest and leisure, including reasonable limitation of working hours and periodic holidays with pay'.

In the contemporary world, these rights are more generally honoured in the breach than in the observance. On 2008 figures, the World Bank estimates that 22 per cent of the world's population live in conditions that match its definition of 'extreme poverty' (that is, they live on the equivalent of less than US$1.25 per day at 1993 purchasing power parity). Secure access to sufficient food, clean water, and basic health-care remain endemic challenges for many in the world's poorer countries. According to UNICEF, 24,000 children die of preventable poverty-related illnesses every day. More detailed information can be found in Pogge (2004, pp. 1–2) or the World Bank's poverty index.

In view of these persistent challenges, social and economic rights have been dismissed as 'manifesto rights', that is, rights that represent an aspiration or a goal perhaps, but rights that cannot in fact be met. As was discussed in Chapter 1, Cranston's (1967) savage critique holds that the inclusion of so-called manifesto rights diminishes the integrity of human rights declarations. The argument is that while rights against torture, say, are absolute, manifesto rights can be violated without the same sort of moral condemnation legitimately following. One of the reasons that rights against torture can be understood to be absolute, and represent a different moral standard, is that they can be understood in terms of a perfect obligation in Kant's sense of the term – that is, the right corre-lates to a perfect duty, held by everyone and performable by everyone (O'Neill, 1996).

On Cranston's view, the sorts of rights that pass his test of what it is to be a human right are realizable by legislation and are within the power of governments, as the relevant duty-bearers, to effect. Where that is not the case then the right does not seem to be much use to the rights-bearer. In Chapter 2 we noted a similar argument made by Burke: it is the good itself, and not the abstract right to it, that is important, and to Burke it was unclear how the abstract right helped procure the good.

A related but more sophisticated argument is advanced by Onora O'Neill:

> Only if we jettison the entire normative understanding of rights in favour of the aspirational view, can we break the normative link between rights and their counterpart obligations. If we take rights seriously and see them as normative rather than aspirational, we must take obligations seriously. If, on the other hand, we opt for a merely aspirational view, the costs are high. For then we also have to accept that where human rights are unmet there is no breach of obligation, nobody at fault, nobody who can be held to account, nobody to blame and nobody who owes redress. (2005, p. 430)

How should we respond to such a challenge? O'Neill is right to think that most theorists will reject the path of adopting an aspirational or manifesto account of social and economic rights. The costs of doing so are significant. But the alternative path, on O'Neill's reading, is not viable. The thought here is not just that the obligations associated with social and economic rights cannot be met, but that they cannot be specified without an institutional structure that would identify relevant duty-bearers and assign appropriate duties. Thus, people can have welfare rights that have the status of human rights, but if a) human rights are held by all, and b) not all live under relevant institutions, then c) it is, on O'Neill's analysis, incoherent to think of these rights as human rights.

The contemporary human rights regime does indeed recognize an institutional structure – a world of sovereign states (see Chapter 4). States are both the primary agents of human rights obligations, and the agent against whose power human rights are designed to protect. The language affirming socio-economic rights in the UDHR and the ICESCR very strongly implies that these are rights state-centric rights. For example, Article 22 of the UDHR reads:

> Everyone, as a member of society, has the right to social security and is entitled to realization, through national effort and international co-operation and *in accordance with the organization and resources of each State*, of the economic, social and cultural rights indispensable for his dignity and the free development of his personality. (Emphasis added)

That being the case, we should expect the content of the human right to welfare in Sweden to be different to the human right to welfare in Niger. Yet the majority of defenders of human rights against poverty direct their arguments towards the justification of trans-border obligations.

O'Neill (2001) argues that states are the primary agents in global justice because only states have the capacity to assign and enforce the performance of necessary tasks by capable agents. However, the paradoxical status of states as both agent of human rights and most likely threats to human rights signals a degree of conceptual confusion at the heart of human rights, and is compared by O'Neill to putting foxes in charge of hen houses:

> It is true enough that those who are to achieve progressively the full realization of human rights must have capacities to do so – but it does not follow that those with (a good range of) the necessary capacities can be trusted to do so. (2005, p. 435)

There are two problems being run together here. One is a concern about the possibility of knowing the content of counterpart obligations to rights in a way that allows us, when a right has been violated, to know who is to blame and may be held to account for it. The other is a worry about the prudence of a system that, insofar as these obligations are assigned, it is by default to a set of agents that may not discharge them effectively, either because of a lack of capacity or a lack of good faith. I will return to the second of these later on.

With regard to the first point, the difference between rights to welfare and rights not to be tortured, for instance, is that in the case of the right not to be tortured we can see pre-institutionally who the relevant duty-bearer is, for it is everyone. Everyone can discharge the counterpart duty not to torture, and they can do so without the need for an institutional structure to be created to assign and manage responsibilities. Moreover, if a person were to be tortured, it would be clear who the rights-violator is; the person or persons who acted to carry out the torture would themselves be responsible.

Welfare rights are not like this. Say that a person has a right to food. If that is true, and it is a human right, then all persons have a right to food. But who are the duty-bearers? It cannot be the case that all persons, everywhere, are simultaneously responsible for the counterpart duties to all other persons' rights to food – this moves us no further forward in understanding to whom we should make a claim when we are in need of food. If I have more food than I strictly need, and I know that there are literally millions of others who do not have enough to eat, to which of the millions do I owe my surplus food? The very absurdity of the questions indicates that something has gone wrong here.

One way that we might try to understand what has gone wrong in this argument is to think of the duties correlative to rights as positive or negative. On this model, positive duties are those that require action on the part of the agent, negative duties require only that the agent refrain from acting. Some restrictive readings of natural rights hold that the only sorts of rights that persons have are negative rights, that is, rights whose correlative duties require the forbearance of other agents (Hart, 1967). Libertarians also hold that only negative duties carry definitive normative force (Nozick, 1974).

We might think that this helps us understand what is going on in the confusion over the allocation of counterpart duties with respect to social and economic rights, as follows. Civil and political rights, 'real rights', we might say, are negative rights – they are rights not to be treated in ways that violate our inherent dignity. The right not to be tortured is an example; all that is required for the fulfilment of that right is that all others refrain from violating it. The very negativity of this right is crucial to its universality. All agents can fulfil a negative duty simultaneously; there need be no ambiguity, therefore, about the allocation of the duty. In Kant's terms, this would be a perfect duty.

The right to food, on the other hand, is, like social and economic rights generally, a positive right; its fulfilment depends upon positive action by some other agent(s). It is not enough that others simply refrain from preventing me obtaining food, there needs to be some actual action undertaken to facilitate my access to food. But if that is so, then it is not a duty that can be performed by all simultaneously, and thus it cannot be a universal duty. In Kant's terms, this would be an imperfect duty.

Conventional morality considers perfect duties to be more morally weighty than imperfect duties, though this conclusion arguably proceeds from a false view of the Kantian distinction between perfect and imperfect duties. For Kant (and Kantians), perfect duties are those that always must be performed if we are to be just. Imperfect duties are also morally weighty, but the agent has some discretion as to the circumstances in which these ought to be performed (O'Neill, 1996). We do generally think it is more morally bad that someone actively kill another person – thus violating her negative right not to be killed, which right can be respected by all simply by their forbearance – than for a person to fail to help another person by giving her food, even when we know that the person is dying of starvation (Thomson, 1986). It might be a good thing if a person were to help another by giving her food, but it does not seem to be as strict a moral demand as the prohibition on killing another person.

Negative rights, then, are argued to be more morally significant than positive rights. Social and economic rights are not simply manifesto rights, they are also secondary sorts of human rights, if they are human rights at all. But this way of thinking about social and economic rights would be fundamentally mistaken, as Henry Shue (1980) has demonstrated. Two points in his argument are particularly worth bringing out. The first relates to the claim that social and economic rights are less important than civil and political rights. The second relates to the claim that only forbearance is needed to protect negative rights, whilst action is needed to protect positive rights.

Shue begins with the proposition that if there are any rights at all, then these must include basic rights to security. Shue uses 'basic' rights to refer to universal minimum rights; he deliberately does not base his argument on the assumed validity of the UDHR. I take it, though, that his argument can be understood to justify human rights, if not necessarily so extensive a list of human rights as are found in the International Bill of Rights. We have basic rights to security, Shue says, because the enjoyment of any right is dependent on our being reasonably secure from threats to our life, liberty, bodily integrity, and so on (1980, pp. 20–2). But it turns out that '[t]he same considerations that support the conclusion that physical security is a basic right support the conclusion that subsistence is a basic right' (1980, p. 24). He goes on, 'Deficiencies in the means of subsistence can be just as fatal, incapacitating, or painful as violations of physical security' (1980, p. 24). For Vandana Shiva this speaks to the 'indivisibility of so-called 'first' (civil and political) and 'second' (social, economic and cultural) generation rights'. As she puts it: 'Freedom from hunger is no less a human right than freedom of speech. Without the former, the latter does not exist' (1999, p. 88).

The claim that protection of negative rights requires only negative correlative duties can also be rejected. The example of torture seems to be a classic case of a negative right. But in fact torture as a human rights problem is not a product of lots of individuals spontaneously and discretely engaging in the practice of torture. Torture is both an industry and an institutional practice. There are manuals and implements available to instruct and equip would-be torturers, who are very often members of institutional structures, such as government or military agencies (Shue, 2005). To protect the right of someone not to be tortured, then, requires an infrastructure of police and courts, which require funding and quite substantial action to be effective.

> [I]t may be possible *to avoid violating* someone's rights to physical security yourself by merely refraining from acting in ways that would constitute violations. But it is impossible to *protect* anyone's rights to physical security without taking, or making payments toward the taking of, a range of positive actions. (Shue, 1980, p. 37)

The protection of so-called negative rights, like the protection of so-called positive rights, requires action. Insofar as we accept the general applicability to honour a positive duty to protect the right to physical security on the grounds that it is of paramount importance, then we equally have reason to accept the general applicability of a positive duty to protect the right to subsistence. We have positive duties to protect at least some social and economic rights.

We can now return to O'Neill's point that the counterpart obligations are underspecified, that the relevant duty-bearer is unclear, in the case of human rights arguments concerning global poverty. O'Neill does an excellent job of drawing attention to a lack of clarity and to sloppy thinking in the human rights and global justice literature, but I think John Tasioulas is right when he says that she has overstated the significance of the problem of counterpart duties:

> O'Neill is taking a difference of degree – relating to how much we can typically know about counterpart obligations independently of institutional structures – and converting it into a difference of kind, i.e. that welfare rights are institutionally-dependent for their very existence, whereas liberty rights are not. (Tasioulas, 2004, p. 16)

We can, then, reject the view that welfare rights are mere 'manifesto rights', but there is still some distance to go before we have adequately answered the challenge of understanding the nature of the rights that persons in severe poverty have, and the extent and allocation of the counterpart duties.

Pogge, poverty and rights

Thomas Pogge has tried to address that challenge, and has been remarkably influential in the debate. Pogge insists that we should stop talking about poverty in terms of 'helping' the poor; the truth is that we have duties arising from human rights. If we fail to honour these, we are not being uncharitable, we are being unjust. His account of human rights represents a departure from previous thought in at least two respects. First, he sets the benchmark for concern about human rights in terms of whether or not they have been fulfilled, rather than whether or not they have been violated. Second, he primarily conceives of human rights obligations as negative duties not to uphold unjust coercive institutions that foster the underfulfilment of human rights. Both of these points require unpacking.

The idea that we should think of human rights in terms of whether or not they are fulfilled, and that this should displace the legalistic framework of thinking about whether or not human rights are violated, is a response to the social reality of many the world's poorest states, in which the underfulfilment of human rights to such goods as education, stable, secure and adequate food supplies, stable and secure access to clean water, as well as protection of civil and political rights, can be a common problem.

It also broadens the terms in which we understand responsibility for human rights. If human rights are conceptualized in terms of violation, then this implies an interactional understanding of responsibility, wherein direct interaction between agents accounts for the causation of a human rights violation. But a broadly institutional view, wherein the interactions of agents are mediated through institutions, can account for the cause of human rights underfulfilment more widely (Pogge, 2002, pp. 59–70).

Pogge has been criticized for positing a clean distinction between an interactional and an institutional account that he cannot in fact sustain (Besson, 2003), and has softened some of the apparently inconsistent implications arising from his earlier insistence on 'official disrespect' as being a feature of human rights (Pogge, 2007), but his account is intended to be a reasonably moderate one that steers a path between exclusively interactional and exclusively institutional conceptions of the morality of human rights (2002, pp. 44–50). The decisive feature of the argument is the claim that institutional relationships mediate individual agents' relationships, and that, to the extent that such institutions are implicated in the underfulfilment of human rights, individual agents are likewise implicated.

The advantage of this approach is that it seems to better capture the character of the challenge of protecting social and economic rights. The purpose of human rights standards, on Pogge's view, is not (only) to constrain government or individual actions, but also to set constraints on the 'design of basic rules of our common life' (2002, p. 47). The influence of Rawls' thought is evident here: Rawls (1971) construes social justice as a set of principles that establish the basic rules of common life within states. Pogge's conception of human rights essentially applies this way of thinking to the global level.

What Pogge is defending is a sufficientarian standard of human rights, defined in probabilistic terms (Pogge, 2002, pp. 49–50), that is, it matters that people's human rights are generally secure. Aberrant instances of malnutrition are thus not instances of human rights underfulfilment, widespread instances of malnutrition are. This overcomes a worry about the viability of Pogge's human rights threshold, and speaks to concerns raised by scholars such as Abdullahi An-Na'im (2001) about the applicability of the legalistic paradigm of human rights to post-colonial states where human rights monitoring and protection structures are under-resourced (cf. Clapham, 1999).

But it also has some counter-intuitive implications for what is and is not thus judged to be a human rights issue. Leif Wenar (2005) gives the example of a government that enacts the kidnap and torture of a small number of its citizens, but generally has an effective police and courts service that ensures that instances of kidnap and torture are rare, and does not customarily kidnap or torture its citizens. On Pogge's probabilistic standard of human rights, it does not look as though a human right has been violated. Thus, Wenar argues,

> Probabilistic considerations do have a place within human rights doctrine. Yet the unnatural ring of Pogge's language should make us suspect that probabilities cannot plausibly be built into the very definition of human rights as Pogge recommends. (Wenar, 2005, p. 289)

This is an important criticism, but it does not seem to speak conclusively against Pogge's project. It is open to Pogge to say that there are negative duties mediated through institutions, and that these stand in addition to negative interactional duties, which would register the government's kidnapping and torture of citizens as a human rights violation, however many were involved. As Pogge himself observes: 'A commitment to human rights goes along with interactional moral commitments; but this is no reason to identify the former with the latter' (2002, p. 65). The reverse presumably also applies. Elizabeth Ashford seems to judge this correctly when she says that 'human rights are claims directly on private individuals as well as social institutions, but ... the institutional account provides a particularly perspicuous account of the nature of many of the duties generated by human rights' (Ashford, 2004, p. 185).

The institutional dimension of human rights also leads some commentators to observe an affinity with the political conception of human rights canvassed in Chapter 4 (for example, Tasioulas, 2004). Insofar as Pogge understands human rights as setting limits to the operations of institutions, it can be said that he too takes a functional view of human rights. Like the adherents of the political view, Pogge is certainly significantly influenced by Rawls in his thinking and in his preference for a political rather than a moral justification for human rights duties, though critical of Rawls' approach to global justice (2002, pp. 104–8). Nevertheless, he explicitly defends a 'moral' view of human rights, in that the legitimacy of a human rights claim is independent of there being particular human rights recognized in international law. Pogge (2002, p. 64) makes much of Article 28 of the UDHR, which states that 'Everyone is entitled to a social and international order in which the rights and freedoms set forth in this Declaration can be fully realized'. But his argument is not dependent upon this, rather, this ancillary argument shows that there are grounds supportive to his position within widely accepted and authoritative human rights standards.

A bit more needs to be said to clarify the difference that Pogge's conception of human rights makes to individual duties with respect to human rights. Pogge draws an analogy with slavery to help clarify this point. On a conventional (interactional) understanding of human rights, it seems that so long as I own no slaves myself, then I have not violated anyone's rights (2002, p. 66). But if I buy goods produced by slave labour, such as sugar, and if I pay taxes to a government that upholds laws that make slavery possible and enforceable, and benefit from the protection of my own property that the governments' laws also make possible, then I in fact contribute to the maintenance of an unjust institution, which is coercively enforced, and which makes possible the unjust (and human rights-violating) institution of slavery.

What is particularly morally powerful, from Pogge's point of view, is that this participation of mine in the institutional order that makes slavery possible, is the violation of a *negative duty*. Thus Pogge's account 'can go well beyond minimalist libertarianism without denying its central normative tenet: that human rights entail only negative duties' (2002, p. 66). Indeed, not only libertarians will be affected by this; we often understand negative duties to be more stringent moral demands than positive duties. On Pogge's account, I can have duties related to people's social and economic rights in other countries, not as positive duties, but as negative duties. Understood in this way, 'human rights give you claims not against all other human beings, but specifically against those who impose a coercive institutional order upon you' (2002, p. 67). The counterpart duty of such a right is that all human beings have a negative duty not to uphold or maintain institutions that are coercively imposed and that contribute to the underfulfilment of human rights.

A central part of the story here is the empirical claim that global institutional arrangements are a crucial factor in the widespread underfulfilment of human rights. Pogge is committed to this claim, and thus holds that ordinary citizens in wealthy countries are themselves *causally* implicated in the underfulfilment of human rights:

It is convenient for us citizens of wealthy countries, and therefore common, to ignore such interdependencies – to explain the severe underfulfilment of human rights in so many countries by reference to local factors domestic to the country in which it occurs. This *explanatory nationalism* ... diverts attention from the question of how we ourselves might be involved, causally and morally, in this sad phenomenon. (Pogge, 2002, p. 49)

Given the pervasiveness of global institutions, such as markets, inter-governmental organizations that regulate global markets, and intergovernmental structures that uphold the division of the world into a system of sovereign states, it looks likely to be virtually impossible for ordinary citizens to avoid participating in institutions that can be said to be complicit in an unjust order. If that is true, then, how can we honour our negative human rights duty? Pogge offers this answer:

> I might honor my negative duty, perhaps, through becoming a hermit or an emigrant, but I could honor it more plausibly by working with others toward shielding the victims of injustice from the harms I help produce or, if this is possible, toward establishing secure access [to human rights] through institutional reform. (2002, p. 66)

If institutional arrangements that foster the underfulfilment of human rights are pervasive, then it looks highly likely that most people will in fact fail to honour their negative human rights-respecting duty most of the time. Becoming a hermit is hardly a viable option for the major-ity, and if the global institutional order is itself inhospitable to the widespread fulfilment of human rights, then emigration is not a possi-bility either. That leaves 'shielding the victims' or working towards 'institutional reform', what Pogge calls 'compensatory duties'. Rowan Cruft (2005b) has rightly pointed out that these do not look like negative duties after all, but Pogge (2005a) replies that the primary duty is the negative duty not to participate in upholding unjust institutions, and that it is because of the failure to honour this negative duty that 'derivative positive duties' arise. Of course, we might wonder at the reasonableness of a negative duty that it is prac-tically impossible to honour, and think that the 'derivative' character of the positive duties is just a conceit. Cruft notes a further creeping demandingness to the structure of our human rights duties as Pogge conceives it, since it seems likely that the effectiveness of the nega-tive duty must imply 'other-directed precautionary duties. These are duties to take action to ensure that *other people* comply with their negative duties' (Cruft, 2005b, p. 32).

Pogge, though, adopts a familiar line to insulate his argument from demandingness critiques. He says:

The word 'compensate' is meant to indicate that how much one should be willing to contribute toward reforming unjust institutions and toward mitigating the harms they cause depends on how much one is contributing to, and benefitting from, their maintenance. (Pogge, 2002, p. 50)

Thus, the extent of one's compensatory duties is a function of one's complicity. This suggestion tracks some intuitively appealing moral norms – essentially it seems to say, 'you are liable for the costs of your portion of the problem'. But the problem here is enormously complex, and it seems implausible to think that one could calculate, via some sort of ethical algorithm, our individual portions of the causal responsibility, and compute from that our portions of the costs (cf. Appiah, 2010, O'Neill, 1996). What Pogge intends here is better understood as our complicity in *a way of life* that is structurally dependent on relations with others that are harmful.

Pogge's work has been enormously influential. Much of the recent philosophical literature in this field begins from the premise that debates about whether there *are* social and economic rights are settled. The live questions now concern what these rights entail in terms of correlative duties, who are the relevant duty-bearers, and why agents have these duties. A wealth of material has been published, and much of it responds to Pogge's argument in one way or another (see, *inter alia,* essays collected in Pogge, 2001; Caney, 2004; Tasioulas, 2004; Brock and Moellendorf, 2005; Føllesdal and Pogge, 2005; Jaggar, 2010). Rather than rehearsing these, I will spend the remainder of this chapter looking at some important criticisms that have been raised in relation to the project of thinking about global poverty in terms of human rights.

Poverty, agency and harm

As noted above, Pogge rejects what he calls 'explanatory nationalism', that is, the view that severe and extreme poverty are, or are mostly, the consequence of factors internal to poor countries. But critics suggest that he and others are mistaken in supposing that global poverty can be 'solved' by redistributing resources from rich countries to poorer countries, and/or by reforming global institutions such as the IMF and the WTO. This is an oft-made move – what Mills (2010) calls 'explanatory internationalism' – whereby scholars deploy a contrast between the 'minor' sacrifices required by the rich to provide the resources required to meet the needs of the poor (1 per cent of global GDP comes up very often as a figure).

Joshua Cohen (2010) raises serious doubts about the empirical claims being made in general in these types of arguments and in detail in Pogge's argument. His central claim is that it is a mistake, and a dangerous one at that, to speak of solutions to global poverty as magic formulae; indeed, it may be a mistake to speak of 'global' poverty at all, insofar as doing so rather masks the difference between poverty in India, Brazil, the Democratic Republic of Congo, East Timor, and so on.

Pogge (2002) has drawn particular attention to the 'resource curse', that is, the norms of sovereignty and resource ownership that accord authority over natural resources within a country to the government of that country, which Pogge argues incentivizes exploitative authoritarian government in weak, resource-rich states (cf. Wenar, 2008b; 2010). As a corrective to this, Pogge proposes what he calls a 'global resources dividend', essentially a tax on the extraction of natural resources, payable to a global fund that is used for development assistance, distributed either via governments or NGOs (cf. Hayward, 2005b; Cohen, 2010).

The resource curse may be a valid explanatory variable, but Cohen's point is that it is simply misleading to suggest that this, or any global principle, is *the* explanatory variable. What is needed, and Cohen is surely right about this, is careful and specific social scientific work to identify context-appropriate development measures. This is not to say that philosophy has no role to play – on the contrary, philosophy is needed both to clarify the bases of moral responsibility and to articulate reasons why the persistence of extreme poverty in conditions other than radical scarcity represents an injustice (Cohen, 2010, pp. 40–1) – but that philosophers should not misrepresent the causes of poverty in doing so.

This argument dovetails neatly with a concern raised elsewhere by Leif Wenar (2011). To say that a person ought to perform a duty is to presuppose that the content of that duty is knowable. So, to be able to say what any individual agent's portion of the duties to solve global poverty would be, one would have to know how much of whatever type of resource is needed to solve global poverty. But in fact, we do not. We are not completely in the dark either; we know that some types of development strategies have worked well in some countries and communities, but that the very same strategies have failed elsewhere (though we do not always understand why). Wenar (2011) is particularly perspicuous on the complexity of what he calls 'the donor's question' – the question of how much (money, time or other resource) the donor is obliged to give to which mediating agent (for example, an NGO) to effect which measure of change (in which country, community, for which people?), to honour their obligations with respect to the problem 'global poverty'.

The fact that there is not a single coherent answer to the question 'how can we solve global poverty?', let alone the question 'what should I, as an individual, do?' should not surprise us. The world is remarkably diverse along multiple axes. But the point of this critique is that the terms in which debates about global poverty and human rights have been pursued implies the reverse. It implies that there is such a thing as 'global poverty' rather than problems of insecure and unsustainable access to adequate food, water, healthcare, education and livelihoods, for various reasons, in various places. It presents a picture of a world divided into rich and poor, and deflects attention from enormous disparities of wealth within poor countries.

We might also note that the issue of 'solving global poverty' is rather a different one from the issue of human rights against global poverty, but the two are conflated in much of the literature. If we take it to be true that severe poverty in some parts of the world represents an injustice, given significant wealth elsewhere, then presumably we are concerned with the just distribution of resources. In other words, the question of justice here rests on how the total cake should be divided up. It is not obvious that the appropriate way to address this question is through the conceptual architecture provided by human rights.

Another important criticism concerns the direction of the argument. It is striking that people in developing countries barely feature as agents in this argument at all. '"We", rues Pogge (speaking of and to the West), are harming the global poor' (Chandhoke, 2010, p. 69). Why, Chandhoke wonders, are the obligations of rich elites within developing countries not discussed more? And why are 'the poor' not themselves engaged in debate? These questions could be put to any of a number of theorists of global justice. Pogge has answered this charge as follows:

> If I address myself mostly to the world's affluent, it is not because I see the poor as passive subjects rather than as agents, but because I don't take myself to have any standing to advise them. I do have such standing vis-à-vis citizens of the affluent countries, which derives from the moral values they profess. (Pogge 2010, p. 209)

We might take this as a sensible approach to a division of labour. Western moral philosophers have expertise in moral arguments and intuitions, particularly those operative in Western states, which also tend to be the most affluent, so they should get on with the business of articulating the problem in those contexts. This is fair enough as far as it goes. But more could be said. The very conceptualization of poverty that is at work in these debates presupposes a great deal about the lives, values and aspirations of actual agents living in communities defined as poor, whilst not reflecting on their agency. Mills (2010) sees in this the continuation of a long and invidious tradition of unfavourably comparing non-white peoples' impoverished lives to an idealized European embodiment of 'success'. Francis Mading Deng (2009, but writing in 1998) likewise expresses frustration with the Western projection of Africa as 'poor'. Here, he is reflecting on the Dinka of Southern Sudan's changing conceptions of wealth and poverty, a change he attributes significantly to responses to the experience of catastrophic armed conflict in the region:

> [T]he Dinka not only yearn for peace and security but have become keenly aware of the need to improve their lot and try to engage in development, previously alien to their culture, but now voiced with an almost obsessive sense of purpose. And yet, not once did any of the chiefs and elders interviewed describe their condition as one of poverty. (2009: 29)

As I have argued elsewhere (Woods, 2012), quite apart from the troubling reification of peoples and countries that the discourse of 'global poverty' engenders, if the arguments advanced in support of duties held by wealthy citizens fail to register *as agents* the rights-bearers to whom these duties are owed, then the foundations of the obligations are undermined. The arguments are based on the claim that rights-bearers are agents: their agency is crucial to the justification of rights. This has implications, too, at the level of moral psychology, for the recognition of rights-claimants as 'one of us', in the sense of 'one of us rights-holders' (see Chapter 3).

A final line of criticism worth noting, focusing on the concept of harm, has been advanced against Pogge's thesis and applies more generally to arguments that hang on a relation of harm between affluent agents and poorer agents mediated by institutions (for example, Caney, 2005; cf. Risse, 2005). What is intriguing here is that critics have held both that the argument from harm does not do enough, and that it does too much. Another point of divide here is the extent to which the legacy of colonialism does or should weigh in the explanation of harm and the allocation of duties.

Chandhoke (2010) criticizes the priority that Pogge accords to moral responsibility within an institutional framework. The central concern here is that by making this foundational to the justification of counterpart obligations for human rights, it seems to follow that no human right is violated, or at least, no obligations follow, if harm occurs independently of the shared institutional framework. Thus, if I participate in the global economy by buying a pair of trainers that I have reason to believe have been produced with child labour, then I participate in a shared institutional scheme with the child and have derivative positive obligations to the child (which could be discharged indirectly by, say, campaigning for an end to child labour rather than by directly compensating the specific child) that arise from my failure to honour the negative duty not to participate in such human rights-disrespecting institutions. But if a child is forced to labour in an isolationist state, and the goods produced do not reach my national economy, then I seem to have no human rights-related obligations to that child. From the point of view of the two children, it is not obvious why one has a strong claim to my taking some action, but the other does not.

As Chandhoke points out, 'the problem is that in many cases of severe poverty ... it cannot be conclusively established that poverty is the result of decisions of Western-dominated global institutions' (2010, p. 72). Having made the negative duty not to harm others through unjust institutions the bedrock of his account of human rights, Pogge seems to place the obstacle of a high burden of proof in the path of those who would seek to justify obligations. This is puzzling, because it seems that an uncontroversial premise has ended up delivering deeply controversial results (as, for example, in the case of the two children described above). A direct argument for positive duties now begins to look more consistent.

Pogge (2010) counters that Chandhoke has misunderstood his argument, and that nowhere does he say that the argument from negative duties implies that an argument cannot or should not be made that justifies positive duties as well. The argument for positive duties does seem more likely to suffer from the deep uncertainty about the allocation of counterpart obligations identified by O'Neill (above). But Pogge is right that nothing in his argument rules out the type of approach that Chandhoke suggests. However, Chandhoke is right that Pogge's argument is shaped by his commitment to liberalism and liberal principles of justice. Indeed, the vast majority of scholars working in this literature are liberals of one stripe or another. Liberal assumptions about causation, harm and legitimate coercion underpin the excitement around an argument from harm; that liability for harm generates duties, the performance of which can be legitimately coerced, and is an important principle in a moral system that requires strong justifications for coercion.

This helps to explain why liberal readings of the argument from harm have worried critics that it is over- rather than under-inclusive of cases that generate human rights-related obligations. Alan Patten (2005) highlights what he sees as a lack of clarity in Pogge's work as to what sorts of relations or interactions constitute harm. To harm someone implies placing them in a worse state than they would otherwise be in, which in turn applies some 'baseline' against which a judgement can be made that harm has occurred. This baseline could be 'diachronic', that is, it could compare the situation with a given point in the past, or 'subjective', that is, comparing the situation with a hypothetical assessment of what would have been otherwise (Patten, 2005, p. 22). Pogge prefers the latter. But Patten's worry is that this renders the definition of harm inherently unstable. Different interpretations will lead to divergent conclusions as to whether a person has been harmed or not. Harming, causing harm, and failing to help appear to be conflated, but libertarians, whom Pogge seeks to engage with the argument from harm, are committed to the view that these are distinct, and will have distinct moral weightings in an argument about obligations. Patten concludes:

> He [Pogge] may be able to reach the strong conclusion from an injunction against causing harm, but it is not the minimal injunction that libertarians acknowledge. Instead, it is an injunction that has built into it the moral imperative of assisting people who are in dire need. It is proper, in my view, for this imperative to play a role in our thinking about duties to the global poor. But in the end, it may be better to be up front about this obligation than to stretch the concept of harm awkwardly to make space for duties of assistance. (2005, p. 27)

Conclusion

Debates about social and economic rights have moved significantly beyond the defence of them as more substantive and important than mere 'manifesto rights'. That is not to say that the protean character of human rights does not continue to generate claims that give rise to this charge, but powerful arguments have been marshalled in support of 'basic rights' to subsistence, or welfare, or against severe and extreme poverty. That said, O'Neill's concerns about the underspecification of the allocation of counterpart duties may still stand to a greater or lesser extent.

Recent work on social and economic rights has been dominated by the approach developed by Pogge. The idea that persons have a negative duty not to uphold coercively imposed institutions that foster the under-fulfilment of human rights is a remarkably elegant piece of philosophical argument. In the judgement as to whether or not it is valid, much will hang on the ways in which harm is understood, the extent to which persons can really be under a negative duty that it is virtually impossible for them to perform, and how clearly and efficaciously we can identify the content of the derivative positive duties.

Critics of this approach question the empirical claims underpinning the general principle and the striking direction of the argument in terms of the agents being addressed. This is an argument by the affluent, to the affluent, about what they should do for the poor. To some, that is amongst the most controversial features of this debate. To others, that is the direction of argument that is most urgently needed given the massive discrepancy between the values affirmed in affluent states and the (in)action that can be observed.

9 Environmental Human Rights?

'A healthy environment is a human right.' (Amnesty International, 2009)

Introduction

In the early twenty-first century we face a looming environmental crisis. The depletion of non-renewables, such as fossil fuels, is actually less of a concern than the threat to renewable environmental resources, such as a stable climate and biodiversity. If Shue is right that human rights protect against 'standard threats' to human dignity (see previous chapter), then we might well find that environmental problems turn out to be amongst the standard threats that human beings face in the twenty-first century. In recent years there have been calls for the protection of 'environmental human rights' from NGOs and activist groups (such as Amnesty International, above), as well as philosophical defences of such rights from within the academic community. These have sometimes been conceived in broad terms, for example, as a human right to a 'decent' environment, and sometimes in very specific terms, as in a human right to water, or to the ownership of specific natural resources. The global reach of human rights seems *prima facie* well suited to addressing the global scope of environmental problems like climate change and biodiversity loss.

This is a fairly new area of research in political philosophy and in law as well as being an emerging political practice. The United Nations Environment Programme has been leading discussions of a Draft Declaration on Human Rights and the Environment. The Office of the High Commissioner for Human Rights has also mandated an Independent Expert to report on the nascent practice of environmental

162

human rights around the globe. As yet, no international agreement affirming environmental human rights specifically exists, but the principle that human rights and environmental sustainability are related is unequivocally affirmed in the Millennium Development Goals. Moreover, the UN Declaration on the Rights of Indigenous Peoples, the African Charter on Human and Peoples' Rights, and several national constitutions all include human or constitutional rights that can be interpreted as environmental human rights (Hayward, 2005a). There is also a growing body of empirical evidence demonstrating the human rights impacts of ecologically unsustainable economic practices, both globally and at local and national levels (see, *inter alia*, Zarsky, 2002; Picolotti and Taillant, 2003; for an overview, see Woods, 2010, pp. 3–25).

However, exploring the idea of environmental human rights raises a number of difficult normative and conceptual questions. Which agents (can) have human rights? Can there be rights claims and corresponding duties that hold across generations? Does the concept of human nature encompass non-human nature? Are the two distinct? Are the values from which human rights arise complementary, conflicting or neutral with respect to environmental values? What sorts of goods do environmental human rights protect? Are these best protected by *environmental human rights*, or by an argument about the implications of other human rights, or by other means entirely?

These questions need to be addressed if we are to make sense of the idea of environmental human rights. I tackle the discussion in three stages. First, I survey various ways of conceptualizing environmental human rights. Second, I look for points of coherence and tension between environmental values and human rights. Finally, I include a brief discussion of the most recent application of debates about human rights and the environment: climate change and human rights.

Ways of conceptualizing environmental human rights

Environmental human rights do not fit neatly into any one of the three 'generations' of rights (see Chapter 1). Or rather, depending on how environmental human rights are understood, they could fit within any of them (Boyle, 2008). Environmental human rights may be understood as civil and political rights, protecting access to information about proposed development projects and giving communities or individuals powers to raise questions about, or lodge objections to, likely environmental impacts, protecting rights to environmental protests, and so on.

Something like this approach animates Robyn Eckersley's (1996) proposal for a green-inflected 'immanent critique' of liberal rights.

Understood in these terms, environmental human rights have the potential to be of enormous significance politically. Since the death of the environmental activist Ken Saro-Wiwa in Nigeria in 1995 it has been clear that there is an acute need to protect the security of environmental activists. Saro-Wiwa, together with eight other activists from the Movement for the Survival of the Ogoni People, a Nigerian environmental justice group protesting at the drilling activities of Shell in the Niger Delta, was executed for inciting the murder of four Ogoni leaders who supported Shell. The convictions were widely condemned as unsafe.

From a philosophical point of view, however, the Saro-Wiwa case, and others like it (see Barry and Woods, 2012), seem to be more about drawing on fairly traditional civil and political rights to protect environmental interests, rather than introducing a substantively new conception of a human right. A rather more philosophically challenging version of the argument accords civil and political rights to non-human nature and/or to future humans, which would mandate the representation of future persons' environmental interests in democratic decision-making via proxies (Beckman, 2008).

A second way of thinking about human rights would be as a species of social and economic rights. Here there may be more that challenges conventionally accepted notions of what human rights are (though, as we have seen, there is much to debate within that). Thinking of human rights in this way, we could say that persons have a human right to a 'clean', 'healthy', 'decent', 'unpolluted' or 'safe' environment (respectively, The Dalai Lama, 2009; Amnesty International, 2009; Hayward, 2005a; Hancock, 2003; Nickel, 1993). Or we could say that human beings have rights to particular goods, such as (clean) water (Alvarez, 2003) or ecological space (Hayward, 2007), or against particular harms, such as climate change (Caney, 2010). What connects these arguments to the argument for other social and economic rights is the thought that protection of these goods is a precondition for the exercise of other rights, and that positive and coordinated action is needed to deliver these rights.

A less often pursued route to thinking about environmental human rights would be to define them as a group right or solidarity right (see Chapter 1). Examples here include Jan Hancock's (2003) defence of the rights of peoples to ownership of natural resources, which he sees as being particularly important for ensuring that sustainable development projects that affect indigenous peoples really are ecologically sustainable. Another example would be to posit future humans as a group who have collective environmental rights that place counterpart obligations on the present. I will say more about this idea in relation to climate change in the third section of the chapter.

Implicit in all of this are different answers to the question of who would be the rights-holder(s). With respect to first- and second-generation rights, a plausible answer would be individual human beings, but not necessarily only currently living human beings. However, as already noted, one could also defend the view that non-human nature has rights. Animal rights are the most familiar examples of such arguments (see, for example, Regan, 1985; Singer, 1975; Feinberg, 1974).

As we saw in Chapter 3, it may be difficult to give clear secular reasons that justify human rights but are able to restrict the possession of rights only to human beings. If the grounds for holding that human rights are justified are related to the agency of the being who has these rights, and if it is also true that there are human beings who seem not to fully have the capacity for agency but have these rights, then there probably are good reasons for thinking that higher apes, and perhaps quite a number of other animals, have rights of equal protections along with human beings. But the argument gets more complicated if we think that the justification for human rights relates to having special moral value. An ecocentrist could hold that ecosystems have special moral value and thus ought to enjoy the protections of certain rights. Finally, a particularly important part of the idea of environmental human rights lies in the claim that future generations, either individually or collectively, can be rights-bearers.

The motivation for drawing on the framework of human rights is often to generate justifying reasons for the protection of some environmental good from uncontested premises. Indeed, many theorists take the status and validity of human rights to be thoroughly uncontroversial. For example, Tim Hayward's account of constitutional environmental rights 'takes as its premise that human rights have a justification and legitimacy which precludes their being rejected' (2005a, p. 35). That being the case, it is not surprising to find that theorists of environmental human rights have mostly tended to assume in their arguments that rights-holders are individual human beings. It is worth looking at a few different strategies in some detail.

Prior to a few recent book-length defences of the idea of environmental human rights (Hancock, 2003; Hayward, 2005a; Hiskes, 2009), the most significant philosophically focused discussion of environmental human rights is James Nickel's 1993 paper defending the human right to a 'safe' environment, justified on the basis of fundamental human interests. The interest-based approach is fairly standard within the literature on environmental human rights: As well as Nickel, Hayward (2005a) and Simon Caney (2010) take this route, whereas Aaron Lercher (2007) is a rare example of a theorist who defends an environmental human right grounded in will theory. The claim is that the interest in environmental goods is of sufficient moral weight to generate counterpart obligations that apply to people, governments or corporations. These obligations are mostly negatively construed – that is, these agents have obligations not to act in ways that will present an unacceptable risk to the safety of the environment.

'Safe' and 'unacceptable risk' are deliberately vague terms. Nickel draws on the language of the International Bill of Rights – in particular Article 25 of the UDHR, which proclaims the right to a 'standard of living adequate to ... health and well-being'. There follows a list of goods: education, food, etc. The environment is not mentioned, but if we accept the claim that an unsafe environment presents a risk to one's health and well-being that has the seriousness of other threats recognized in human rights, then there seems no reason not to think that the right to a safe environment might be implied in, or reasonably extrapolated from, the UDHR.

The key point that needs to be demonstrated, then, is that an unsafe environment is a threat to human rights. Again, the ambiguity of the term is important here. A polluted environment is not necessarily an immediate threat to an individual's (or a family's) dignity, health or well-being. But then, neither is the absence of a job necessarily. Temporary unemployment for an otherwise reasonably well resourced person, who has savings or other means of subsistence or access to welfare to fall back on, is quite obviously not a human rights concern. But chronic unemployment resulting from discrimination, say, or from a depressed economy, and in the absence of welfare services for support, is very likely to be a human rights issue.

Likewise, aberrant pollution, say a temporary oil spill that is quickly, thoroughly and responsibly cleaned up, should most likely not be considered a human rights issue: it does not seem to be the case that such an incident would constitute a threat to human dignity, nor undermine a person's autonomy, or compromise their well-being in a significant way. It may undermine their health, particularly if they have underlying respiratory conditions, but this will be a temporary threat.

On the other hand, frequent oil spills that are not cleared up quickly, thoroughly and responsibly, are very likely to pollute irrigation and drinking water and release toxins into the air, and the impacts of this, if unchecked, will compound over time. This will be very likely to constitute a threat to the health and well-being of people, particularly children, who by virtue of having smaller bodies begin to experience ill-effects at lower concentrations of toxins (Shrader-Frechette, 2007). The pollution of irrigation water threatens food supplies and the local agricultural industry, which in turn destabilizes the economy. All of this will have a plausible impact on other aspects of human rights, and thus constitutes a threat to human dignity.

There is a dissatisfying generality and uncertainty to this kind of argument. What the argument crucially depends upon is there being a critical threshold in environmental (un)safety, the passing of which constitutes a threat to human rights. Below that threshold, it may be bad that (say) there is a small oil spill, but it is not a bad of the magnitude of human rights issues.

However, recall Griffin's defence of the device of a threshold in the justification of human rights in Chapter 3:

> Is the threshold line sharp? Of course not. That is why it is not enough simply to object that the threshold I define is 'vague'. Most terms are vague, if only at the edges. The degree of vagueness is what is crucial. What matters here is whether the vagueness is so great that it cripples important thought. Will a society have to do work to make the threshold sharper? Yes. Will contingent matters such as the wealth of a society influence the placing of the line? They need not, but they might. Have societies dealt with comparable threshold problems before? Often. (Griffin, 2010, p. 748)

Nickel's defence is not quite so robust as this, but the thought is the same:

> How safe must the environment be? The total elimination of all risks is impossible ... A better approach is to specify that the environment, or the level of safety from environmental risks, should be satisfactory or adequate for health ... The fact that terms such as 'satisfactory' and 'adequate' are vague is not a significant problem in this context ... International human rights typically set broad normative standards that can be interpreted and applied by appropriate legislative, judicial, or administrative bodies at the national level. (Nickel, 1993, p. 285)

In relying on the global, local and national institutions to interpret critical thresholds, the human right to a safe environment is not qualitatively different to the human right to education, say, or even freedom of expression. That said, critical thresholds in environmental safety may be more difficult to define than like thresholds in relation to other goods.

Nevertheless, the basic structure of Nickel's proposed right to a safe environment is endorsed in other formulations of environmental human rights. Hayward (2005a) argues that the right to an environment adequate for health and well-being should be enshrined in the constitution of every liberal democracy, on the grounds that this is consistent with the implementation of existing accepted human rights. As Hayward (2005a, p. 31) notes, the 'declaratory formulation' he, Nickel and others adopt is entirely consistent with other iterations of human rights. There is scope for flexibility within this for different nation-states to interpret the necessary and sufficient conditions for this standard of adequacy, and again the concept of there being a critical threshold below which no environment should be allowed to fall seems to be implied.

That perhaps speaks to a critical difference, though. The concept of thresholds in other human rights applies to the rights-bearer: the moral minimum standard set by human rights is a critical threshold below which a person should not be allowed to fall. Thus, it sets minimum standards for education, health, well-being, free speech, democratic participation, respect by the courts, and so on. In the case of environmental human rights what is at stake is the minimum environmental conditions to which a human being can be exposed. There is a generality to this right, that in some respects is similar to the generality of freedom of expression – the test of which is surely not just whether a person does say what they wish to say, but also whether they feel able to in the context of the general political and civil environment (see Miller, 1996) – but it is also different from this insofar as it relates to physical goods.

Another salient feature of the structure of environmental human rights proposals relates to the justification and character of environmental human rights duties. Nickel takes such duties to be a function of the seriousness of the threats that they protect against. Kristin Schrader-Frechette (2007) presents an argument that betrays the influence of Rawlsian thought: her position is that where people have benefitted from participation in cooperative social institutions that generate environmental impacts, there is an institutional justification for their having derivative environmental human rights duties within the sphere of that institution. The primary focus of this is an argument about the duties that arise within states, but this example is also suggestive of the potential for a global-level argument that tracks the logic of Thomas Pogge's work on an institutional account of human rights (see Chapter 7). Indeed, Hayward's (2005a) constitutional environmental rights are explicitly indebted to Pogge's model. This informs a tendency for environmental human rights to be negatively conceived (as they are in Nickel without the institutional architecture being so explicit), with the failure to uphold negative duties triggering derivative compensatory duties. This strategy is also observable in debates about climate change and human rights (see below). These are duties to prevent human beings being exposed to conditions that have crossed the critical threshold.

Richard P. Hiskes (2009) conceives environmental human rights in a very different way. For him, human rights derive their functionality from a 'community of justice'. They are expressive of the relational condition of human beings: human identity, understood here as linked to an awareness of (the need for) human dignity, is constituted by 'the shared self-understandings of the participants embodied in their institutional arrangements' (Sandel, 1982, p. 173; also in Hiskes, 2009, p. 14). Michael Sandel's thought is an important marker for this approach, as is Rorty's anti-foundationationalist vision of human rights (see Chapters 5 and 3 respectively).

However, while Sandel and other communitarians (and, as Hiskes points out, the early natural rights critic Burke) see the community as historically constructed and shaped, Hiskes' conception of the community is importantly future-oriented, and that innovation is owed to Avner de-Shalit's (1995) communitarian theory of intergenerational justice. De-Shalit sees the community as extending both forwards and backwards in generations and in time, and the individual's sense of identity as being connected to the intergenerational community. There are affinities in de-Shalit's work with a tradition in environmental ethics of understanding environmental obligations in terms of a notion of stewardship, rather than assuming a moral time horizon that is co-terminous with individual lives (see Attfield, 1999 for an introduction). Hiskes' innovation is to add to this intergenerational vision of a community of justice the concept of human rights as a crucial part of the institutions, traditions and practices that are expressive of the community identity. Human rights protect the conditions that make community possible and are simultaneously justified by the community as (partly) constitutive of the sense of self that can be sustained within it.

The individual human being, then, has an identity that is understood to be relationally constituted – that is, in relation to past, present and future fellow members of her community, and, most interestingly, to her environment. Though he does not use the phrase, Hiskes' thought embraces the idea that humans are inherently ecologically embedded beings, which, of course, they are, but this is not something that is overtly recognized in the theories of human nature that have otherwise been invoked to justify human rights (Woods, 2010).

De-Shalit also sees humans as embedded within intergenerational communities that share the goal of sustaining the community, which, as a precondition, mandates sustaining the physical environment in which the community lives. Hiskes interprets this as a norm of 'reflexive reciprocity', whereby the present owes the future the duty of preserving the environment which allows the future to fulfil its duty of sustaining the community (Hiskes, 2009, pp. 57–61). This is a shared interest, thus Hiskes is offering an interest-based account of a kind, but the interests are conceived in thick moral terms that embrace a communitarian account of the self, in contrast to the other interest theorists surveyed thus far in this chapter. The threshold standard is also potentially higher in Hiskes' thought than in either Hayward's or Nickel's, since the current generation has a duty to protect the future from 'emergent harms or risks': here the time horizon of moral obligations is fundamentally reconceived. Hiskes himself is aware of the extent to which he is departing from familiar paths:

> Environmental human rights ... clearly constitute a newly emergent human right, one especially tied to the concept and practice of social justice, specifically environmental justice aimed at future generations. This is a new understanding of both human rights and of environmental justice, one that relies heavily on the acceptance of several other new or otherwise controversial conceptualizations ... The concepts of a relationally defined self-identity, emergent harms or risks, and reflexive reciprocity ...are not the terms usually found in a characterization of the foundation of human rights or in defense of a new right. (Hiskes, 2009, p. 144)

In moving away from what are taken to be uncontroversial premises, Hiskes has presumably lost part of the strategic advantage that is otherwise gained for the project of promoting environmental justice by adopting the language of human rights. As Nickel points out, this is 'a valuable normative asset' (1993, p. 283) which represents a medium for articulating moral demands that are sometimes poorly understood if expressed in other terms, such as environmental virtues (see below). Nevertheless, Hiskes' willingness to explore a controversial notion of human rights potentially offers him resources that are not available from within a more conventional understanding of human rights – I return to this below.

But it also brings with it a feature of the argument that from a liberal perspective can be seen as a cost. The community is not conceived in fully cosmopolitan terms in Hiskes' argument, nor could it be, really, given the thickness of the community necessary to motivate the fairly strong account of identity in play here. But that means that the intergenerational goal of preserving the community is to some extent parochial rather than, or certainly more than, it is global. Thus, the liberal has two potential avenues of critique. One is that there is a conceptual tension between the parochialism of intergenerational human rights and the universalism of conventionally understood temporally limited human rights. Hiskes moves between the justification for human rights coming from a particular intergenerational community and the duties arising being owed to humanity *as a group*, which he postulates as a novel kind of group right (2009, pp. 148–51), though one that is obviously quite different from the idea of group rights canvassed in Chapter 1.

The other critique open to the sceptic is a doubt that Marcel Wissenburg (1998) has pressed in relation to de-Shalit's conception of community, which applies against Hiskes' human rights argument as well: the selfish non-procreator seems to have no reason whatever to honour environmental duties justified in this way, and the reasons to act even for those who have children seem to depend upon a relational conception of the self that is not uncontroversial. In fairness, though, Hiskes is aware of the controversy. Moreover, from the point of view of a significant strand of environmental thought, an account of human rights that embraces a relational sense of self will be more hospitable to environmental values than a narrowly liberal one.

Environmental values and human rights

A critical question for the validity of environmental human rights from an environmental ethics point of view is whether the human rights framework is hospitable to environmental values. We will mostly look at this from the perspective of environmental ethicists. Amongst the few human rights theorists who have given serious consideration to this question, Carl Wellman (1999) is sceptical about the prospects for accommodating the holistic character of environmental values within the analytical confines of human rights theory. What environmental values are is of course itself a matter for debate. One way of approaching this puzzle is to explore the extent to which environmental human rights could cohere with values found on a spectrum that ranges from ecocentrism to anthropocentrism.

Ecocentrists generally regard the environmental crisis as an ethical crisis as well as a political and economic one, which is to say that the prevalence of environmentally unsustainable patterns of living is indicative of flawed moral thought and practice as well as politics or economics. It follows from this that the remedy to environmental problems lies not (only or primarily) in articulating and advocating different policies, but rather, in defining and promoting different values. Central to this argument is the distinction between instrumental and intrinsic value. Anthropocentrists, it is claimed, value non-human nature only instrumentally, as a resource to be used or consumed to achieve particular ends, whereas ecocentrists argue that nature has intrinsic value – value independent of the uses it can or does have for humans (O'Neill, 1993; Rolston, 2003; cf. Norton, 2003).

The anthropocentric attitude of instrumental valuation is explained variously as the product of the dominance of economic rationality (Hancock, 2003); the modernist disenchantment of the natural world, proceeding from the insights of Francis Bacon and Isaac Newton, and culminating in the industrial revolution (Marshall, 1995); or the continuation of patriarchy beyond the social sphere and into human – non-human relations (Salleh, 1997). Whatever the causal root of this attitude, the resultant human chauvinism facilitates a lack of care and respect for the environment that has paved the way for the policy choices that have created the environmental problems now faced.

The solutions proposed by ecocentrists to these problems vary in detail, but some broad themes are discernible. Most importantly, nature is to be recognized as having intrinsic value. The consequence of this would be that there would be a presumption in favour of preserving a given feature of nature, rather than a presumption in favour of human use of the environment being acceptable (Naess, 2003). Second, humans are to be recognized as necessarily a part of, rather than apart from, non-human nature. The community of moral concern is therefore radically altered and expanded to include animals, plants, ecosystems, rocks and sands (Leopold, 1968). Understood in this way, human identity is inherently relational. A central plank of liberal moral philosophy is also challenged, that is, the understanding of the human agent as autonomous, which autonomy is crucial for moral freedom. In contrast, we find ecocentrists posit a condition of 'relative autonomy', wherein human beings are indeed capable of purposive action, but that action is necessarily constrained by a social and an ecological context (Eckersley, 1992). This explains the rationale for Klaus Bosselmann's (2001) contention that a viable account of environmental human rights must be subject to an ecological limitation: humans do not have rights to goods beyond the sustainable ecological means of the planet. As he puts it, 'individual freedom is determined not only by a social context – the social dimension of human rights – but also by an ecological context' (Bosselmann, 2001, p. 119).

Anthropocentrists, in contrast, reject the argument from intrinsic value, either on the analytical grounds that intrinsic value cannot be demonstrated (O'Neill, 1993), or on the pragmatic basis that it fails to persuade enough people, whereas the anthropocentric argument has broad(er) potential appeal (Norton, 2003). A 'weak' or 'enlightened' anthropocentrism, it is argued, can justify extensive duties of respect for non-human nature without recourse to strong metaphysical claims about non-human value. 'Weak' here refers to the extent of the implications of accepting the anthropocentric premise that humans have value – this need not, and should not on the 'weak' view, entail the claim that *only* human beings have significant moral value (Norton, 2003; Hayward, 1998). The advantage of this approach, then, is that all that need be posited is a human *valuer* and an account of the interests she has in protecting a given standard of environmental sustainability or a given range of environmental goods.

In fact, as John O'Neill (2007) has argued, one could readily accept the purportedly ecocentric story about the relational nature of the self from an anthropocentric point of view. This is significant for the present discussion, because the standard assessment is that an argument from human rights is and should be rejected by ecocentrists (Nickel, 1993). The rationale for this is that a moral philosophy and social and spiritual ontology that posits human nature as the source and determinant of value, privileged and disconnected from the rest of nature, has engendered centuries of environmental degradation (White Jnr, 1967). Insofar as human rights centrally depend upon the claim that humans *qua* humans have unique moral value, this looks from an ecocentric point of view like more of the same. Why would anyone expect the value system that generated catastrophic environmental problems to be capable of generating just solutions?

But central aspects of the ecocentric perspective can be sustained from within an (enlightened) anthropocentric perspective. For example, Hiskes' (2009) account of environmental human rights includes a plausible picture of the self that is valuable, but is also socially and ecologically relational, and sees human interests in the non-human environment as spanning an intergenerational time horizon that better maps longer ecological cycles. If that is so, then the politically and morally significant language of human rights would seem to be available, certainly on an enlightened anthropocentrist account of environmental ethics, and on terms that capture much (though admittedly, not all) of what is important from an ecocentric perspective.

It is less clear that the more recognizably liberal accounts of environmental human rights (for example, Hayward, 2005a) are quite as hospitable to the relational conception of the self. However, it is certainly implicit in any account of environmental human rights that humans are ecologically embedded beings; human rights, recall, protect humans from standard threats to the necessary conditions for agency, or to their dignity. To claim environmental human rights is to say that a minimum standard of environmental integrity is needed for humans to enjoy rights to anything else.

This so far fairly rosy picture ignores a somewhat misanthropic strain within some environmental ethics. For example, Holmes Rolston III, considering what the priority should be if environmental values and human rights conflict, has this to say:

> Given the fact that environmental values have been so precipitously reduced, given that the Zimbabwean population is escalating (the average married woman there desires to have six children) one ought to put black rhinos first, even if this costs human lives. (Rolston, 2003, p. 459)

Leaving aside the unpalatable undertones of this, Robin Attfield (2003) seems to me to get the response to this right: the priority is to work out principles of sustainable development. If that is achieved then, in the long run, philosophical debates about conflicts between human rights and environmental values substantially take care of themselves. However, this answer dodges difficult questions about population ethics. Any move to restrict reproductive freedom can be rejected as a violation of human rights (for example., the right to found a family). Birth rates have been shown to drop significantly in proportion to the rise in women's economic independence and security, which suggests that coercive policies are not necessarily required in all contexts to limit population growth. Nevertheless, the exponential growth in the human population in the past 200 years is itself a serious environmental burden.

In the early twenty-first century we are some considerable distance from sustainable patterns of living. A recently developed framework for capturing this problem is the concept of ecological space, which refers to the total material throughput capacity of the environment – the amount of resources and energy it can produce, the amount of waste it can absorb, whilst maintaining itself. Western people generally take up much more ecological space than do their counterparts in developing countries (for Americans the figure is roughly five times the sustainable benchmark; Europeans are in the region of two times over). The affluent live in ecological debt at the expense of the present poor and all future generations.

The concept of sustainable development, endorsed by the UN in the Millennium Development Goals, promises a win–win scenario for economic growth, the promotion of human rights and the protection of the environment. Sustainable development has been defined as 'development that meets the needs of the present generation without compromising the ability of future generations to meet their own needs' (WCED, 1987, p. 24). Though there have undoubtedly been some successes amongst the thousands of projects associated with Agenda 21, the global action plan agreed at the Earth Summit in Rio de Janeiro in 1992, in reality, despite advances in 'green technology', economic growth has yet to be decoupled from environmental degradation globally and in many contexts locally as well (Barry, 2012).

This failure calls into question the very idea of 'sustainable development' and the overriding assumption at the heart of it: that human rights, economic growth and environmental sustainability are mutually achievable goals (see Davidson, 2012). An important question, then, is whether the human rights of the current and immediately succeeding generations can be fulfilled without unsustainable growth (in the long term, unsustainable growth will impinge on human rights). Even if they can, there is also a real deficit of political will and leadership to achieve this (Shue, 2011). A strong current of the environmental ethics literature deals with the critique of desire-driven consumption that sustains the global economy, a critique that owes a significant debt to the eighteenth-century natural rights theorist, Jean-Jacques Rousseau. Rousseau (1984) saw that increased technological innovation, far from freeing human beings, perversely increased their dependency, as what was a luxury to one generation became a necessity to the next. The virtues of thrift, (self-) sufficiency, and 'treading lightly on the earth' are praised in this strand of environmental ethics (Hursthouse, 2007).

How do human rights as a framework fare in relation to this aspect of environmental ethics? On the one hand, there is nothing within the concept of human rights that licenses ecological debt. On the contrary, the principle of equity, or at any rate fairness, explicit in accounts of ecological space as a normative principle (for example, Hayward, 2007, who proposes a human right to equitable ecological space) implies a pretty radical overhaul of carbon- and other resource-heavy lifestyles. Equity, as in equal per capita entitlements, in fact looks to be problematic because they incentivize population growth at a state level, and because they neglect the different needs of different people – children, pregnant women and disabled people, may all have needs-based grounds for entitlement to greater ecological space. A principle of fairness (understood in Rawlsian terms) addresses this to some degree, but there are potential problems with any method of measuring entitlements to ecological space (cf. Hayward, 2007; Ziegler, 2007). That said, we should not expect any single conceptual approach to solve all practical problems. Conor Gearty (2010) argues that human rights in practice have been a mixed blessing for environmental protection efforts. And yet, the discourse of holding power to account, the means to protect protestors, and the principle of the moral equality of all human beings are powerful concepts for the project of environmental justice.

We should also acknowledge that human rights need not be the totality of an ethical system. Indeed, human rights represent moral minimums, they do not exhaust the range of moral concepts and norms that inform and define principles of justice and notions of virtue. But, if we recall the concerns raised about the protean character of human rights and the increasing hegemony human rights discourse seems to command, we might not treat this point so lightly. Cast in these terms, the minimalism of human rights is itself a concern: human beings could in principle live with quite a bit less biodiversity, and a lot less wilderness than currently exists, and meet human rights. As Wissenburg (1998) puts it, we could choose to live in a 'global Manhattan', perfectly sustainably. There is nothing in the notion of environmental human rights that could register as an objection to that (Woods, 2010). If that is accurate, then there are instrumental reasons for environmental ethicists to be wary of adopting the language of human rights if it is also the case that doing so squeezes the space in which other moral concepts, like environmental virtues, gain traction.

Climate change and human rights

In recent years particular attention has been paid to the problem of climate change. A number of theorists have invoked the concept of human rights to justify duties held by present persons towards future persons (Caney, 2005a, 2010; Hayward, 2007; Aminzadeh, 2007; Humphrey, 2010; Bell, 2011). The question of whether or not future generations can have rights that would generate obligations now is an important one for assessing the usefulness of human rights for environmental protections more generally as well as addressing debates about climate change. Many environmental problems are intergenerational in nature, but I will focus here on climate change as an example.

The impacts of atmospheric greenhouse gases (GHGs) increase exponentially rather than in a linear fashion. For this reason, efforts to protect the present generation from the harmful effects of climate change are unlikely to be sufficient to protect non-overlapping future generations, even were it not the case that we are compounding the problem by adding to the total concentration of carbon in the atmosphere (Page, 2006; Caney, 2010; Gardiner, 2010). Moderate predictions of the likely impacts of climate change give us reason to expect higher mortality rates from tropical diseases such as malaria, which will spread over greater areas, increased severe weather events, increased drought and desertification in sub-Saharan Africa, and forced migration due to rising sea levels in coastal areas and around flood plains. These burdens will most likely disproportionately fall on those already in relatively impoverished circumstances (Page, 2006; Bell, 2011; McKinnon, 2011). Like the global justice literature, the climate change debate is mostly conducted by, and addressed to, Western elites. This is in marked contrast to some other strands of the environmental justice literature, for example, that driven by the so-called 'environmentalism of the poor' (Guha, 2002; Martinez-Alier, 2002).

Amongst the most influential contributors to this debate has been Simon Caney, who initially advanced the claim that 'Persons have a human right not to suffer the disadvantages of climate change' (2005a, p. 786). He has since modified his stance to argue that other, generally accepted human rights are violated by climate change, a position also defended by Derek Bell (2011) and Henry Shue (1999). A plausible claim can be made that at the very least human rights to life, health and physical security are threatened by climate change.

As in the discussion in relation to Pogge's and Shue's positions regarding global poverty, the general strategy here is to build an argument from the least controversial premises possible. Thus, no claims are being made for future generations as bearers of group rights – the justification for counterpart duties is reached through the predictable threat that will be caused to individual human rights in the not so far off future. The influence of Pogge's approach to global poverty is also evident in the structure of the justificatory argument: insofar as present persons have contributed to the problem of climate change through carbon-emitting activities, they are complicit in the *harm* of climate change. It is the failure to observe the negative duty not to harm future persons that generates derivative positive duties to either mitigate or compensate the effects of climate change.

Of course, previous generations also contributed to the problem. To mop up the costs of 'unclaimed emissions', Caney (2005; 2010b) proposes an 'ability to pay' principle that is justified with reference to human rights as well as a harm-based principle. A different approach would be to defend a 'beneficiary pays principle' that allocates duties to the citizens of affluent states on the grounds that the Western industrial revolutions created the inequalities in the global economy today which benefit affluent citizens whilst contributing to climate change (Neumeyer, 2000; Shue, 1999).

For the human rights argument, a great deal hangs on whether duties and rights must be contemporaneous, or whether harms caused at one point in time but impacting significantly later can be properly said to be violations of (human) rights that impose duties now (Gosseries, 2008). Joel Feinberg has argued that future persons have 'contingent rights', that is, rights that are contingent on their coming into existence, but that 'cry out for protection from invasions that can take place now' (1974, p. 171). Ernest Partridge (1990) clarifies the character of this contingency: it is not that we are wondering whether or not there might be future persons – barring calamity, we fully expect there to be future persons. Bell (2011) concludes that as we can be very confident that climate change will constitute a threat to their human rights, we can also be confident about our duties.

Much has been made of Derek Parfit's (1987) 'non-identity problem' in this context, though it is fair to say that the discussion has generated more heat than light. A simple gloss of Parfit's rather complex idea might go as follows. Environmental policy *ECO*, adopted now, would influence the patterns of living of current people, so it would influence which people met and mated and became parents. (In some discussions this is even taken to the level of influencing the precise gametes that are combined in the case of the same parents, influenced, say, by whether the parents drive home from work or take public transport, thus arriving later.) Environmental policy *POLLUTE* would have a different influence, so the offspring that parents produce in the context of policy *ECO* would be different from the offspring that are produced in the context of policy *POLLUTE*. This being the case, Parfit's thesis suggests that we cannot say that the children who grow up after policy *POLLUTE* have been harmed by the environmentally damaging impacts of this policy, relative to what their lives would otherwise have been, because the fact is that their lives *would not otherwise have been*. Their lives would not have been better under policy *ECO*; they would not have been born at all under policy *ECO*, because different offspring altogether would have come into being instead. In short, the non-identity problem suggests that a person cannot be harmed by an event that also caused them to be brought into existence, because the non-factual baseline against which harm is being compared would be non-existence.

We should note that many people who will be alive in the second half of the twenty-first century will already have been born today, hence the non-identity problem, even if it is taken to be significant, is not fatal to the argument that human rights claims justify duties to mitigate or compensate for climate change. Moreover, some, like Parfit himself, take the view that the conclusion to draw from the non-identity problem is that it makes no difference to our moral *obligations* to future generations, it only entails that we cannot say that the justification for those obligations is that future people will be harmed. Others think that the non-identity problem makes a great deal of difference, and use up a lot of ink debating solutions (so far, none proffered have been fully convincing: cf. Tremmel, 2009).

Some fairly absurd and disanalogous analogies have been advanced in the literature to try to demonstrate that future persons can indeed be harmed by non-contemporaneously undertaken actions, and that such actions thus constitute violations of the harmed agents' (human) rights. Examples include Robert Elliot's (1988) idea of a booby-trapped time capsule, or Caney's (2010) idea of a sabotaged bridge. Elliot imagines a time capsule that is booby-trapped at time *t*, such that, when a person opens the time capsule at *t* + 80, the person is injured. This demonstrates that the person setting the booby trap was wrong to do so, even if the injured party was not yet born when the booby trap was set. The underlying claim is that future generations can be harmed by current actions. In Caney's bridge case, he draws an analogy between climate change and the act of a saboteur who damages a bridge that people drive across. The sabotage causes the bridge to collapse, causing the deaths of several people beneath it. Insofar as we recognize that a person ought not to commit the harmful act in the sabotage case, then it follows that persons ought not to engage in acts that will cause harmful climate change, since these similarly threaten fundamental rights.

But climate change is not a deliberate act of sabotage by one agent; rather, it is the cumulative result of many uncoordinated acts that individually would not cause harm to other persons. It is therefore much more like a bridge that has been overused by lots of otherwise moral and law-abiding motorists, whose individual actions alone are not harmful, but whose cumulative impacts unwittingly cross a critical threshold. The profoundly mediated character of causal responsibility for climate change presents a challenge for conventional moral thinking (Attfield, 2009). Theorists such as Caney and Shue see the concept of human rights as an appropriate framework for confronting this challenge.

There has been an interesting shift in the purpose of human rights, or at least in the ends for which they are being invoked. Natural rights in the eighteenth century were proclaimed against the power of centralizing states and hereditary privilege in defence of the liberty and democratic rights of the majority. In the early part of the twenty-first century we find human rights claims being invoked to justify limiting the freedom of affluent citizens to pursue lifestyles that are sustained only at the expense of their poorer fellows amongst the present generations and of all people, but again the poor in particular, amongst future persons.

Can the protean concept of human rights function in this way? It seems to me that the Hiskes (2009) model of environmental human rights is more hospitable to this line of argument than the more familiar (though still, perhaps, contentious) Pogge-esque approach to human rights that dominates this literature. The intergenerational relational self better accounts for the connection between present and future persons than does the attenuated conception of harm or the disanalogous analogies that are used to justify it. Moreover, this communitarian account is more readily open to duties owed by the present generation to the future because of the actions of past generations, thus can easily accommodate responsibility for the costs associated with historical emissions.

The more controversial premises for Hiskes' thought, and the parochialism they engender, may count as reasons to reject his model of environmental human rights if the goal is to piggy-back upon the established normative architecture of human rights as a means of justifying duties. Recall Hayward's position, which 'takes as its premise that human rights have a justification and legitimacy which precludes their being rejected' (2005a, p. 35). Recall, too, the proclamations of natural rights theorists, who held their truths to be 'self-evident'. It may be that in years to come, environmental human rights of one sort or another will be held to be self-evident too.

Conclusion

In this chapter I have looked at the idea of environmental human rights. While it is clear that environmental issues raise human rights concerns in the real world, this does not automatically translate into a seamless harmony between the concept of human rights and environmental justice or environmental ethics in political philosophy. Nevertheless, there has been considerable and growing interest in the concept of environmental human rights, and in drawing on the moral authority of human rights for advancing environmental claims, within political philosophy.

Various ways of conceptualizing environmental rights have been considered. Some account of human interests in environmental goods is the most dominant approach. Hiskes' 'emergent' environmental human rights represent an interesting variation of this. I suggested that his vision of the relational self is more hospitable to environmental values than more analytical notions of human rights. However, given that one purpose of invoking human rights is to draw on the moral authority of an uncontroversial normative architecture, it is unsurprising to find that comparatively less contentious approaches to human rights tend to be adopted. This is particularly the case in the literature on climate change and human rights, which has expanded markedly in the past few years. In this context, as in the debate about global justice, human rights are employed as a means of justifying duties that are held to be owed by the affluent citizens of the world, in this case to their poorer contemporaries, and to future generations. Thus the scope of human rights has expanded considerably beyond that of its eighteenth-century ancestors, now encompassing not only all human beings, but their descendents as well.

Conclusion

'We hold these truths to be self-evident.' (US Declaration of Independence)

Human rights have become so accepted a part of moral and political discourse at a global level, and in many parts of the world at national and local level as well, that their authoritative status is often taken for granted, by politicians, ordinary citizens, activists and political philosophers. Like the American Revolutionaries, many of us hold the truth of human rights to be self-evident. Moreover, it seems appropriate, in some respects, to take this moral authority for granted, for to question the validity of human rights seems to lead us toward implicitly supporting tyrants and torturers. Those who deny the validity of human rights may not find themselves in appealing company.

However, the idea of human rights is controversial. The concept of human rights is a relatively recent human invention, compared to the concept of law or the concept of justice. The idea of natural rights, from which human rights evolved, was a revolutionary one. Human rights were first recognized in international legal and political practice at the UN not following the excitement of revolution, but following the horror of a world war. Nevertheless, they retained something of the revolutionary character of their natural rights ancestors insofar as they proclaimed universal principles that challenged long-standing norms.

Human rights are fundamentally moral rights; they do not depend upon recognition in international or national law for their validity or their normative authority. That may be both a strength and a weakness. It is a strength insofar as human rights can thereby be invoked as a corrective to law and the political authorities that enact and enforce legislation. It is potentially a weakness in that the justification of human rights is thus a matter of moral argument, and that moral argument will typically be addressed to a plurality of agents affirming divergent conceptions of the good. Providing justifying reasons that can be taken to be action-guiding for a diverse and potentially unbounded domain of agents is a difficult task.

The most analytically robust accounts of a justification for human rights employ the tools of secular Western moral and political philosophy. There are a number of unresolved questions in this field at the moment. In Chapter 3 we considered arguments that conform to what has been called the traditional or naturalistic conception of human rights, wherein advocates attempt to derive a justification of human rights from some philosophically robust account of a feature of humanity, such as human dignity or personhood. We also considered the doubts raised by two influential critics of human rights. It seems plausible to say that neither of the critics quite carries their argument: MacIntyre seems to set the bar of the translatability of concepts too high, whereas Rorty seems to take too much on faith with respect to the prospects for a human rights culture without justifying reasons. But the challenges they press against the various attempts to provide foundations for human rights are nevertheless important and difficult. Both the dignity and personhood conceptions of human rights are as yet incomplete projects. It remains to be seen whether a positive account of human dignity can be elaborated that will not prove either under-inclusive or over-inclusive. In contrast to this, in Chapter 4, we looked at the political view, which eschews such abstract philosophical foundations and instead pursues an argument grounded in contemporary human rights practice. This relatively new approach to understanding human rights seems to me to begin from a conception of human rights that is at odds with lived experience of human rights unless seen through the relatively narrow prism of international relations. But, of course, human rights as a global standard have become a significant feature of the world, despite the changing fortunes of human rights discourse at different points in recent history, before and after 9/11.

The relationship between religion and human rights seems to me to be a particularly important topic. Research in this area is being conducted almost along two separate paths. There are scholars working from within the perspective of one or other religious tradition, and then there are scholars working from within a broadly secular liberal perspective. There is a quite literal obstacle of translation in terms of texts that are available only in given languages, but there is a broader and more philosophically interesting issue of translation here regarding the extent to which the sorts of justifying reasons for a commitment to human rights that can be offered from within one tradition can be fully intelligible within another. In some respects this debate continues the issues raised in the analytic search for philosophical foundations: if we all agree that there are (these particular) human rights, do we need to agree on, or at least mutually understand, why we agree? The framers of the UDHR thought, or perhaps hoped, that we could get along reasonably well without that level of deep agreement.

The persistence of these debates is a reflection of the persistence of deeper and long-standing debates about the nature of the self and the sources of value in religious, moral and political philosophy, which impinge upon the question of whether there can be universal values of the sort that human rights purport to recognize. Thorough-going relativism is fairly easily rejected. There do not seem to be either logically consistent or empirically defensible grounds for holding that cultures are so bounded and static as to preclude the possibility of intercultural dialogue and influence. If that is widely accepted, it remains the case that the grounds and content of moral universalism are difficult to specify. It may also be the case that universal values are not only or best realized in terms of universal rights; other moral idioms may be more hospitable to the justification of universal values understood as a matter of practical reason. Against that view, one can press the thought that there is a particular link between the institution of rights and the protection of human dignity.

One part of the difficulty regarding the justification of universalism might be explained with reference to a very human tendency to unconscious bias and self-interest. The framers of the UDHR, no less than the framers of the late eighteenth-century declarations of natural rights, could not help but draw on their own experiences to identify the standard threats to human dignity that call forth the protection of human rights. Feminists, multicultural theorists, post-colonial theorists, theorists of race and queer theorists have all seen in the difference-blindness of liberal universalism the realization not of neutrality but of exclusion. The judgement as to whether or not liberal universalism can be adequately conceived will in part depend upon a judgement about the feasibility of the 'unencumbered self'. That said, the main live debates within multiculturalism are debates within liberalism. However, few liberals defend the idea of collective rights, and at least some proponents of collective rights find reasons to reject liberalism.

Another very much live area of debate within human rights theory is in the field of global poverty and human rights. For the most part the claim that social and economic rights are mere 'manifesto rights' is now rejected. The clean separation between positive rights and negative rights on which this argument significantly relied has been shown to be much less distinct than opponents of social and economic rights supposed. However, if human rights give rise to counterpart obligations, as they must do if they are to be more than just empty rhetoric, then a principle for allocating duties in ways that allow rights-holders to direct their legitimate claims to a particular agent seems to be a necessary condition. That principle is only partially answered in an institutional account of human rights. The institutional account proposed by Thomas Pogge does, however, represent a significant innovation in the development of human rights theory. For example, the standard of underfulfilment rather than violation of human rights as a benchmark, and the conceptualization of human rights duties as negative duties not to uphold unjust institutions, have inspired much critical attention.

This approach to conceptualizing human rights has also been influential in the emerging field of environmental human rights, alongside alternative approaches that draw on and significantly extent the idea of the situated self to encompass an intergenerational perspective and give recognition to the ecological embeddedness of human life. This is an area of human rights theory that arguably extends the protean character of human rights further than any other, for if environmental human rights are ultimately to be effective in the ways their defenders hope, they must imply that future persons can be bearers of rights that give rise to corresponding obligations now. It seems implausible to say that the threats associated with severe environmental problems like climate change do not constitute threats to human dignity. But whether the concept of human rights can or should be used to express the ethical issues at stake in this field is another open question. Whatever the answer, human rights as a field of study within political philosophy is alive and well.

Further Reading

General works

Readers unfamiliar with general debates and concepts within moral and political philosophy will likely benefit from looking at general introductions to these fields. Kymlicka (2002) and Wolff (1996) are both excellent primers for political philosophy. Mackie (1990) and Rachels (2002) clearly explain some central issues in moral philosophy. None of these texts includes substantial discussion of human rights, though Kymlicka does so more than the others. An excellent and fairly short work is Appiah (2005), which defends the principles of cosmopolitan thought but in doing so introduces some arguments and concepts relevant to debates about human rights in an engaging and accessible way. Hayden (ed.) (2001) is a collection of abridged primary texts that have contributed to the development of the philosophy of human rights.

The online and freely accessible *Stanford Encyclopedia of Philosophy* is also an excellent resource for an enormous range of topics in philosophy, and has entries on human rights and on a number of related topics covered in this book.

Chapter 1: What is a Human Right?

General works on the concept of rights can be found in Waldron (ed.) (1984). In addition Jones (1994) and Wellman (2011) discuss both rights and human rights. Nickel (2005) is also useful here. Cranston (1967), Dworkin (1984) and Hart (1967) are important texts.

Chapter 2: A Brief History of Human Rights

Alston et al. (2007), Freeman (2002) and Donnelly (2003) are all classic

186

introductions to human rights, though none is focused exclusively on human rights theory. Alston et al. (2007) is also useful for an introduction to human rights law, along with the excellent Sieghart (1985). Freeman (2002) gives an introduction to the history of human rights. A more extensive and indeed impressive history can be found in Ishay (2008). Histories particularly focusing on the French Revolution and the idea of natural rights can be found in Hunt (2007) and Van Kley (ed.) (1997). Maritain (1948) collects the ideas of members of the UNESCO committee.

Chapter 3: Philosophical Foundations for Human Rights

Freeman (1994) and Mendus (1995) are both article-length discussions that give a useful synthesis of some of the debates in this chapter. Book- and article-length defences of particular positions with respect to the philosophical foundations of human rights include Beitz (2009), Gewirth (1982), Griffin (2008), Rawls (1999b) and Raz (2007). Important lines of criticisms of human rights philosophy are found in Rorty (1993) and MacIntyre (1994). The latter is an important text independently of its relevance to human rights theory. On the concept of human dignity, Arieli (2002) is a useful overview, and Kaufman et al. (eds) (2010) is an excellent collection of essays.

Chapter 4: A Political Conception of Human Rights

Rawls (1993/1999b) is the seminal text for the political conception of human rights. Beitz (2009) and Raz (2007, 2010) significantly extend and develop a Rawlsian approach to human rights. Donnelly (2003) is a good overall introduction to some aspects of human rights politics, and is an example of someone who takes Rawls' own project of domestic justice to be broadly applicable at the global level. Thoughtful criticisms of the political conception can be found in Liao and Etinson (2012) and Gilabert (2011).

Chapter 5: Religion and Human Rights

Perry (2000) is the leading proponent of the view that human rights are ineliminably religious; Kohen (2007) is a carefully argued book-length rebuttal of that view. Freeman (2004) offers a useful introduction to some of the issues at stake in this chapter. On Islam and human rights An-Na'im (2009) and Sachedina (2009) offer contrasting book-length discussions. Othman (1999) and Ghai (2009) are thoughtful contributions to the debate on Asian values, and are both found in collections of essays that are well worth dipping into further.

Chapter 6: Universalism and Relativism

For authoritative statements of liberal and communitarian positions the obvious texts are Rawls (1999a) and Sandel (1982); both are demanding reads but an overview in one of the general political philosophy texts mentioned above may serve as a primer. Parekh's (1999a) paper has been influential, as has Taylor (2009). Teson (1985) is a useful overview of relativism. On feminist approaches to human rights and the concept of women's human rights Bunch (1990), Charlesworth (1995) and Peach (2001) are all engaging. Beasley (1999) is a general introduction to feminist thought; there are also chapters on feminist thought in Kymlicka (2002) and Wolff (1996).

Chapter 7: Minority Groups and Minority Rights

There is a dauntingly large literature on multiculturalism. Cohen (ed.) (1999) includes Okin's 'Is multiculturalism bad for women?' and a number of replies written by leading scholars in the field, including Kymlicka and Parekh. Kymlicka has published extensively on the topic. Young (1990) is another landmark text in this field. Barry's (2001) defence of liberal egalitarianism against multiculturalism is an important critique, as is Phillips' more sympathetic work (2009).

On gay rights Nussbaum (1996) is a (long) article and Ball (2003) is a book-length treatment of the topic, both written with reference to the American context. On queer theorists' ambivalence towards same-sex marriage Ferguson (2007), again written with an American focus, is a thoughtful discussion.

Chapter 8: Global Poverty and Human Rights

Shue (1980) and Pogge (2002) are the two seminal texts discussed at some length in this chapter; a good place to pursue further reading would be either of these. Pogge (2002) also discusses Shue's work. Collections of essays mentioned in the chapter include contributions from many significant authors in this area: Pogge (ed.) (2001), Pogge (ed.) (2004) and Jaggar (ed.) (2010).

Chapter 9: Environmental Human Rights?

Attfield (1999) offers an excellent introduction to environmental ethics. Light and Rolston (eds) (2003) is a large collection of classic essays on environmental issues. Woods (2010) discusses the relationship between human rights and environmental sustainability. Hancock (2003), Hayward (2005a) and Hiskes (2009) all present book-length defences of environmental human rights, while Nickel (1993) is a long article that sets out many of the themes and strategies taken up in the later, longer works. On climate change and human rights Humphrey (ed.) (2010) is a useful collection of essays. Caney (2005a, 2010) has been amongst the most prominent defenders of a human rights-based approach to the problem of climate change.

Bibliography

Alston, Philip et al. (2007) *International Human Rights in Context: Law, Politics, Morals,* 3rd edn (Oxford: Oxford University Press).

Alvarez, Ignacio J. (2003) 'The Right to Water as a Human Right', in R. Picolotti and J.D. Taillant (eds) *Linking Human Rights and the Environment* (Tuscon: University of Arizona Press).

Aminzadeh, Sara C. (2007) 'A Moral Imperative: The Human Rights Implications of Climate Change', *Hastings International and Comparative Law Review,* vol. 30.

Amnesty International (2009) Demand Dignity Campaign Leaflet, available online at http://www.amnesty.org/en/library/asset/AMR20/003/2009/en/ 7f3db66e-aa18-42cd-86f7-9434e0d94a8d/amr200032009en.pdf (accessed 13 June 2012).

An-Na'im, Abdullahi A. (1990) 'Human Rights in the Muslim World: Socio-Political Conditions and Scriptural Imperatives, A Preliminary Inquiry', *Harvard Human Rights Journal,* vol. 3.

An-Na'im, Abdullahi A. (1996) *Toward an Islamic Reformation* (Syracuse University Press).

An-Na'im, Abdullahi A. (2001) 'The Legal Protection of Human Rights in Africa: How to Do More with Less', in A. Sarat and T.R. Kearns (eds) *Human Rights: Concepts, Contests, Contingencies* (Ann Arbor: University of Michigan Press).

An-Na'im, Abdullahi A. (2009) *Islam and the Secular State* (Cambridge, MA: Harvard University Press).

Appiah, Kwame Anthony (2005) *Cosmopolitanism: Ethics in a World of Strangers* (London: Penguin).

Appiah, Kwame Anthony (2010) 'Morality: Aid, Harm, and Obligation', *Boston University Law Review,* vol. 90.

Arendt, Hannah (1971) *The Origins of Totalitarianism* (New York: Meridian Books).

Arieli, Yehoshua (2002) 'On the Necessary and Sufficient Conditions for the Emergence of the Doctrine of the Dignity of Man and His Rights', in D. Kretzmer and E. Klein (eds) *The Concept of Human Dignity in Human Rights Discourses* (Dordrecht: Kluwer).

Arkoun, Mohammed (1993) 'The Concept of "Islamic Reformation"', in T. Lindholm and K. Vogt (eds) *Islamic Law Reform and Human Rights: Challenges and Rejoinders* (Oslo: Nordic Human Rights Publications).

Asad, Talal (1997) 'On Torture, or Cruel, Inhuman and Degrading Treatment', in R.A. Wilson (ed.) *Human Rights, Culture and Context: Anthropological Perspectives* (London: Pluto Press).

Asad, Talal (2003) *Formations of the Secular: Christianity, Islam, Modernity* (Stanford, CA: Stanford University Press).

Ashford, Elizabeth (2007) 'The Duties Imposed by the Human Right to Basic Necessities, in T. Pogge (ed.) *Freedom from Poverty as a Human Right: Who Owes What to the Very Poor?* (Oxford: Oxford University Press).

Attfield, Robin (1999) *The Ethics of the Global Environment* (Edinburgh: Edinburgh University Press).

Attfield, Robin (2009) 'Mediated Responsibilities, Global Warming and the Scope of Ethics', *Journal of Social Philosophy*, vol. 40.

Baaz, Mikael (n.d.) 'Human Rights or Human Wrongs?' Centre for European Research, Göteborg University, Working Paper 06.02.

Baker, Keith Michael (1998) 'The Idea of a Declaration of Rights', in G. Kates (ed.) *The French Revolution: Recent Debates and Controversies* (London: Routledge).

Ball, Carlos A. (2002) *The Morality of Gay Rights: An Exploration in Political Philosophy* (London: Routledge)

Barry, Brian (2001) *Culture and Equality: An Egalitarian Critique of Multiculturalism* (Cambridge: Polity).

Barry, Brian (2002) 'Second Thoughts – And Some First Thoughts Revived', in P. Kelly (ed.) *Multiculturalism Reconsidered* (Cambridge: Polity).

Barry, John (2012) *The Politics of Actually Existing Unsustainability: Human Flourishing in a Climate-Changed, Carbon-Constrained World* (Oxford: Oxford University Press).

Barry, John and Kerri Woods (2012) 'Environment', in M. Goodhart (ed.), *Human Rights: Politics and Practice*, 2nd edn (Oxford: Oxford University Press).

Bauer, Joanne and Daniel Bell (eds) *The East Asian Challenge to Human Rights* (Cambridge: Cambridge University Press).

Blanc, Louis (1848) *The Organization of Work*, Online Library of Liberty, accessed from http://oll.libertyfund.org/title/1166/27620, on 2 July 2012.

Beasley, Chris (1999) *What is Feminism Anyway? An Introduction to Feminist Theory* (London: Allen & Unwin).

Beckman, Ludvig (2008) 'Do global climate change and the interest of future generations have implications for democracy?' *Environmental Politics*, vol.17.

Beitz, Charles R. (2004) 'Human Rights and the Law of Peoples', in D.K. Chatterjee (ed.) *The Ethics of Assistance: Morality and the Distant Needy* (Cambridge: Cambridge University Press) .

Beitz, Charles R. (2009) *The Idea of Human Rights* (Oxford: Oxford University Press).

Benhabib, Seyla (2002) *The Claims of Culture: Equality and Diversity in the Global Era* (Princeton: Princeton University Press).

Bell, Derek (2011) 'Does Anthropogenic Climate Change Violate Human Rights?' *Critical Review of International Social and Political Philosophy*, vol. 14.

Berry, Christopher J. (1997) *The Social Theory of the Scottish Enlightenment* (Edinburgh: Edinburgh University Press).

Besson, Samantha (2003) 'Human Rights, Institutional Duties, and Cosmopolitan Responsibilities', *Oxford Journal of Legal Studies*, vol. 23.

Beyleveld, Deryck (1991) *The Dialectical Necessity of Morality: An Analysis and Defense of Alan Gewirth's Principle of Generic Consistency* (Chicago: University of Chicago Press).

Bielefeldt, Heiner (1995) 'Muslim Voices in the Human Rights Debate', *Human Rights Quarterly*, vol. 17.

Binnion, Gayle (1995) 'Human Rights: A Feminist Perspective', *Human Rights Quarterly*, vol. 17.

Bosselmann, Klaus (2001) 'Human Rights and the Environment: Redefining Fundamental Principles?' in B. Gleeson and N. Low (eds) *Governing for the Environment: Global Problems, Ethics and Democracy* (Basingstoke: Palgrave Macmillan).

Bowring, Bill (2008) 'Misunderstanding MacIntyre on Human Rights', *Analyse und Kritik*, vol. 30.

Boyle, Alan (2008) 'Human Rights and the Environment: A Reassessment', *Fordham Environmental Law Review*, vol. 18.

Brock, Gillian and Darrel Moellendorf (eds) (2005) *Current Debates in Global Justice* (Dordrecht: Springer).

Brock, Gillian and Harry Brighouse (eds) (2005) *The Political Philosophy of Cosmopolitanism* (Cambridge: Cambridge University Press).

Brown, Chris (1997) 'Universal Human Rights: A Critique', *The International Journal of Human Rights*, vol. 1.

Buchanen, Allen (2000) 'Rawls' Law of Peoples: Rules for a Vanished Westphalian World', *Ethics*, vol. 110.

Bull, Hedley (2002) *The Anarchical Society* (Basingstoke: Palgrave Macmillan).

Bunch, Charlotte (1990) 'Women's Rights as Human Rights: Toward a Re-Vision of Human Rights', *Human Rights Quarterly*, vol. 12.

Bunch, Charlotte (1997) 'The Intolerable Status Quo: Violence Against Women and Girls', in *The Progress of Nations 1997* (New York: Unicef).

Burke, Edmund (1987) *Reflections on the Revolution in France* (ed. J.G.A. Pocock) (Cambridge: Hackett).

Caney, Simon (2004) 'Global Poverty, Human Rights and Obligations', in T. Pogge (ed.) *Ethical and Human Rights Dimensions of Poverty* (Geneva: UNESCO).

Caney, Simon (2005a) 'Cosmopolitan Justice, Responsibility, and Global Climate Change, *Leiden Journal of International Law*, vol. 18.

Caney, Simon (2005b) *Justice Beyond Borders* (Oxford: Oxford University Press).

Caney, Simon (2010) 'Climate Change, Human Rights, and Moral Thresholds, in S. Humphreys (ed.) *Human Rights and Climate Change* (Cambridge: Cambridge University Press).

Caney, Simon and Derek Bell (forthcoming) *Global Justice and Climate Change* (Oxford: Oxford University Press).

Card, Claudia (1999) 'Against Marriage', in J. Corvino (ed.), *Same Sex* (Lanham, MA: Rowman & Littlefield).

Chandhoke, Neera (2010) '"How Much Is Enough, Mr Thomas? How Much Will Ever Be Enough?"', in Jaggar (ed.) *Thomas Pogge and his Critics.*

Charlesworth, Hilary (1995) 'Human Rights as Men's Rights', in J. Peters and

A. Wolper (eds) *Women's Rights: International Feminist Perspectives* (New York: Routledge).

Clapham, Christopher (1999) 'Sovereignty and the Third World State', *Political Studies*, vol. 47.

Cobbah, Josiah M. (1987) 'African Values and the Human Rights Debate: An African Perspective', *Human Rights Quarterly*, vol. 9.

Cohen, Joshua (2004) 'Minimalism about Human Rights: The Most We Can Hope For?' *Journal of Political Philosophy,* vol. 12.

Cohen, Joshua (2010) 'Philosophy, Social Science, Global Poverty', in Jaggar (ed.) *Thomas Pogge and his Critics.*

Conti, Mario (2011) 'Statement from Archbisop Mario Conti', Scottish Catholic Media Office, 9 October 2011 (available online at http://www.scmo.org/articles/archbishop-mario-conti-issues-statement-on-marriage.html, accessed 10 October 2011).

Cowden, Mhairi (2012) 'What's love got to do with it? Why a child does not have the right to be loved', *Critical Review of International Social and Political Philosophy*, vol. 15.

Cranston, Maurice (1967) 'Human Rights, Real and Supposed', in D.D. Raphael (ed.) *Political Theory and the Rights of Man* (London: Macmillan).

Cruft, Rowan (2005a) 'Human Rights, Individualism and Cultural Diversity', *Critical Review of International Social and Political Philosophy*, vol. 8.

Cruft, Rowan (2005b) 'Human Rights and Positive Duties', *Ethics and International Affairs*, vol. 19.

Cruft, Rowan (2013) 'Why Is It Disrespectful to Violate Rights?' *Proceedings of the Aristotelian Society*, vol. 103.

Dalai Lama (2009) 'A Clean Environment is a Human Right', available online at http://www.dalailama.com/messages/environment/clean-environment (accessed 20 October 2012).

Daniels, Norman (2011) 'Reflective Equilibrium', *The Stanford Encyclopedia of Philosophy (Spring 2011 Edition)*, Edward N. Zalta (ed.), URL = <http://plato.stanford.edu/archives/spr2011/entries/reflective-equilibrium/>.

Davidson, Stewart (2012) 'The Insuperable Imperative', *Capitalism, Nature, Socialism*, vol. 23.

Deng, Francis M. (2009) 'The Cow and the Thing Called "What": Dinka Cultural Perspectives on Wealth and Poverty', in W. Twinning (ed.), *Human Rights: Southern Voices* (Cambridge: Cambridge University Press).

de-Shalit, Avner (1995) *Why Posterity Matters: Environmental policies and future generations* (London: Routledge).

Dershowitz, Alan (2004) *Rights from Wrongs: a Secular Theory of the Origins of Rights* (New York: Basic Books).

Donnelly, Jack (1982) 'Human Rights and Human Dignity: An Analytic Critique of Non-Western Conceptions of Human Rights', *The American Political Science Review*, vol. 76.

Donnelly, Jack (1998) 'Human Rights: A New Standard of Civilization?' *International Affairs*, vol. 74.

Donnelly, Jack (1999) 'Human Rights and Asian Values: A Defense of "Western" Universalism', in J. Bauer and D. Bell (eds) *The East Asian Challenge to Human Rights* (Cambridge: Cambridge University Press).

Donnelly, Jack (2003) *Universal Human Rights in Theory and Practice* (Ithaca, NY: Cornell University Press).

Donnelly, Jack (2007) 'The Relative Universality of Human Rights', *Human Rights Quarterly,* vol. 29.

Dower, Nigel (1996) 'Europe and the Globalisation of Ethics', in P. Dukes (ed.) *Frontiers of European Culture* (Lewiston, NY: Edwin Mellen Press).

Düwell, Marcus (2010) 'Human Dignity and Human Rights', in P. Kaufmann et al. (eds) *Humiliation, Degradation, Dehuminization* (Dordrecht: Springer).

Dworkin, Ronald (1984) 'Rights as Trumps', in J. Waldron (ed.) *Theories of Rights* (Oxford: Oxford University Press).

Eckersley, Robyn (1992) *Environmentalism and Political Theory: Toward an Eco-centric Approach* (London, UCL Press).

Eckersley, Robyn (1996) 'Greening Liberal Democracy: The Rights Discourse Revisited', in B. Doherty and M. de Geus (eds) *Democracy and Green Political Thought: Sustainability, Rights and Citizenship* (London: Routledge).

Elliot, Robert (1988) 'The rights of future people', *Journal of Applied Philosophy*, vol. 6.

Elshtain, Jean Bethke (1999) 'The Dignity of the Human Person and the Idea of Human Rights: Four Inquiries', *Journal of Law and Religion*, vol. 14.

Ernst, Gerhard and Jan-Christoph Heilinger (eds) (2011) *The Philosophy of Human Rights: Contemporary Controversies* (Berlin: De Gruyter).

Feltham, Brian (2003) 'A Role in Practical Reasoning for People's Beliefs about Value', *Critical Review of International Social and Political Philosophy*, vol. 6.

Feinberg, Joel (1970) 'The Nature and Value of Rights', *Journal of Value Inquiry*, vol. 4.

Feinberg, Joel (1974) 'The Rights of Animals and Future Generations', in W. Blackstone (ed.) *Philosophy and Environmental Crisis* (Athens, Georgia: University of Georgia Press).

Ferguson, Ann (2007) 'Gay Marriage: An American and Feminist Dilemma,' *Hypatia*, vol. 22.

Finnis, John (1980) *Natural Law and Natural Rights* (Oxford: Oxford University Press).

Finnis, John (1997) 'Law, Morality, and "Sexual Orientation"', in J. Corvino (ed.) *Same Sex: Debating the Ethics, Science, and Culture of Homosexuality* (New York: Rowman & Littlefield).

Floyd, Rita (2011) 'Why We Need Needs-Based Justifications of Human Rights', *Journal of International Political Theory*, vol. 7.

Føllesdal, Andreas (2005) 'Human Rights and Relativism', in A. Follesdal and T. Pogge (eds), *Real World Justice* (Dordrecht: Springer).

Forst, Rainer (2012) 'The Justification of Human Rights and the Basic Right to Justification: A Reflexive Approach', in C. Corradetti (ed.) *Philosophical Dimensions of Human Rights* (Dordrecht: Springer).

Foucault, Michel (1984) *The Foucault Reader* (New York: Pantheon).

Fraser, Arvonne S. (1999) 'Becoming Human: The Origins and Development of Women's Human Rights', *Human Rights Quarterly*, vol. 21.

Fraser, Nancy and Axel Honneth (2003) *Redistribution or Regeneration?* (London: Verso).

Freeman, Michael (1994) 'The Philosophical Foundations of Human Rights', *Human Rights Quarterly*, vol. 16.

Freeman, Michael (1995) 'Are There Collective Human Rights?' *Political Studies*, vol. 43.

Freeman, Michael (2002) *Human Rights* (Cambridge: Polity).

Freeman, Michael (2004) 'The Problem of Secularism in Human Rights Theory', *Human Rights Quarterly*, vol. 26.

Frey, R.G. (1988) 'Moral Standing, the Value of Lives, and Speciesism', *Between Species: A Journal of Ethics,* vol. 4.

Fukuyama, Francis (1989) 'The End of History', *The National Interest*, Summer.

Gaita, Raimond (2000) *A Common Humanity: Thinking about Love and Truth and Justice* (London: Routlegde).

Galeotti, Anna Elisabetta (2006) *Toleration as Recognition* (Oxford: Oxford University Press).

Gardiner, Stephen (2010) *A Perfect Moral Storm: The Ethical Tragedy of Climate Change* (Oxford: Oxford University Press).

Gardner, John (2008) '"Simply in Virtue of Being Human": The Whos and Whys of Human Rights', *Journal of Ethics and Social Philosophy*, vol. 2.

Gearty, Conor (2010) 'Do Human Rights Help or Hinder Environmental Protection?', *Journal of Human Rights and the Environment*, vol. 1.

Geras, Norman (1995) *Solidarity in the Conversation of Humankind: The Ungroundable Liberalism of Richard Rorty* (London: Verso).

Gewirth, Alan (1976) 'Action and Rights: A Reply', *Ethics*, vol. 86.

Gewirth, Alan (1979) 'The Basis and Content of Human Rights', *Georgia Law Review*, vol. 13.

Gewirth, Alan (1982) *Human Rights: Essays on Justification and Applications* (Chicago, IL: University of Chicago Press).

Gewirth, Alan (1984) 'Are There Any Absolute Rights?' in J. Waldron (ed.) *Theories of Rights: Oxford Readings in Philosophy* (Oxford: Oxford University Press).

Ghai, Yash (2009) 'Universalism and Relativism: Human Rights as a Framwork for Negotiating Interethnic Claims', in W. Twining (ed.) *Human Rights, Southern Voices* (Cambridge: Cambridge University Press).

Ghanea-Hercock, Nazila (2000) 'Faith in Human Rights: Human Rights in Faith', in J. Thierstein and Y.R. Kamalipour (eds) *Religion, Law and Freedom: A Global Perspective* (Greenwood Press).

Gilabert, Pablo (2011) 'Humanist and Political Perspectives on Human Rights', *Political Theory*, vol. 39.

Glendon, Mary (1994) *Rights Talk: The Impoverishment of a Political Discourse* (New York: Free Press).

Gosseries, Axel (2008) 'On future generations' future rights', *Journal of Political Philosophy,* vol. 16.

Griffin, James (2008) *On Human Rights* (Oxford: Oxford University Press).

Griffin, James (2010) 'Human Rights: Questions of Aims and Approach', *Ethics*, vol. 120 .

Griffin, James (2011) 'Human Rights: Questions of aim and approach', in Ernst and Heilinger (eds) *The Philosophy of Human Rights* (a revised version of his 2010 paper).

Griffiths, Anne (2001) 'Towards a Plural Perspective on Kwena Women's Rights', in J.K. Cowan et al. (eds) *Culture and Rights: Anthropological Perspectives* (Cambridge: Cambridge University Press).

Hancock, Jan (2003) *Environmental Human Rights: Power, Ethics and Law*, (London: Ashgate).

Hart, H.L.A. (1967) 'Are There Any Natural Rights?' in A. Quinton (ed.) *Political Philosophy* (Oxford: Oxford University Press).

Hassan, Riffat (1996) 'Religious Human Rights and the Qur'an', *Emory International Law Review*, vol. 10.

Hayden, Patrick (2001) *Philosophy of Human Rights* (New York: Paragon).

Hayward, Tim (1998) *Political Theory and Ecological Value* (Cambridge: Polity Press).

Hayward, Tim (2005a) *Constitutional Environmental Rights* (Oxford: Oxford University Press).

Hayward, Tim (2005b) 'Thomas Pogge's Global Resources Dividend: A Critique and An Alternative', *Journal of Moral Philosophy*, vol. 2.

Hayward, Tim (2007) 'Human Rights versus Emissions Rights: Climate Justice and the Equitable Distribution of Ecological Space', *Ethics and International Affairs*, vol. 21.

Henkin, Louis (1995) 'Human Rights and State Sovereignty', *Georgia Journal of International and Comparative Law*, vol. 25.

Henkin, Louis (1999) 'That 'S' Word', *Fordham Law Review*, vol. 68.

Henle, R.J. (1980) 'A Catholic View of Human Rights: A Thomistic Reflection', in A.S. Rosenblum (ed.) *The Philosophy of Human Rights: International Perspectives* (London: Aldwych Press).

Hiskes, Richard P. (2009) *The Human Right to a Green Future* (Cambridge: Cambridge University Press).

Hobbes, Thomas (1984) *Leviathan* (Oxford: Oxford University Press).

Hohfeld, Wesley N. (1919) *Fundamental Legal Conceptions as Applied in Judicial Reasoning* (New Haven, CT: Yale University Press).

Hope, Simon (2011) 'Common Humanity as a Justification for Human Rights Claims', in Ernst and Heilinger (eds) *The Philosophy of Human Rights.*

Humphreys, Stephen (ed.) (2010) *Human Rights and Climate Change* (Cambridge: Cambridge University Press).

Hunt, Lynn A. (2007) *Inventing Human Rights: A History* (New York: Norton & Co).

Huntington, Samuel P. (1993) 'The Clash of Civilizations?' *Foreign Affairs*, vol. 72.

Hursthouse, Rosalind (2007) *On Virtue Ethics* (Oxford: Oxford University Press).

Hussain, Hishammuddin Tin (2001) 'Human Rights – The Asian Perspective', in R.G. Patman (ed.) *Universal Human Rights?* (Basingstoke: Palgrave Macmillan).

Inoue, Tatsuo (1999) 'Liberal Democracy and Asian Orientalism', in J. Bauer and D. Bell (eds) *The East Asian Challenge to Human Rights* (Cambridge: Cambridge University Press).

Ishay, Micheline R. (2008) *The History of Human Rights: From Ancient Times to the Globalization Era* (Berkeley, CA: University of California Press).

Jackson, Robert (2000) *The Global Covenant* (Oxford: Oxford University Press).

Jaggar, Alison (2005) '"Saving Amina": Global Justice for Women and Intercultural Dialogue', in A. Follesdal and T. Pogge (eds) *Real World Justice* (Dordrecht: Springer).

Jaggar, Alison (ed.) (2010) *Thomas Pogge and His Critics* (Cambridge: Polity).

Jennings, Jeremy (2011) *Revolution and the Republic: A History of Political Thought in France since the Eighteenth Century* (Oxford: Oxford University Press).

Jones, Peter (1994) *Rights (Issues in Political Theory)* (London: Macmillan).

Jones, Peter (2000) 'Human Rights and Diverse Cultures: Continuity or Discontinuity?', *Critical Review of International, Social and Political Philosophy*, vol. 3.

Kant, Immanuel (2004) *Fundamental Principles of the Metaphysics of Morals*, available online at http://www.gutenberg.org/ebooks/5682 (accessed 13 June 2012).

Kaplan, Abraham (1980) 'Human Relations and Human Rights in Judaism', in A.S. Rosenblum (ed.) *The Philosophy of Human Rights: International Perspectives* (London: Aldwych Press).

Kaufmann, P. et al. (eds) (2010) *Humiliation, Degradation, Dehumanization* (Dordrecht: Springer).

Kohen, Ari (2007) *In Defense of Human Rights: A Non-Religious Grounding in a Pluralistic World* (Abingdon: Routledge).

Korsgaard, Christine M. (1996) *The Sources of Normativity* (Cambridge: Cambridge University Press).

Kymlicka, Will (1996) *Multicultural Citizenship: A Liberal Theory of Minority Rights* (Oxford: Oxford University Press).

Kymlicka, Will (1999) 'Liberal Complacencies', in J. Cohen (ed.) *Is Multiculturalism Bad for Women?* (Princeton: Princeton University Press).

Kymlicka, Will (2002) *Contemporary Political Philosophy* (Oxford: Oxford University Press).

Kukathas, Chandran (1992) 'Are There Any Cultural Rights?' *Political Theory*, vol. 20.

Kukathas, Chandran (1998) 'Liberalism and Multiculturalism: The Politics of Indifference', *Political Theory*, vol. 26.

Kukathas, Chandran (2003) *The Liberal Archipelago: A Theory of Diversity and Freedom* (Oxford: Oxford University Press).

Laborde, Cecile (2005) 'Secular Philosophy and Muslim Headscarves in Schools', *Journal of Political Philosophy*, vol. 13.

Langlois, Anthony J. (2001) *The Politics of Justice and Human Rights: Southeast Asia and Universalist Theory* (Cambridge: Cambridge University Press).

Leopold, Aldo (1968) *A Sand County Almanac* (New York: Oxford University Press).

Lercher, Aaron (2007) 'Are There Any Environmental Rights?', available online at http://www.lib.lsu.edu/faculty/lercher/Are%20There%20Any%20 Environmental%20Rights.pdf (accessed 12 April 2005).

Liao, S. Matthew (2006) 'The Right of Children to be Loved', *Journal of Political Philosophy*, vol. 14.

Liao, S. Matthew and Adam Etinson (2012) 'Political and Naturalistic Conceptions of Human Rights: A False Polemic?' available online at: http://www.smatthewliao.com/wp-content/uploads/2012/06/LiaoEtinson PoliticalAndNaturalisticConceptionsOfHumanRights.pdf, published in *Journal of Moral Philosophy*, vol. 9.

Light, Andrew and Holmes Roston III (eds) (2003) *Environmental Ethics: An Anthology* (Oxford: Blackwell).

Locke, John (1988) *Two Treatises of Government* (ed. P. Laslett) (Cambridge: Cambridge University Press).

Loobuyck, Patrick (2005) 'Liberal Multiculturalism', *Ethnicities*, vol. 5.

Loobuyck, Patrick (2010) 'The Moral Requirement in Theistic and Secular Ethics', *Heythrop Journal*, vol. 51.

Lynch, Tony (2001) 'Gaita: A Common Humanity' (Review) *Australian Journal of Philosophy*, vol. 4.

Macedo, Stephen (2000) *Diversity and Distrust: Civic Education in a Multicultural Society* (Cambridge, MA: Harvard University Press).

MacInytre, Alasdair (1994) *After Virtue* (London: Duckworth).

MacInytre, Alasdair (1999) *Dependent Rational Animals* (London: Duckworth).

MacInytre, Alasdair (2008) 'What More Needs to be Said? A Beginning, Although Only a Beginning, at Saying It', *Analyse und Kritik*, vol. 30.

Mackie, J.L. (1984) 'Can There Be A Rights-Based Moral Theory?' in Waldron (ed.) *Theories of Rights*.

Mackie, J.L. (1990) *Ethics: Inventing Right and Wrong* (London: Penguin Books).

MacKinnon, Catharine A. (1993) 'Crimes of War, Crimes of Peace', in S. Shute and S. Hurley (eds) *On Human Rights: The Oxford Amnesty Lectures 1993* (New York: Basic Books)

Macklin, Ruth (2003) 'Dignity is a useless concept', *British Medical Journal*, vol. 327.

MacLeod, Sorcha and Douglas Lewis (2004) 'Transnational Corporations: Power, Influence, Responsibility', *Global Social Policy*, vol. 4.

MacPherson, C.B. (1962) *The Political Theory of Possessive Individualism: Hobbes to Locke* (Oxford: Clarendon Press).

Manokha, Ivan (2009) 'Foucault's Concept of Power and the Global Discourse of Human Rights', *Global Society*, vol. 23.

Maritain, Jacques (ed.) (1948) *Human Rights: Comments and Interpretations* (Geneva: UNESCO).

Markovic, Mihailo (1981) 'Philosophical Foundations for Human Rights', *Praxis International*, vol. 4.

Marshall, Peter (1995) *Nature's Web: Rethinking Our Place on Earth* (London: M.E. Sharpe).

Martinez-Alier, Joan (2002) *The Environmentalism of the Poor: A Study of Ecological Conflicts and Valuation* (Cheltenham: Edward Elgar).

Marx, Karl (1978) 'On the Jewish Question', in R.C. Tucker (ed.) *The Marx-Engels Reader,* 2nd edn (London: Norton).

Mayer, Ann Elizabeth (1993) 'A Critique of An-Na'im's Assessment of Islamic Criminal Justice', in T. Lindholm and K. Vogt (eds) *Islamic Law Reform and Human Rights: Challenges and Rejoinders* (Oslo: Nordic Human Rights Publications).

McClelland, J.S. (1996) *A History of Western Political Thought* (London: Routledge).

McCrudden, Christopher (2008) 'Human Dignity and Judicial Interpretation of Human Rights', *Oxford Legal Research Papers*, vol. 24.

McKinnon, Catriona (2011) 'Climate Change Justice: Getting Motivated in the

Last Chance Saloon', *Critical Review of International Social and Political Philosophy*, vol. 14.

Mendus, Susan (1989) *Liberalism and the Limits of Toleration (Issues in Political Theory)* (Basingstoke: Macmillan).

Mendus, Susan (1995) 'Political Theory and Human Rights', *Political Studies*, vol. 43

Mendus, Susan (2002) 'Choice, Chance and Multiculturalism', in P. Kelly (ed.) *Multiculturalism Reconsidered* (Cambridge: Polity).

Mendus, Susan (2011) 'Should Religion be Special?', available online at: http://www.york.ac.uk/politics/our-staff/sue-mendus/ (accessed 12 March 2012).

Merry, Sally Engle (2001) 'Changing rights, changing culture', in J.K. Cowan et al. (eds) *Culture and Rights: Anthropological Perspectives* (Cambridge: Cambridge University Press).

Merry, Sally Engle (2005) *Human Rights and Gender Violence* (Chicago: University of Chicago Press).

Meyer, Michael J. (1989) 'Dignity, Rights and Self-Control', *Ethics*, vol. 99.

Mill, John Stuart (1985) *On Liberty* (London: Penguin).

Miller, Chris (ed.) (1996) *The Dissident Word: The Oxford Amnesty Lectures 1995* (New York: Basic Books).

Miller, David (2005) 'Cosmopolitanism: A Critique', *Critical Review of International Social and Political Philosophy*, vol. 5.

Miller, David (2006) 'Multiculturalism and the Welfare State: Theoretical Reflections', in W. Kymlicka and K. Banting (eds) *Multiculturalism and the Welfare State* (Oxford: Oxford University Press).

Mills, Charles W. (2010) 'Realizing (Through Racializing) Pogge', in Jaggar (ed.) *Thomas Pogge and his Critics*.

Modood, Tariq (1998) 'Anti-Essentialism, Multiculturalism and the Recognition of Religious Groups', *Journal of Political Philosophy*, vol. 6.

Modood, Tariq (2005) 'Remaking Multiculturalism after 7/7', Working Paper, Open Democracy.

Modood, Tariq (2007) *Multiculturalism: A Civic Idea* (Cambridge: Polity).

Moore, Margaret (2008) 'Global Justice, Climate Change and Miller's Theory of Responsibility', *Critical Review of International Social and Political Philosophy*, vol. 11.

Morsink, Johannes (2009) *Inherent Human Rights: Philosophical Roots of the Universal Declaration* (Philadelphia: University of Pennsylvania Press).

Murphy, Liam B. (1993) 'The Demands of Beneficence', *Philosophy and Public Affairs*, vol. 22.

Naess, Arne (2003) 'The Deep Ecological Movement: Some Philosophical Aspects', in A. Light and H. Rolston III (eds) *Environmental Ethics: An Anthology* (Oxford: Blackwell).

Nagel, Thomas (1995) 'Personal Rights and Public Space', *Philosophy and Public Affairs*, vol. 24.

Nasr, Seyyed H. (1980) 'The Concept and Reality of Freedom in Islam and Islamic Civilization', in A.S. Rosenblum (ed.) *The Philosophy of Human Rights: International Perspectives* (London: Aldwych Press).

Neumeyer, Eric (2000) 'In Defence of Historical Accountability for Greenhouse Gas Emissions', *Ecological Economics*, vol. 33.

Neumeyer, Eric (2003) 'Is Respect for Human Rights Rewarded? An Analysis of Total Bilateral And Multilateral Aid Flows', *Human Rights Quarterly*, vol. 25.

Nickel, James (1993) 'The Human Right to a Safe Environment: Philosophical Perspectives on its Scope and Justification', *Yale Journal of International Law*, vol. 18.

Nickel, James (2005) *Making Sense of Human Rights* (Oxford: Wiley/Blackwell).

Nietzsche, Friedrich (1982) 'The Gay Science', in W. Kaufmann (ed.) *The Portable Nietzsche* (London: Penguin Books).

Norton, Bryan (2003) 'Environmental Ethics and Weak Anthropocentrism', in A. Light and H. Rolston III (eds) *Environmental Ethics: An Anthology* (Oslo: Nordic Human Rights Publications).

Nozick, Robert (1974) *Anarchy, State, Utopia* (New York: Basic Books).

Nussbaum, Martha (1996) 'Lesbian and Gay Rights', in M. Leahy and D. Cohn-Sherbok (eds) *The Liberation Debate: Rights and Issue* (London: Routledge).

Nussbaum, Martha (1997) 'Capabilities and Human Rights', *Fordham Law Review*, vol. 66.

Nussbaum, Martha (2001) *Women and Human Development: The Capabilities Approach* (Cambridge: Cambridge University Press).

Nussbaum, Martha (2008) *Liberty of Conscience: In Defense of America's Tradition of Religious Equality* (New York: Basic Books).

Nussbaum, Martha (2011) *Creating Capabilities* (Cambridge, MA: Harvard University Press).

Nussbaum, Martha and Jonathan Glover (eds) (1995) *Women, Culture and Development: A Study of Human Capabilities* (Oxford: Oxford University Press).

Oh, Irene (2007) *The Rights of God: Islam, Human Rights and Comparative Ethics* (Washington, DC: Georgetown University Press).

OHCHR (no date) 'What are Human Rights', available online at http://www.ohchr.org/EN/Issues/Pages/WhatareHumanRights.aspx (accessed 20 October 2013).

Okin, Susan Moller (1998a) 'Feminism, Women's Human Rights and Cultural Differences', *Hypatia*, vol. 13.

Okin, Susan Moller (1998b) 'Feminism and Multiculturalism: Some Tensions', *Ethics*, vol. 108.

Okin, Susan Moller (1999) 'Is Multiculturalism Bad for Women?' in J. Cohen (ed.) *Is Multiculturalism Bad for Women?* (Princeton: Princeton University Press).

Okin, Susan Moller (2002) 'Mistresses of their Own Destiny: Group Rights, Gender, and Realistic Rights of Exit', *Ethics*, vol. 112.

Okin, Susan Moller (2005) 'Forty Acres and a Mule for Women: Rawls and Feminism', *Philosophy, Politics and Economics*, vol. 4.

O'Neill, John (1993) *Ecology, Policy and Politics: Human Well-Being and the Natural World* (London: Routledge).

O'Neill, John (2007) *Markets, Deliberation and Environmental Value* (London: Routledge).

O'Neill, Onora (1996) *Towards Justice and Virtue* (Cambridge: Cambridge University Press).

O'Neill, Onora (2001) 'Agents of Justice', *Metaphilosophy*, vol. 32.

O'Neill, Onora (2004) 'Global Justice: Whose Obligations?' in D.K. Chatterjee (ed.) *The Ethics of Assistance: Morality and the Distant Needy* (Cambridge: Cambridge University Press).

O'Neill, Onora (2005) 'The Dark Side of Human Rights', *International Affairs*, vol. 81.

Othman, Norani (1999) 'Grounding Human Rights Arguments in Non-Western Culture: *Shari'a* and the Citizenship Rights of Women in a Modern Islamic State', in J. Bauer and D. Bell (eds) *The East Asian Challenge to Human Rights* (Cambridge: Cambridge University Press).

Page, Edward (2006) *Climate Change, Justice and Future Generations* (Cheltenham: Edward Elgar).

Paine, Thomas (1999) *Rights of Man: Being a Reply to Mr Burke* (Boston, MA: Dover).

Panikkar, R. and R. Panikkar (1982) 'Is the Notion of Human Rights a Western Concept?', *Diogenes*, vol. 30.

Parekh, Bhiku (1999a) 'Non-ethnocentric Universalism', in T. Dunne and N.J. Wheeler (eds) *Human Rights in Global Politics* (Cambridge: Cambridge University Press).

Parekh, Bhiku (1999b) 'A Varied Moral World', in J. Cohen (ed.) *Is Multiculturalism Bad for Women?* (Princeton: Princeton University Press).

Parekh, Serena (2004) 'A Meaningful Place in the World: Hannah Arendt on the Nature of Human Rights', *Journal of Human Rights*, vol. 3.

Parfit, Derek (1987) *Reasons and Persons* (Oxford: Oxford University Press).

Partridge, Ernest (1990) 'On the Rights of Future Generations', in D. Scherer (ed.) *Upstream/Downstream: Issues in Environmental Ethics* (Philadelphia: Temple University Press).

Patten, Alan (2005) 'Should We Stop Thinking About Poverty in Terms of Helping the Poor?', *Ethics and International Affairs*, vol. 19.

Patten, Alan (2009) 'Survey Article: The Justification of Minority Rights', *Journal of Political Philosophy*, vol. 17.

Peach, Lynda Joy (2001) 'Are Women Human? The Promise and Perils of "Women's Rights as Human Rights"', in L.S. Bell et al. (eds) *Negotiating Culture and Human Rights* (New York: Columbia University Press).

Perry, Michael J. (1992) 'Is the Idea of Human Rights Ineliminably Religious?', *University of Richmond Law Review*, vol. 27.

Perry, Michael J. (2000) *The Idea of Human Rights: Four Inquiries* (Oxford: Oxford University Press).

Perry, Michael J. (2005) 'A Right to Religious Freedom? The Universality of Human Rights, The Relativity of Culture', *Roger Williams University Law Review*, vol. 10.

Phillips, Anne (2009) *Multiculturalism without Culture* (Princeton: Princeton University Press).

Picolotti, Ramona and Jorge Daniel Taillant (eds) (2003) *Linking Human Rights and the Environment* (Tuscon: University of Arizona Press).

Pluhar, Evelyn B. (1987) 'The Personhood View and the Argument from Marginal Cases', *Philosophica*, vol. 39.

Pogge, Thomas (ed.) (2001) *Global Justice* (Oxford: Blackwell).

Pogge, Thomas (2002) *World Poverty and Human Rights* (Cambridge: Polity), 2nd edn, 2007.

Pogge, Thomas (ed.) (2004) *Ethical and Human Rights Dimensions of Poverty* (Geneva: UNESCO).

Pogge, Thomas (2005a) 'Severe Poverty as a Violation of Negative Duties', *Ethics and International Affairs*, vol. 19.

Pogge, Thomas (2005b) 'Cosmopolitanism: A Defence', *Critical Review of International Social and Political Philosophy*, vol. 5.

Pogge, Thomas (2010) 'Responses to the Critics', in Jaggar (ed.) *Thomas Pogge and His Critics*.

Rachels, James (2002) *The Elements of Moral Philosophy* (Maidenhead: McGraw-Hill).

Raphael, D.D. (ed.) (1967) *Political Theory and the Rights of Man* (London: Macmillan).

Raz, Joseph (1986) *The Morality of Freedom* (Oxford: Oxford University Press).

Raz, Joseph (2007) 'Human Rights without Foundations', *Oxford Legal Studies Research Paper*, 14.

Raz, Joseph (2910) 'Human Rights Without Foundations', in J. Tasioulas and S. Besson (eds) *The Philosophy of International Law* (Oxford: Oxford University Press).

Rawls, John (1993) 'The Law of Peoples', in S. Shute and S. Hurley (eds) *On Human Rights: The Oxford Amnesty Lectures 1993* (New York: Basic Books).

Rawls, John (1999a) *A Theory of Justice*, Revised Edition (Oxford: Oxford University Press).

Rawls, John (1999b) *The Law of Peoples* (Cambridge, MA: Harvard University Press).

Rawls, John (2005) *Political Liberalism* (New York: Columbia University Press).

Regan, Tom (1985) 'The Case for Animal Rights', in P. Singer (ed.) *In Defense of Animals* (New York: Basil Blackwell).

Renteln, Alison (1985) 'The Unanswered Challenge of Relativism and the Consequences for Human Rights', *Human Rights Quarterly*, vol. 7.

Risse, Mattias (2005) 'How Does the Global Order Harm the Poor?', *Philosophy and Public Affairs*, vol. 33.

Rolston III, Holmes (2003) 'Value in Nature and the Nature of Value, in A. Light and H. Rolston III (eds) *Environmental Ethics: An Anthology* (Oxford: Blackwell).

Rorty, Richard (1989) *Contingency, Irony and Solidarity* (Cambridge: Cambridge University Press).

Rorty, Richard (1993) 'Human Rights, Rationality, and Sentimentality', in S. Shute and S. Hurley (eds) *On Human Rights: The Oxford Amnesty Lectures 1993* (New York: Basic Books).

Rorty, Richard (1999) *Philosophy and Social Hope* (London: Penguin Books).

Rosen, Michael (2012) *Dignity: Its History and Meaning* (Cambridge, MA: Harvard University Press).

Rousseau, Jean-Jacques (1984) *A Discourse on Inequality* (ed. M. Cranston) (London: Penguin Books).

Rousseau, Jean-Jacques (1993) *The Social Contract* (London: Dent).

Sachedina, Abdulaziz (2009) *Islam and the Challenge of Human Rights* (Oxford: Oxford University Press).

Said, Edward (2001) 'The Clash of Ignorance', *The Nation*, 22 October.

Salleh, Ariel (1997) *Eco-feminism as Politics: Nature, Marx and the Postmodern* (London: Zed Books).

Sandel, Michael (1982) *Liberalism and the Limits of Justice* (Cambridge: Cambridge University Press).

Sandel, Michael (1984) 'Introduction', in Sandel (ed.) *Liberalism and its Critics* (New York: New York University Press).

Schaber, Peter (2011) 'Human Rights without Foundations?' in G. Ernst and J.C. Heilinger (eds) *The Philosophy of Human Rights* (Berlin: De Gruyter).

Scott, Joan Wallach (1997) *Only Paradoxes to Offer: French Feminists and the Rights of Man* (Cambridge, MA: Harvard University Press).

Sen, Amartya (1997) 'Human Rights and Asian Values', 16th Morgenthau Memorial Lecture on Ethics and Foreign Policy, Carnegie Council on Ethics and International Affairs.

Sen, Amartya (2002) 'East and West: The Reach of Reason', *New York Review of Books*, vol. 47.

Sen, Amartya (2005) 'Human Rights and Capabilities', *Journal of Human Development*, vol. 6.

Sen, Amartya (2012) 'The Global Reach of Human Rights', *Journal of Applied Philosophy*, vol. 29.

Shah, Niaz (2006) 'Women's Human Rights in the Koran: An Interpretive Approach', *Human Rights Quarterly*, vol. 28.

Sharma, Arvind (2003) 'The Religious Perspective: Dignity as a Foundation for Human Rights Discourse', in J. Runzo et al. (eds) *Human Rights and Responsibilities in the World Religions* (Oxford: One World Publications).

Shiva, Vandana (1999) 'Food Rights, Free Trade, and Fascism', in M. Gibney (ed.) *Globalizing Rights: The Oxford Amnesty Lectures 1999* (Oxford: Oxford University Press).

Shklar, Judith (1985) 'Putting Cruelty First', in her *Ordinary Vices* (Boston: Belknap Press).

Shrader-Frechette, Kristin (2001) 'MacIntyre on Human Rights', *The Modern Schoolman*, vol. 79.

Shrader-Frechette, Kristin (2007) 'Human Rights and Duties to Alleviate Environmental Injustice: The Domestic Case', *Journal of Human Rights*, vol. 6.

Shue, Henry (1978) 'Torture', *Philosophy and Public Affairs*, vol. 7.

Shue, Henry (1980) *Basic Rights: Subsistence, Affluence and US Foreign Policy* (Princeton, NJ: Princeton University Press).

Shue, Henry (1999) 'Global Environment and International Inequality', *International Affairs*, vol. 75.

Shue, Henry (2005) 'Torture in Dreamland: Disposing of the Ticking Bomb', *Case Western Journal of International Law*, vol. 37.

Shue, Henry (2011) 'Face Reality? After You! A Call for Leadership on Climate Change', *Ethics and International Affairs*, vol. 25.

Sieghart, Paul (1985) *The Lawful Rights of Mankind: Introduction to the International Legal Code of Human Rights* (Oxford: Oxford University Press).

Singer, Marcus G. (1985) 'On Gewirth's Derivation of the Principle of Generic Consistency', *Ethics*, vol. 95.

Singer, Peter (1972) 'Famine, Affluence and Morality', *Philosophy and Public Affairs*, vol. 1.

Singer, Peter (1975) *Animal Liberation: Towards an End to Man's Inhumanity to Animals* (London: Avon Books).

Singer, Peter (2005) 'Ethics and Intuitions', *Journal of Ethics*, vol. 9.

Singham, Shanti Marie (1994) 'Betwixt Cattle and Men', in D. van Kley (ed.) *The French Idea of Freedom* (Stanford: Stanford University Press).

Spelman, Elizabeth (1990) *Inessential Women* (Boston: Beacon Press).

Stammers, Neil (1999) 'Social Movements and the Social Construction of Human Rights', *Human Rights Quarterly*, vol. 21.

Steiner, Hillel (1994) *An Essay on Human Rights* (Oxford: Blackwell).

Stoeker, Ralf (2010) 'Three Crucial Turns on the Road to an Adequate Understanding of Human Dignity', in P. Kaufmann et al. (eds) (2010) *Humiliation, Degradation, Dehumanization* (Dordrecht: Springer).

Sweet, William (2003) 'Solidarity and Human Rights', in W. Sweet (ed.) *Philosophical Theory and the Universal Declaration of Human Rights* (Ottawa: University of Ottawa Press).

Tasioulas, John (2004) 'The Moral Reality of Human Rights', in T. Pogge (ed.) *Ethical and Human Rights Dimensions of Poverty* (Geneva: UNESCO).

Tasioulas, John (2010) 'Taking Rights out of Human Rights', *Ethics*, vol. 120.

Tasioulas, John (2011) 'On the Nature of Human Rights', in Ernst and Heilinger (eds) *The Philosophy of Human Rights*.

Taylor, Charles (1987) *Sources of the Self* (Cambridge, MA: Harvard University Press).

Taylor, Charles (1994) 'The Politics of Recognition', in A. Gutman (ed.) *Multiculturalism* (Princeton: Princeton University Press).

Taylor, Charles (2007) *A Secular Age* (Cambridge, MA: Harvard University Press).

Taylor, Charles (2009) 'Conditions of an Unforced Consensus on Human Rights', in O. Savić et al., *Politics of Human Rights* (London: Verso)

Teson, Fernando (1985) 'International Human Rights and Cultural Relativism', *Virginian Journal of International Law*, vol. 25.

Thomson, Judith Jarvis (1986) 'Killing, Letting Die and the Trolley Problem', in W. Parent (ed.) *Rights, Restitution, and Risk: Essays in Moral Theory* (Cambridge, MA: Harvard University Press).

Tremmel, Jörg (2009) *A Theory of Intergenerational Justice* (London: Earthscan).

Tyson, Brad, and Said, Abdul Aziz (1993) 'Human Rights: A Forgotten Victim of the Cold War', *Human Rights Quarterly*, vol. 15.

Van Der Ploeg, P.A. (2002) 'Minority Rights and Educational Authority', *Journal of Philosophy of Education*, vol. 32.

van Kley, Dale (ed.) (1997) *The French Idea of Freedom: The Old Regime and the Declaration of Rights of 1789* (Stanford: Stanford University Press).

Waldron, Jeremy (ed.) (1984) *Theories of Rights: Oxford Readings in Philosophy* (Oxford: Oxford University Press).

Waldron, Jeremy (1987) *Nonsense Upon Stilts: Bentham, Burke and Marx on the Rights of Man* (London: Routledge).

Waldron, Jeremy (1993) 'A Right-Based Critique of Constitutional Rights', *Oxford Journal of Legal Studies*, vol. 13.

Waldron, Jeremy (2009) 'Dignity, Rank and Rights: The 2009 Tanner Lectures', NYU School of Law, Public Law Research Paper No. 09–50.

Waltz, Susan (2004). 'Universal Human Rights: The Contribution of Muslim States', *Human Rights Quarterly*, vol. 26.

WCED (1987) Report of the World Commission on Environment and Development: Our Common Future (available online at http://www.un-documents.net/wced-ocf.htm, accessed 3 March 2995).

Wellman, Carl (1999) *The Proliferation of Rights: Moral Progress or Empty Rhetoric?* (Boulder: Westview).

Wellman, Carl (2000) 'Solidarity, the Individual, and Human Rights, *Human Rights Quarterly*, vol. 22.

Wellman, Carl (2011) *The Moral Dimensions of Human Rights* (Oxford: Oxford University Press).

Wenar, Leif (2005) 'The Nature of Human Rights', in A. Follesdal and T. Pogge (eds) *Real World Justice* (Dordrecht: Springer).

Wenar, Leif (2008a) 'John Rawls', *Stanford Encyclopedia of Philosophy_(Fall 2008 Edition)*, E.N. Zalta (ed.), URL = <http://plato.stanford.edu/archives/fall2008/entries/rawls/> (accessed 6 January 2013).

Wenar, Leif (2008b) 'Property Rights and the Resource Curse', *Philosophy and Public Affairs*, vol. 36.

Wenar, Leif (2010) 'Realistic Reform of International Trade in Resources', in A. Jaggar (ed.) *Thomas Pogge and his Critics*.

Wenar, Leif (2011) 'Poverty is no Pond', in P. Illingworth and T. Pogge (eds) *Giving Well, The Ethics of Philanthropy* (Oxford: Oxford University Press).

Wheeler, Nicholas J. (2000) *Saving Strangers: Humanitarian Intervention in International Society* (Oxford: Oxford University Press).

White Jnr, L. (1967) 'The Historical Roots of Our Ecologic Crisis', *Science*, vol. 161.

Williams, Bernard (1972) *Morality: An Introduction to Ethics* (Cambridge: Cambridge University Press).

Williams, Bernard, with J.C. Smart (1973) *Utilitarianism: For and Against* (Cambridge: Cambridge University Press).

Williams, Bernard (1987) 'The Standard of Living: Interests and Capabilities', in G. Hawthorn (ed.) *The Standard of Living* (Cambridge: Cambridge University Press).

Williams, Bernard (1985) *Ethics and the Limits of Philosophy* (London: Routledge).

Williams, Eric (1994) *Capitalism and Slavery* (Chapel Hill, NC: University of North Carolina Press).

Wilson, Richard A. (ed.) (1998) *Human Rights, Culture and Context: Anthropological Perspectives* (London: Pluto Press).

Wiredu, Kwasi (1990) 'An Akan Perspective on Human Rights', in A. An-Na'im (ed.) *Human Rights in Africa: Cross-Cultural Perspectives* (Washington DC: The Brookings Institute).

Wissenburg, Marcel (1998) *Green liberalism: The Free and Green Society* (London: UCL Press).

Wolff, Jonathan (1996) *An Introduction to Political Philosophy* (Oxford: Oxford University Press).

Wollstonecraft, Mary (2007) *Vindication of the Rights of Women* (Oxford: Oxford University Press).

Woods, Kerri (2010) *Human Rights and Environmental Sustainability* (Cheltenham: Edward Elgar).

Woods, Kerri (2012) 'Whither Sentiment? Compassion, Solidarity and Disgust in Cosmopolitan Thought', *Journal of Social Philosophy*, vol. 43.

Young, Iris Marion (1990) *Justice and the Politics of Difference* (Princeton: Princeton University Press).

Young, Iris Marion (2002) *Inclusion and Democracy* (Oxford: Oxford University Press).

Zarsky, Linda (ed.) (2002) *Human Rights and the Environment: Conflicts and Norms in a Globalized World* (London: Earthscan).

Ziegler, Rafael (2007) 'Tracing Global Inequality in Eco-space: A Comment on Tim Hayward's Proposal', *Journal of Moral Philosophy*, vol. 4.

Index